Innocents Abroad Too

Innocents Abroad Too

JOURNEYS AROUND THE WORLD
ON SEMESTER AT SEA

Michael Pearson

 SYRACUSE UNIVERSITY PRESS

Syracuse University Press, Syracuse, New York 13244-5160
Copyright © 2008 by Michael Pearson

All Rights Reserved

First Edition 2008

08 09 10 11 12 13   6 5 4 3 2 1

Maps reproduced with permission of Donald Emminger,
graphic designer, Old Dominion University.

The paper used in this publication meets the minimum requirements of
American National Standard for Information Sciences—Permanence of
Paper for Printed Library Materials, ANSI Z39.48–1984.∞™

For a listing of books published and distributed by Syracuse University Press,
visit our Web site at SyracuseUniversityPress.syr.edu.

ISBN-13: 978-0-8156-0909-4
ISBN-10: 0-8156-0909-4

Library of Congress Cataloging-in-Publication Data
Pearson, Michael, 1949–
Innocents abroad too : journeys around the world on semester at sea / Michael Pearson. — 1st ed.
p. cm.
Includes bibliographical references.
ISBN 978-0-8156-0909-4 (cloth : alk. paper)
1. Pearson, Michael, 1949—Travel. I. Title.
PS3616.E255Z46 2008
818'.6—dc22
2008027915

Manufactured in the United States of America

 Since I turned nineteen years old, all of my great adventures have been with the same companion. Because of her, travel and love are inextricably linked for me. If I've spent much of my life dreaming and roaming like Don Quixote, she has been a Sancho Panza far more slim, beautiful, and wild-hearted than the original. In her eyes and laughter and tears, the world has flashed by in a blur that made dreams and wakefulness no more separate than windmills and giants. Traveling around the world with her has been a waking dream, one that is inside of me still—and always will be. To her, this book is dedicated.

One must travel to learn.

—Mark Twain, *The Innocents Abroad*

Michael Pearson is a professor of creative writing at Old Dominion University. He has written reviews and travel stories for a variety of magazines and newspapers. He is also the author of *Imagined Places: Journeys into Literary America,* which was listed by the *New York Times Book Review* as a Notable Book of 1992; *John McPhee,* a biographical critical study; *A Place That's Known,* a collection of essays; *Dreaming of Columbus: A Boyhood in the Bronx,* a memoir; and *Shohola Falls,* a novel.

Contents

Prefatory Note

Most people never get to circumnavigate the globe by ship. I had the good fortune to do it twice with the Semester at Sea program, first in 2002 and again, taking a somewhat different course, in 2006. Only about one in ten Americans even has a passport; therefore, it seems like a stroke of extraordinary luck to have traveled as much as I have in the first decade of the twenty-first century. Each year tens of thousands of college students do a study abroad program in a specific country. Semester at Sea is different: it takes students on a 100-day voyage to ten countries around the world.

I was fortunate to be born in a place that induced—really compelled—the desire to travel. I grew to young adulthood in the 1960s in the Bronx, the only mainland borough of New York City and a place that produced dreams of escape to rival, I would guess, those spawned by classics like *The Count of Monte Cristo*. At some point during the decade of the sixties, the Bronx transformed itself in my mind from home to prison. For me, all roads led *from* the Bronx. The only way to go was *out*. Jump the walls, leave the squat brick buildings behind, and discover where my real home was in the world.

What kept me alive with hope and anticipation throughout my adolescence were reading and the dream of writing. As Orhan Pamuk explained his vocation in his Nobel Prize acceptance speech, "A writer is someone who spends years patiently trying to discover the second being inside him, and the world that makes him who he is . . . the person who shuts himself up in a room, sits down at a table, and, alone, turns inward." Pamuk goes on to say that a writer's secret is not inspiration but stubbornness and endurance. As a young man—in love from the start with the isolation and seductive loneliness of the writing life—I suspected I had the necessary stubborn streak in me. If the Bronx and the Catholic education that inevitably accompanied it in my neighborhood gave me anything, it was patience and a belief in an afterlife, and for me that didn't mean heaven but a life beyond the pizza places and bars on Bedford Park Boulevard and Villa Avenue.

In this respect, travel and writing became, early in my life, intimately connected. Experience and imagination fed one another. Both were necessary parts of who I was, or, more accurately, who I wanted to be as I lay in my bed in my apartment in the Bronx, listening to the roar of the buses on the avenue and feeling in my spine the vibrations of the D train that rumbled beneath the sidewalk. Years later, when I first read William Butler Yeats's "The Circus Animals' Desertion," I instantly recognized his metaphors of a ladder and the foul rag-and-bone shop of the heart as my own separate instincts to imagine life from the privacy of my room and, at the same time, to fling open the door and roam through it, uncovering all the secrets that the world had to offer.

My father warned me years ago about having my cake and eating it too, but as soon as I knew I wanted to write, I knew I wanted to live a life of both the imagination and experience, as well. Travel writing does not merely allow those two impulses to coexist, it demands that they do. Wordsworth characterized poetry as emotion recollected in tranquility. Such an idea could serve as a workable definition of serious travel writing, too. The travel writer must leap into the world. Motion is essential. Without experience, there is no writing. It cannot simply rise of its own accord from the imagination. But experience is not enough. There must be the stillness that comes after experience, the contemplation of it, the recollection of the fury of life in tranquility. For the travel writer, there is always the adventure and then, after the crossing to safety, the making of meaning.

In 1869, Mark Twain published his first successful book, *The Innocents Abroad*. It changed the nature of travel writing, announcing the new role of the travel writer as someone who had to come to terms with both the cluttered world and a new phenomenon, the tourist industry. Twain's title was perfect for his subject, but it was even more wide-ranging and resonant than he might have imagined. And that's why (with some trepidation) I've appropriated his title and added *Too*. Twain's title describes the position of the traveler—always—an innocent abroad. *Innocent* can mean being upright and blameless, but it also suggests the fact that the traveler can never know enough about a foreign place or culture to be anything but naïve. The traveler must recognize the limits of his or her vision. The first step in a journey may start with some degree of arrogance, but for it to continue and become a true journey, there must be humility. How can any of us ever see the *other* much more clearly than Adam Delano saw Benito Cereno in Melville's masterful short story? Perhaps as travelers, we should strive to be innocents abroad in another way, open-hearted and honest, unmalicious and childlike, gazing with eyes undulled by too much glib sophistication. Conrad said our goal is to see. It was then. And still is.

In the fall of 2002 and the fall of 2006, I sailed on two different ships, each time traveling more than 22,000 nautical miles. I visited sixteen countries on those two journeys. In 2002, the ship sailed from Canada to Japan, China, Hong Kong, Vietnam, Malaysia, India, Kenya, South Africa, Brazil, and Cuba. In 2006, the ship left San Diego, sailed to Mexico to board the students, and then went to Hawaii, Japan, Hong Kong, Vietnam, Myanmar, India, Egypt, Turkey, Croatia, and Spain. One of the main reasons I wanted to sail again in 2006 was to go through the Suez Canal, to visit the land of the pharaohs and to see Istanbul, the only city that straddles Europe and Asia.

I wasn't alone by any means. My wife, Jo-Ellen, was by my side the whole way, and we journeyed with dozens of other professors, staff, older passengers, and approximately 600 college students each trip. One voyage came in the wake of 9/11 and the other in the midst of the war in Iraq. Both seemed precarious times to travel, especially as an American citizen. But jeopardy was part of the essential nature of travel—as were comedy and drama. We had all in equal measure—death and burial at sea, imprisonment, hospitalization, the specter of pirates, students who had been sent home found stowing away on the ship, meetings with Fidel Castro and Desmond Tutu, love affairs, marriages, a ship of saints and sinners, the felicitous and the foolhardy.

The word *travel* has its roots set complexly in the ancient meaning of the word *travail*. It is associated with pain and anguish and hard work—even with the labor of childbirth. And this makes sense to me, for travel should be about bringing new things to life, and that's never easy. Travel is not only about seeing new places but about seeing oneself anew. "The whole object of foreign travel is not to set foot on foreign land," G. K. Chesterton suggested. "It is to at last set foot on one's own country as a foreign land!" That's what I hoped finally to do in my journeys around the world, to avoid becoming what one of the characters in *Barton Fink* calls the writer: "just a tourist with a typewriter." I wanted to be more than a sightseer. I hoped to become a traveler who would return home with a new way of regarding what I had left behind.

Acknowledgments

The writer of any book owes many debts, primarily to those who offered encouragement, criticism, and guidance. My deep appreciation goes to Michele Rubin of Writers House, Mary Selden Evans and Mona Hamlin of Syracuse University Press, Don Emminger of Old Dominion University Graphic Design, and Michael Knight of the Helene Wurlitzer Foundation. I also want to thank Semester at Sea for taking me on as a hired hand twice. I am grateful to the hundreds of students who shared their experience of traveling the world with me and the many people in the more than a dozen countries who we encountered along the way. And, of course, once again, to Jo-Ellen for . . . everything.

2002

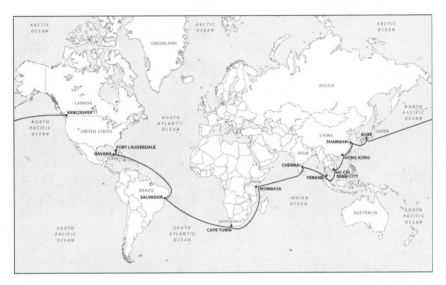

2002. *Created by Donald Emminger, graphic designer, Old Dominion University.*

Beginnings

Have you ever found yourself staring at a map the way you would gaze at a star-strewn sky, the way a man might regard an attractive woman—with longing and anticipation? Since I was a boy, I have loved the mysterious lines of maps, countries colored as fantastically as rainbows, the soft blue of the seas framing all we can hope to know, or a landmass with the lovely and frightening whiteness of Antarctica disappearing into the emptiness of the margins, into what we may not wish to know.

I loved maps the way my boyhood companions loved baseball and football. Words like *China* and *India* had the power to make my heartbeat quicken, an attraction as beautiful and confusing as first love. Maps are symbols of possibility, perhaps, of the hope that we can shape our destiny, or at least figure out where we might be heading. They suggest, as well, that there may be locations not described in the lines of latitude and longitude, places yet undiscovered. Maps are simple representations of the complex world, signposts for wayfarers, metaphors for what we seek—escape from all that is known, a glimpse of the extraordinary, a new sense of self, a discovery of home.

Our first experiences with travel are likely an attempt to lose our innocence, and then later, perhaps, to regain it. Our earliest journeys may be to fill a blank page and our later ones to erase some of the marks we have made in the world and that the world has made on us. One way or the other, travel is about innocence lost or recaptured, about changing the way we see ourselves and how we live our lives. If even true travel doesn't transform us permanently, it usually allows us to leave personal history behind. When we travel, there is only History and the characters we make of ourselves. Our lives become a new page—a blank one—for experience to write upon. As travelers, we are in the world *now,* in the immediate and present sensation, not drifting in the past or yearning for (or fearing) the future.

In late August 2002, when my wife, Jo-Ellen, and I flew from New York City to Vancouver, British Columbia, to embark on a voyage around the world on the SS *Universe Explorer* with the Semester at Sea program, the shadow of 9/11 stretched out behind us and before us, a dark world from which there seemed no return. On that ship, with more than 700 students, faculty, staff, adult passengers, and children, we sailed into a world of new hazards, where we might be despised not for anything we did but just for being Americans, where language barriers existed but the vocabulary of terror appeared to be the lingua franca.

Maybe because it would have been easier to stay at home, we took off on our 105-day voyage around the globe. Our sons were grown, we had been married two-thirds of our lives, my mother-in-law died three years before, and my own mother had passed away a few weeks after September 11, 2001, just shy of her ninetieth birthday. My mother had been a passionate reader and traveler. More than any other adult I had ever known, she had been as curious as a child. Everything in the world fascinated her, filled her with wonder, it seemed. The attacks on 9/11 could have been an attack on her spirit, for after them she appeared to lose interest in living. Her attention became unfocused, and, willing herself to be gone, she left us forever.

We sold our house in Virginia Beach, gave most of our furniture to our sons, put what remained in storage, and left. In part, I think, I wanted to leave to see if I could find my mother in the world or, more truly, find her passionate spirit. I needed to know how much the world had changed. I needed to bring back that message for her.

Our new home, the SS *Universe Explorer*, was 617 feet long and 84 feet wide. It weighed 23,500 tons, was eight stories high, had a pool, a library, classrooms, two dining halls, an exercise room, and a half-court basketball area surrounded by netting so that the ball would not sail into the Pacific Ocean during an afternoon game. It was a tough old ship, once built for battle despite its makeover as a floating university. And if Melville were right that meditation and water are forever wedded, then my new home would offer a place to make some sense of the traveler's true theme—*time*—the source of all happiness and sadness. All travel writing, ultimately, is about *time,* about stopping it or giving meaning to its fragments. At one point or another, I suppose, everyone feels the need to travel, the desire to disappear and return newborn. It's the wish to be a stranger in a strange land, to break the iron grip of the familiar. Like most people, I was a character in a Hawthorne story haunted by a secret sin. Or Huck shaking off the shackles of domesticity. Cacciato escaping, dreaming of Paris. Finally, I guess, my reasons for wanting to go, for needing to go, were mine. Life. Death. Disappointments. Dreams. My motives weren't exotic. And, besides, the reasons for leaving probably don't matter as much as the journey. The meaning is always in the journey.

A Ship at Sea

We spent three days in late August 2002 roaming around the cycling and walking paradise of Vancouver, British Columbia. Most afternoons we spent in Stanley Park, one of the largest urban parklands in the world, a tree-shaded, rolling landscape framed by five miles of seawall. The embankment stretched along the Strait of Georgia that led into the Pacific Ocean, and the park was shadowed by expensive high rises and the distant North Shore Mountains. It was an old gold rush town, renovated and preserved into what Timothy Leary might have conjured as a vision of the ideal city in one of his LSD dreams. A magnet for bikers and hikers and health food advocates, the city also attracted drug enthusiasts and the homeless. It was a paradise, no doubt, but one stroll far enough down the gritty Granville Street or into the gentrified and Disneyesque Gastown would let anyone know the snake had slithered into town along with yuppies.

Our ship docked not in the upscale downtown harbor but a mile or so away from the tourist ships. That meant we walked past junkies making drug deals in the entryways to rundown apartment buildings as we headed back and forth to buy last-minute items for the voyage. We sailed out, the ship's horns blaring, on August 31, 2002, heading west, leaving what remained of Eden in our wake.

From that moment on, for the next two weeks, the sea was our home. Each morning Jo-Ellen and I propped ourselves against the ship's rails and let the salty spray mist against our skin like incense from a religious service without a minister. Over time, I suppose, the sea has grown more pungent with the salt of the continents. In my mouth, it left the taste of another world, but a familiar one. After a few days, the vastness of the ocean made me long for the familiar distractions of the land just as the land had once made me yearn for the uncluttered sea. The second day out, at noon, Jo-Ellen sighted a whale's spout, and she pointed out to me the curve of black back breaking the smooth surface of the water. We watched and waited. For hours. For days. The ocean compels such attention, something akin to humility, I think, or at least a looking beyond self. On land, usually, we look to filter out and distinguish among individual images that crowd our consciousness, but on the ocean we strain to see the specific among the seeming sameness. Frost had it right, of course, when he suggested that there was only one way to look when confronted with the vastness of the ocean: "The people along the sand / All turn and look one way. / They turn their back on the land. / They look at the sea all day."

The ocean makes you feel as old as time itself. For the ancient Greeks, the sea was an endless river that circled the planet, a stream between the end of the earth and the beginning of heaven. The Pacific is not only the largest ocean but the deepest and, maybe, the most misapprehended. First it was misunderstood by a man who struggled with it on his way around the world in the early sixteenth century—Ferdinand Magellan. As Daniel Boorstin explains in *The Discoverers*, "During the whole three months and twenty days during which they sailed about twelve thousand miles through the open ocean, they had not a single storm. Misled by one experience, they named it Pacific." Magellan, like Columbus, was a discoverer *malgré lui*, a man whose greatest discovery may have been one he missed. Magellan thought he found a mild, pacific ocean, but he had sailed into what is most likely the Earth's largest, most turbulent body of water. Boorstin calls it Magellan's "greatest and most unwilling discovery." According to many historians, misnamed oceans aside, Magellan's journey was probably a more fantastic feat than any done by Columbus or Vespucci, two other famous misnamers. As Boorstin points out, Magellan "would face rougher seas, negotiate more treacherous passages, and find his way across a broader ocean." Magellan was a skillful seaman. He was proud and brave, setting out in the fall of 1519 in five barely seaworthy ships with 250 men on a voyage that had never been done before, or at least never chronicled. He held his crew together through mutinies and starvation and various disasters, but, it should be remembered, he himself didn't complete the circumnavigation. Magellan was killed near the

Philippines, cut down by poisoned arrows and scimitars when he held his ground so that his men could escape. Only eighteen of his crew—none rising to historical fame—returned to Seville three years later.

I was thinking of Magellan the next evening when Captain Ryan, in his lilting Irish tones, told a meeting of the entire ship's company, "We're just a sliver of steel in this wide, wide ocean." Off the starboard bow the following morning, a rainbow—pale green, yellow, and rust—streamed from a dark ribbon of the sky. Behind us, the sun bled through a carpet of clouds, and the sea was immeasurably beautiful. I wondered for a moment what lost sailors must have made of such omens, how Magellan's crew, years into their voyage, would have interpreted those signs. I thought for certain that Captain Ryan's warning had been simple Irish hyperbole, but in eight hours we awoke to ten-foot swells, spumes of spray dancing along the ridgeline of whitecaps that exploded to the horizon. It could have been romantic, an Impressionist's sky, the sea a quilt of light blue and steel grey, but most of the voyagers were too sick to appreciate it. Half the faces I saw around the ship were pasty yellow or pale green. During my first class, at least a half a dozen students walked out of the rolling room, narrow-eyed, jaw muscles popping as if they despised me. At first, I thought that was exactly the case. But as the sea rose and fell with a sickening regularity in the picture window of my classroom on the port side, I realized that I wasn't the worst teacher in the world—as I had at first suspected—but that my lessons were no match for nausea. At least I was able to comfort myself with the belief that my teaching didn't cause nausea. And given that I had to hold tight to the podium just to stand upright and was feeling queasy myself, I was perfectly satisfied with that meager achievement.

Unlike Magellan, I didn't have to deal with mutinies those first few days out, just an audience that rose and fell and changed hue before my eyes. Once I got used to the fact that nausea produced a look on someone's face that could easily be mistaken for apathy or hatred, then I was better able to control my impulse to hide in my cabin before class began. In the first place, the cabin was little bigger than my walk-in closet at home. The porthole (which could not be opened) looked out on to a metal stairway and a lifeboat beyond it. It was a nice reminder that if the waves got much bigger, the ship might capsize and then we'd all have our own little boats to bounce around in. However, the porthole had one advantage: you could, if you looked between steps and around the corner of the lifeboat, catch a glimpse of the ocean. The second reason the cabin wasn't an attractive sanctuary was that it was crowded with books and papers for class. But most importantly, perhaps, Jo-Ellen and I knew intuitively that spending more time than necessary in a 10 x 15 space might not help marital bliss.

Unlike Magellan, I didn't have to deal with starvation either. Food was never much of a problem for anyone onboard. Surely, there were plenty of complaints about the quality of it but never a complaint that there wasn't enough. The dining halls (two cafeterias that resembled high school lunchrooms) were always crowded—breakfast, lunch, and dinner (and a good source told me that 10 P.M. snack time was jammed as well). Students piled rice and pasta and slices of bread on top of one another in tottering leaning towers of carbohydrates that could have gotten them auditions as jugglers at the circus. It seemed they were determined to eat their way out of nausea or else recoup in calories every penny they could of the high cost of the trip. Fish and meat and potatoes all swam in the same light brown river of gravy. Three or four desserts balanced on the edge of most trays. In the first few weeks, previously svelte young women with flat stomachs jiggled into the dining halls like Turkish belly dancers. By the time we reached Japan, some had turned into sumo wrestlers. Others appeared ready for a twelve-step program, for in the evenings one of the dining halls was turned into a pub. Pub Night, which seemed to be about every night, was a strangely American phenomenon, a fraternity party on the high seas. It was a nightly drinking game. Many students drank as many beers and wine coolers as possible in the allotted time. Each student was in theory permitted two tickets, but that didn't stop some from buying tickets from other students. For these it became a chugging contest. At the end of the night, someone always ended up, in the students' terms, "sex-iled" from their rooms, left to drift around the corridors or on the decks, ghostlike, until the roommate took the sock off of the door handle. Some couples were more considerate of their roommates, and they squirmed into lifeboats or onto some vacant space on the floor of the theater. The next morning, red-eyed and ashen but vaguely smiling, they stumbled into the main hall where Core Geography class was held.

In the second week, shortly before we landed in Japan, the staff captain, Harry Sylvester, a tall, grey-bearded man with ironic eyes and a smile that could silence a room of 700 people, offered the students and passengers some admonitions.

"If you have to abandon ship, women and children first applies," he said, eyeing the college men in the first rows of the student union.

A white-haired professor sitting in the row in front of me turned to his wife and whispered into her ear, "Are there no perks on this ship for being tenured?"

"Doors are heavy," Sylvester continued. "Close them. If they're open and you have your finger on them, they could close. They probably will close and that will leave you with, if you're lucky, a smarting or broken finger. If you're not lucky, the finger will be severed. If this happens, try to remember to pick up your finger and put it on ice. That will make it easier for the doctor to sew it back later on."

He looked over at Dr. Jo Jackson, a slim woman in her late forties, who scrunched her shoulders together, smirked, and said, "I'll try to get some extra ice from the kitchen."

Sylvester told us about "Mr. Skylight" and "Code Blue" (medical emergency codes for the crew), and then he paused after saying "Mr. Mob." He looked slowly around the room, as if he were searching for the right young man to fix his eyes upon.

"That's *man overboard*," he said, "and God help you if you slip into the sea. The chances are *not* good that we're getting you back—dead or alive. It could very well be the last we ever see of you. A few years ago aboard a Semester at Sea voyage, a young man took it into his mind that he wanted to rappel from the deck of the ship and touch the water. Because I'm a kind man, I'll assume that alcohol was a contributing factor in that decision. If those are the kind of decisions you're capable of making, your first decision should be never to drink."

There was an audible gasp from many of the students in the audience, not, it seemed, from the thought of a young man rappelling from the ship but at the suggestion that they refrain from drinking.

Sylvester went on. "It was midnight. The young man had consumed enough wine, I suppose, to make this rappelling seem to be a fine idea. Or maybe he was naturally stupid. I can't really say for sure. What I know for certain is that he fell into the sea, into the pitch blackness of the night sea. I want you to imagine that for a moment."

Sylvester paused again for a few seconds so that all the people in the union could imagine themselves in the black water with the lights of the ship fast receding. It made my heart sink to think of the cold water and the hot adrenaline rush of despair.

"Someone happened to see him fall," Sylvester said, "and, most certainly, that piece of luck saved him. The ship performed a figure-eight maneuver and, miraculously, we retrieved him a few hours later. He was sent home at the next port. That was unpleasant for him, I'm sure, but the alternative would have been far worse. We don't want to search for you in the dark sea, and we don't want to call your parents to say that you've been lost overboard—so if any idea seems stupid to you, it is. Don't do it!"

After Sylvester dismissed us from the union, the faculty spent much of the rest of the evening sharing horror stories they had heard about past voyages, tales of students killed in a bus accident in India, pickpockets, armed robberies, rapes, drug busts. One woman recounted the story of a young man on a voyage a few years before who had been depressed at the start of the journey. In port in Venezuela, he jumped from the highest point he could find on the ship to his death on the concrete dock below. She told the story as if she had been there to see him commit suicide, describing the shadow of his body as it fell to the earth and the terrible bone-shattering thud it made as he hit the hard ground. "A bloody note was pinned to his chest," she said.

It was only a few days before we would arrive in Kobe, and during that time, we studied the ocean, each other, and the recent history of Japan. Our interport lecturers emphasized the Japanese inclination toward respect and civility. Our historians described the quiet suffering they said was intrinsic to the culture. We were all prepared, perhaps, for some encounter with the history of heartache in Japan, with a Buddhist acceptance of it, but I think we assumed it would have the arm's-length feel of history to it, the manageable distance of an academic abstraction. We didn't expect it to take on the personal shape it did.

Japan

You can almost guess from the map that Japan is a country of calculated spaces and deep reserve. It's about the size and shape of California, if that state were shaken free from the mainland by an earthquake and left to drift lonely in the Pacific Ocean. But unlike California, which seems overcrowded by most normal standards, Japan is a country so densely populated (in 2002 about 126 million) that manners are likely a key to survival rather than the extracurricular activity they often appear to be in the United States.

Our course across the Pacific Ocean from Vancouver to Kobe was 4,500 miles. For those two weeks, we paid attention to the warnings of the ship's staff and lost no one to the sea, but before we were to depart from Japan, we would leave one student behind—in prison.

Japan is a mysterious, difficult country to understand. Historically, it has kept foreigners out, and in a way it still does. It's not easy to sum up such a place. In the north, it has a climate like Maine's. In the south, like Florida's. Unlike the United States, there are very few truly poor people in Japan and relatively few extraordinarily rich. There is a genuine middle class. The Japanese are not known for their inventions, but they refine technological products with artful efficiency. Even their food products in stores like Sogo are museum-quality works of art. Many say that Japan is an efficiency-bewitched place, everything done with such precision and order that it could make a man develop a twitch. There's little question, though, that they have a knack for improving the original, whatever that item may be—cell phones, computers, cars, or iPods. As Pico Iyer says, "It's common to hear that Japan has created a promiscuous anthology of the world's best styles."

The country consists of more than 3,000 islands and about 60 volcanoes resting along the Pacific Ring of Fire. Most of what exists in Japan comes from somewhere else. Even their constitution was written by Americans some sixty years ago. In what often seems to be the chaos of Asia, Japan is a model of order. The Japanese may be more like Germans than any other people on earth. The larger the crowds, the more safe and orderly the movement of people, it seems. One standard joke about Japan is that if an American reaches out his hand to point something out to a friend, he'll knock over a dozen Japanese in the process. Most likely, those Japanese will skillfully sidestep the hand and bow politely, though.

It's difficult for an American to make sense of the contradictions— Shinto shrines and Pachinko parlors, a forest of neon and Buddhist temples, geishas and gaudy teenage girls, manga and martial arts. It is a country where hanami festivals are ever popular, celebrating the cherry blossom as a reminder of the beauty of life but also its impermanence. Buddhism is an integral part of Japanese culture, and Buddhists see the world as a vale of suffering. For Buddhists, all pain in the world is caused by desire, and only when the self and desire are set aside can someone be content.

With these thoughts in mind, I headed with Jo-Ellen and a group of students to Hiroshima. The bus from Kobe took five hours, a lot longer than the bullet train but much cheaper, too. My nonfiction writing class had read *Hiroshima,* John Hersey's account of the consequences of the atomic bomb, and most of us were thinking, I suspect, of some image from that book as we rode along the unremarkable landscape of the Japanese highway. Hersey recounts the story of the dropping of the bomb at 8:15 A.M. on August 6, 1945, from the perspective of six individuals who lived in the city of 250,000 people. Of those quarter of a million inhabitants, approximately 100,000 were killed with the first blinding burst of light. One hundred thousand more were injured and many thousands died in the days that followed. Hersey describes the "noiseless flash" of the bomb, what to many observers seemed to be a "sheet of sun," and he goes on to chronicle the fires that followed to consume the city. It is a picture of hell and a portrait of six individuals who lived through it.

As I sat in the bus, my head pressed against the window, looking for anything out of the ordinary in the prosaic road, I thought of my mother and how I had discussed *Hiroshima* with her the first time I had read it in high school. It was a book we could talk about only when my father was not in the vicinity. I also thought of Toshiko Sasaki, a twenty-year-old single woman who had lived at home with her mother, father, and three siblings, and one of the six Hersey follows. When the bomb struck, she had been in her job as a clerk in the personnel department of the East Asia Tin Works. At 8:15 A.M., Miss Sasaki had sat down at her place in the plant office and was in the act of turning her head to speak to a young woman at an adjacent desk. Miss Sasaki, who was severely injured but survived the bombing, sat 1,600 yards from ground zero. It was early afternoon when our bus approached the city, and I opened Hersey's book to the paragraph that described the moment of impact for the young clerk.

> Everything fell, and Miss Sasaki lost consciousness. The ceiling dropped suddenly and the wooden floor above collapsed in splinters and the people up there came down and the roof above them gave way; but principally and first of all, the bookcase right behind her swooped forward and the contents threw her down, with her left leg horribly twisted and breaking underneath her. There, in the tin factory, in the first moment of the atomic age, a human being was crushed by books.

As we came into the city, it seemed ordinary enough at first glance. If we expected to see immediately what Kenzuburo Oe described as "a nakedly exposed wound inflicted on all mankind," we were to be disappointed. Hiroshima is a modern city built on a grid system, with convenient trams and an unexpected nightlife. Hiroshima Castle was carefully reconstructed in 1958, and the Shukkein Garden is a typical Japanese oasis in the city, a mannered park of ponds, streams, miniature bridges, and clusters of pines. The city is located at the confluence of the Ota and Motoyasu rivers and had been rebuilt in the concrete, steel, and glass image of everything we had seen in Japan. But in the heart of the city, a haunting reminder of August 6, 1945, and all that remains of the old city, stood the A-Bomb Dome. The former Industrial Promotion Hall had been close to the hypocenter when the bomb dropped. The twisted girders and the skeleton of the building have been preserved by UNESCO as a reminder, left as Oe suggested as a nakedly exposed wound.

Jo-Ellen and I, along with a dozen students, walked to the Cenotaph, erected in memory of the victims of the bomb, and we marched solemnly through the museum, forcing ourselves to stare at the photographs of the rubble and charred bodies. Two memories stay with me from that day. It was the first time (although not the last on the journey) that I had been in a museum in which history was not written by Americans or friends of America. Most of us spent our school years reading history written by the victors. Being the victor in this museum was inglorious. I felt a complicated sense of shame for my country, for its history, for the little I had endured in my life. Gazing at the photographs of burnt children, their flesh the color of dark ash and their skin bubbled like hardened lava, I remembered vividly a moment in my own childhood. I was about nine or ten years old, and one day when I was rummaging through a bedroom closet, I found my father's Seventy-fourth Battalion Yearbook from 1943–1944. Beside the fresh-faced Seabees that smiled from the black-and-white photographs, there were images of bombed-out beachfronts, mangled palm trees, razed huts, and twisted metal on the island of Tarawa. All of these images fascinated me, as I recall, but one, when I came upon it after seeing pictures of my smiling, slim, and blond-haired father, held me in thrall. It was a photograph of a Japanese soldier's head placed on a tatami mat. The head, charred black, and the eyes burnt into scarred empty sockets, had been carefully placed in the sunlight so that its own shadow stood behind it like a circle of dried blood. The mouth was frozen open in a silent but never-ending scream, the teeth still white against the scorched skin.

For my father and many young men of his generation, Japan was this: kamikaze pilots, lost years on sun-bleached islands, nightmares of bodies left unrecognizable by flame throwers. Many, like my father, didn't talk about those years but remembered so vividly they would never even think about buying a Japanese-made car for the remainder of their lives. The Peace Memorial Museum showed me photographs that reminded me of that Navy album of my dad's, and it reminded me how I felt at nine years old, even if then my love for my father confused the meaning of those corpses in my mind.

Outside the dome, Jo-Ellen and I met a man who had been a seven-year-old child living in Hiroshima when the bomb dropped. That would have made him thirteen years younger than Toshiko Sasaki. In an epilogue written forty years after the dropping of the bomb, Hersey recounted what had happened in the intervening years to the six *hibakusha*, the A-bomb victims, whose stories he had told. In 1957 Toshiko Sasaki took the vows of poverty, chastity, and obedience and entered the French Catholic order of Auxiliatrices du Purgatoire, Helpers of Souls, as Sister Dominique Sasaki. Hersey's stories of the six survivors had a strange twist, it seemed to me. The fundamental effect of the bomb on those who survived was to make them more humane. Instead of making them bitter and selfish, their suffering had deepened their sympathy for others, made them more compassionate.

The survivor of the A-bomb who sat before us in the shade of the twisted metal and rubble of the Dome had the kind of smile that suggested he had been surprised by fate once and could never be shocked out of his equilibrium again. He looked older than most sixty-four-year-old Americans do. Not much taller than an adolescent, he was wizened and bent by something more powerful than mere years, it seemed. Three of his front teeth were missing. His eyes glittered in the sunlight that streamed, broken, through the remnants of the roof and building of the A-Bomb Dome, and they shone with an understanding and acceptance of the first principle of Buddhism—that life means suffering. As he spoke with us, translated by a young woman on the street, he spoke softly and smiled shyly the entire time. He said something like this:

> That was another lifetime ago, but I can see it as if it were yesterday. My mother and sister were both alive. My father had already died as a soldier in battle. Without my mother, we would never have stayed alive. We thought the world had come to an end, but she wouldn't let us die. And so we didn't. We lived through the fire and the days of sadness that followed. And I've lived this long now, remembering and coming back to see. To make certain it was not just a nightmare. And to meet others who come back to see. All that's left is to remember.

As he spoke to us, I realized that he was History. Hersey had understood that in his book, what many historians never fully grasp, that history is the individual story, the accumulation of individuals' stories, not a compendium of dates and facts. This man was what the story of the bomb was about, the individual standing against the faceless flash of a technology sparking out of control. Somehow he had survived destruction, and somehow Hiroshima and Japan had as well, rebuilding the cities and the country with a quiet courage and reserve and determination.

As we left him and I glanced over my shoulder, he was still smiling, an unfocused gaze in his eyes, and he reminded me for an instant of a child, of the ten-year-old Toshio Nakamura in Hersey's *Hiroshima*, whose voice ended the 1946 version of the story:

> The day before the bomb, I went for a swim. In the morning, I was eating peanuts. I saw a light. I was knocked to little sister's sleeping place. When we were saved, I could only see as far as the tram. My mother and I started to pack our things. The neighbors were walking around burned and bleeding. . . . Next day I went to Taiko Bridge and met my girl friends Kikuki and Murakami. They were looking for their mothers. But Kikuki's mother was wounded and Murakami's mother alas was dead.

The word *alas* seemed a part of every twisted girder and scarred brick within sight of the old man who had spoken to us. The word *alas* rose like a sigh from the very ground where he sat.

In Kyoto, the next day, we saw another Japan. Kyoto, a city founded in 794 as Heian-kyo, the capital of peace and tranquility, is bounded on three sides by mountains and bisected by the Kamo River. It is a city of gardens, castles, Buddhist temples, and Shinto shrines. It moves to a gentler rhythm than other large cities in Japan like Tokyo or Osaka. As big as Kyoto is, there's a sense of an ancient world alive in it. It's a city of tea ceremonies, an enclave for geishas, and the home of the Philosopher's Walk. The famous path wanders along the base of the Higashiyama Mountains, following the Shishigatani Canal. It meanders past Shinto shrines and Buddhist temples, and it's not difficult to spend a day along the path forgetting that any neon advertisements or high-rise buildings exist in Japan. Named for a Kyoto University philosophy professor, Nishida Kitaro, who used the cherry-tree-lined walk for his daily hikes until his death in 1945, the path is like stepping back in time. It obliges you to consider your place in the world, to reflect on everything and everyone around you.

Jo-Ellen and I spent the better part of the day walking or sitting on benches watching tourists and philosophers stroll along. Part of the time, Jo-Ellen tried on kimonos and I watched, silently admiring how beautiful she looked. She paraded in front of me and did her best to bow in the right coy geisha fashion. With her blonde hair and sky blue eyes, her freckles, her soft Irish beauty, she looked as far from Japanese as one could get. She laughed as she twirled in one kimono after another, the particles of sunlight flashing from her slender dancing frame. What struck me then about her, this woman I had known since she was seventeen years old, was her lack of vanity, that she really didn't know how beautiful she was, how much the atmosphere in the shop changed when she entered it, how much she transformed the world by her presence in it. I realized at that moment, looking at her, that I could very happily stay on the Philosopher's Path with her forever without one second of regret.

That night we drank beers in an Irish pub in Kobe. The waiter, a Japanese kid with a spiked hairdo and a pink streak running through it, wondered aloud if Jo-Ellen were the woman who had starred in the TV show *Moonlighting*.

"Isn't that you?" he asked. "That's you. Isn't it? I know it's you."

"You mean Cybill Shepherd?" I said. "She's too young to be Cybill Shepherd."

"No, that's not me," Jo-Ellen told him. She had heard it before. She draped her jacket over the back of the booth. She wasn't wearing a kimono. Besides being modest, she's a practical woman. The kimono was too expensive.

We both ordered Guinness, but the bar didn't serve it, so we settled for two Asahis and listened to the middle-aged Irish-American guys on acoustic guitars who were singing Beatles songs on the small stage in front of us.

For the moment, this seemed as accurate a picture of Japan as we could get—some strange land between a Shinto shrine and a bullet train. The waiter came back, perhaps to make sure Jo-Ellen hadn't lied to him about being Cybill Shepherd. For a few minutes he stood by our table, telling us his story. He had been a bouncer in Queens, New York, had gotten into some trouble, and decided it would be smart to start over again in the motherland of the Rising Sun. He fit in better than he would have at first supposed, he said. He had found some country in between America and Japan, I assumed. He had found a bar, at least, that seemed as American as it did Japanese. Half the people in the place were American or European men. The other half, draped on the arms of the men, were young Japanese women. Directly outside of the bar was the otherworldliness of modern Japan. Everything moved in a crowded dreamlike quiet in the eerie artificial light. Horns didn't honk and people didn't shout up to apartment windows as they might in Queens.

When we left the Irish pub, Kobe was ablaze in colored lights and flashing signs. A few yards down the street, outside an upscale noodle restaurant, a dozen men were laughing and shouting. It seemed that only drunk men or baseball fans made loud noises in Japan. The businessmen, briefcases at their feet, stood in a semicircle near the edge of the sidewalk. They were tossing a compatriot into the air, singing some phrase as they did it, laughing like schoolboys when they caught him again. The man being tossed turned to us as he landed in their arms. "This is the happiest day of my life," he cried. He had just retired from his job, and his coworkers were launching him into a new life.

"Come, come," they beckoned me to join them.

And I did, tossing him into the air as Jo-Ellen watched from the sidewalk. I stood there in their half-circle, shouting with these Japanese businessmen like one of the boys at summer camp.

The next day, our last in Kobe before we sailed out of port on our way to China, I read Yukio Mishima's short story "Martyrdom" to get ready for a class the following morning. My goal in my literature course was to find work by writers who reflected the cultures we were encountering. I couldn't have guessed as I looked over the Mishima story that morning how freakishly close his tale would come to our own experience. I had read a few of Mishima's novels and knew a bit about his dark, unconventional life. His real name was Kimitaka Hiraoka. Like many writers, he wrote under a pseudonym. But his reasons for doing so were probably quite a bit different than Mark Twain's or George Eliot's. Some say Mishima used the name to hide his young age when he began to write. Others suggest he wanted to keep his writing a secret from his father, a governmental clerk, a hard man with an attraction to military discipline, a father who took pleasure in ferreting out any "unmanly" interest in literature. Mishima lived a dual existence—perhaps like many writers—but within the strict codes of honor and conformity that make up an essential part of the Japanese heritage. Mishima's hidden homosexuality, for instance, must have seemed at times to him an unbearable burden. He was a man of deep secrets and complicated ambivalences. And surely with good cause. His relationship with his grandmother—who brought him up until she died in his early adolescence—bordered on bondage. Later, his relationship with his mother hinted at the incestuous. Fanatically patriotic and conservative, he probably never got over his guilt for not serving in the military during World War II. Because of an incorrect diagnosis, he was declared unfit for duty and instead worked in a factory while his peers saw the war to its bitter conclusion. Much like Professor Fugimaya, the main character of his short story "Act of Worship," Mishima, once he became a famous writer, had a "swarm of followers to whom he was a god." With those followers, he formed the Shield Society, a private army that was apparently organized to protect the emperor and to restore the samurai way and the old Japanese values.

Mishima spent most of his adult life living in two worlds. He was a married man with two children but he roamed the gay bars of Tokyo. He was a mama's boy who turned himself into an ardent bodybuilder. He was a prolific artist who fiercely wanted to live in the world of action rather than the imagination. He always sought the place where art and action converged. His books were often autobiographical or prophetic, leading him, ultimately, toward the moment on November 25, 1970, when, at the age of forty-five, he committed seppuku, ritual suicide. On that day, Mishima and a handful of his followers took a high-ranking general hostage on the Ichigaya military base and demanded to be heard by a gathering of the soldiers. He encouraged them to rise up and save Japan from businessmen and Western influences. "We watched Japan become drunk on prosperity," he had once remarked, "and fall into an emptiness of spirit." He wanted to be a martyr to his notion of the ideal Japan. After the soldiers jeered him off the balcony, Mishima praised the emperor and went inside the general's office to disembowel himself. One of Mishima's followers, Masakatsu Morita, tried three times to put him out of his agony by beheading him, but he failed each time. Another man, Hirojasu Koga, had to finish the job and then, after Morita failed to commit seppuku, Koga beheaded him as well.

Mishima's story "Martyrdom" was no less surreal than the writer's own death. The narrative hints at a suppressed homosexuality and chronicles a bizarre adolescent brutality. It had all the markings of a story about modern Japan—about peer pressure, conformity, and the culture of the mob—but it also reflected Mishima's bewildering attraction to what he saw as the relationship between beauty and death. As a boy, a picture he found of the martyrdom of Saint Sebastian had evoked a powerful erotic response in him. A fanatical love of beauty had led him to a fascination with martyrdom. In his story "Martyrdom," the mysterious bonds between spirituality and cruelty, beauty and death, brutality and sexuality, are summed up in the final scene where a prank becomes tragic and in turn, perhaps, miraculous.

I had just finished reading the story "Martyrdom" when Jo-Ellen came into our cabin and told me the rumor she had heard. The story had begun to circulate that David, one of the students on the ship, had been imprisoned in Japan. All I knew of David was that he came from South America and spoke English with an innocent decorum. Reading "Martyrdom" and hearing about David's imprisonment was one of those eerie coincidences that might not pass muster for fiction but that is fit to mention in nonfiction because it was true. By the time the story circulated to me, I heard that David had been in a fight after a night of clubbing in Kobe. Most of the faculty and many of the students were ready to believe that a privileged and perhaps arrogant Semester at Sea student had drunkenly attacked a demure Japanese man who was quietly minding his own business.

The story of the fight had all the elements of a kung fu melodrama— or maybe the conclusion of a Mishima story. By all accounts, David had been in a hotel elevator with another student when a young Japanese man entered with his girlfriend. For some reason, the man felt that David had insulted the girl. When the elevator door opened to the lobby, the young man stepped out, handed his wallet and cell phone to his companion, and ran back toward David with his arms poised to attack. David defended himself with a karate kick that pinned the young man's hand to the frame of the elevator. As if he were a character caught up in the surreal world of "Martyrdom," David's kick had severed one of the young Japanese man's fingers. That night David found himself in jail, tied to a chair, interrogated for hours.

A week later, after his father had flown from South America and hired a lawyer, when our ship had arrived in Hong Kong and most onboard assumed David was lost for the rest of the voyage, the Japanese officials came to the conclusion that he had only been defending himself. He was released and rejoined the ship. That's when I got to know David and found him to be as gentle and quietly polite as many of us might have imagined any respectful, carefully mannered Japanese person to be. We had a long way to go, but I had already discovered one of the first lessons of the journey: there was no uncomplicated way to define a culture. The real world was as mysterious and baffling as fiction could be, hanged corpses could disappear in a Mishima story, and fingers might fly off hands in the milky fluorescent light of a Japanese night. But perhaps David had discovered the deeper lesson—one that many people in Japan had learned years ago—that the world requires a payment from each of us.

China

The shadow of 9/11 had faded a bit by the time we reached China, but we had a more specific loss to deal with in Shanghai, our first port there. The day after we docked, one of our passengers, Barry, a ninety-two-year-old man who had sailed on Semester at Sea many times before, died. Lloyd Lewan, the executive dean onboard, a bearded, friendly bear of a man, spoke for the entire ship, booming out in his gravelly voice: "He was where he wanted to be, doing what he wanted to do. On his eighteenth voyage with us. We should all be as lucky to live our lives and end them as Barry did."

Barry's body was cremated in China. I never found out the cause of his death; maybe old age, or perhaps eighteen voyages around the world seemed enough for him, this as good a time as any to stop traveling. I didn't see Barry in his usual place in the cafeteria for about a week before he died. But I do remember that Dr. Jo, the physician onboard, a lithe woman who didn't look much older than the students, had lost her ever-present smile. Ordinarily, she skipped and smiled her way around the ship, more dance instructor, it seemed, than medical doctor. But now she moved swiftly and somberly past all of us. The night before he passed away, a death watch fell like a silence over the entire community. Along with May, his sprightly, bright-eyed ninety-two-year-old wife, the ship's community mourned his loss at sea. We gathered at twilight on the aft of the ship, sang "Amazing Grace," remembered Barry, and cast his ashes into the East China Sea. The *Universe Explorer* circled the moonlit water like the devious-cruising *Rachel* at the end of *Moby-Dick,* as if in search of a missing child lost at sea.

Barry's death made me think of my mother. It reminded me not only of the impermanence of everything but of the permanence of death for those who have lost someone. What had hit me the hardest in my mother's death was that I would never see her again on earth. I would never be able to call her and hear her excited response to one of my adventures or listen to her tell of her first sighting of Lake Como or her memories of Yosemite. Never have her gaze at me wide eyed after asking a question about a book she had just read and wanted my "expert" opinion on. There are only a few people in each of our lives who listen with genuine fascination to all our thoughts and experiences. For someone, Barry was that person, as my mother had been to me. For someone, his death meant he was gone forever.

Shanghai seemed even stranger than it might ordinarily have in the light of Barry's death. For many years, Shanghai had been called the "whore of the Orient," a town for scar-faced gangsters and the hedonistic rich, prim missionaries and slick-haired pimps, and it was still a place of extremes. But now those extremes seemed mainly abject poverty clashing with high-rise wealth. The glass façades of office buildings glinted in the smoke-clogged sunlight, and the city throbbed with commerce. I was reading Wei Hui's *Shanghai Baby* right before we got off the ship. The novel was banned and publicly burned in China when it was first published, maybe because it offered such a convincing description of the heart of one of China's most famous cities: "Shanghai is a city obsessed with pleasure. . . . All sorts of vehicles and pedestrians, all their invisible desires and countless secrets, merge with the flow like rapids plunging through a deep gorge. The sun shines down on the street hemmed in on both sides by skyscrapers—the mad creations of humans towering between sky and earth. The petty details of daily life are like dust suspended in the air. They are the monotonous theme of our materialist age."

After the sharp lines of modern Japan, Shanghai seemed to Jo-Ellen and me like a foreign planet. We tramped down the gangway of the ship and walked a few yards to a gate that opened to the screaming center of the city. It was a like Japanese pachinko parlor, an uncontrolled blast of sound. Bicycles, cars, trucks, motorbikes—all competed for the narrow streets. Horns honked, bells rung, engines roared, the sidewalks were cluttered with bikes, littered with debris. Meat and fish and vegetable aromas mixed with the sour smell of cats and garbage. Jo-Ellen held my

hand, and we dashed for our lives across a street that was a blur of traffic. On sidewalks we were tugged by street vendors— "Sixty yuan! No?
Name your price? What price? You tell me price! How much you pay?"
Women brandished calculators like magic wands. "Come look! You come
look my stuff!" Schoolgirls and women walked along arm in arm. Men
and women hawked phlegm and spit into ash cans or onto the blackened
streets. Mothers held children aloft so that they could urinate or defecate
into garbage cans in crowded shopping areas. Streetlights were mere sug-
gestions in Shanghai, little more than a recommendation for those who
had nothing better to do with their time. Red or green, just colors, nothing
to sincerely consider when crossing a thoroughfare.

By the mid–nineteenth century, the British and French took a sleepy
fishing town of 50,000 and transformed it into a major port of over a million people. Shanghai, a name that means "by the sea," was a city built
on trade—mainly opium, silk, and tea—and it became a synonym for
vice, known for opium dens, gambling houses, and brothels. When the
Chinese Communist Party took over the city in 1949, they cleaned up
the opium dens and houses of prostitution and worked on getting rid of
the pervasive slums. And they did a good job. In the process, they may
have erased its wild and forbidden charm. But in the 1990s, the central
government began to redevelop the city. Now there is a building frenzy
in a place with a population density that must rank close to the highest in
the world—more than 14 million in a 6,000 square kilometer area—but a
more incredible 7 million in the 220-square kilometer central city.

Jo-Ellen and I spent only one day in Shanghai, but it was enough
to feel that we were no longer close to orderly Japan. When we passed
through the gate leading from the port to the center of the city, we knew
we had left America far behind, that we had opened the door to a world
that was different from anything we had ever seen before. Too often in
America, I feel as if I am nowhere and anywhere. It doesn't seem to matter if I'm in a parking lot in Virginia Beach or a mall in Kansas City or
driving along a street in the suburbs of Atlanta: it all feels like the same
place. Who can distinguish one Burger King from another, one Levit-
town from its scion, one generic strip of American roadway in the South
from its second cousin in the North? It's what Walker Percy called the

"losangelization" of America, and it makes many feel as dislocated as if they were in one of those new beach developments in the Outer Banks of North Carolina, where every house looks exactly like its neighbor for mile upon dreamlike mile, and a disoriented newcomer can spend hours looking for his own townhouse. In Shanghai, we had entered a world that—for good or ill—was distinct. It took our breath away with the specificity of its smoky air and dirt, its jackhammers and shrieking street vendors, its soaring newness and deep-rooted destitution.

The next morning we flew to Beijing, the capital of the People's Republic of China, into the heart of the nation of forbidden places. The long history of Beijing mirrors the story of China itself, a tale of upheaval and change. Recorded settlement goes back three thousand years. Called Yanjing during the Liao dynasty, the city had its name changed to Dadu by Ghenghis Khan. His followers burned the city to the ground and his men slaughtered every living creature they could find. When the Ming dynasty took over in the fourteenth century, the city became Beiping (a name that refers to northern peace), and in the early fifteenth century it became the capital again and was named Beijing. In the last two hundred years, the story of struggle and change has been much the same—battles with French and English troops, conflicts among warlords, struggles with Japanese invaders, and clashes between Chiang Kaishek's Nationalist Party and Mao Zedong's Communist Army. Contemporary China is no longer the sleeping giant. The Communists organized the unwieldy land, and now it is transforming itself into a Communist-capitalist hybrid that threatens to gobble up the resources of the world.

The plane trip showed a land of vast reaches, and the airport suggested a country of shouts rending the polluted air, a place where people charged blindly into each other's spaces. Gone was the careful sidestepping of Japanese culture. *Demure* is not a word easily translated into Chinese. China has an area roughly the same size as the United States, but, in 2002, with 1.2 billion people, it had five times as many citizens. While many people living in a confined space seems to have made the Japanese decorous nearly to a fault, it has shaped the Chinese into an often aggressive and noisily argumentative people.

In 2002, people were still calling Beijing the "bicycle kingdom," a city of 10 million bikes, one for every other person or so. So I wasn't surprised by the cicada-like whir of bike tires as I stood on my first street corner in the city and breathed in the thick, sooty air. But I was surprised that I did not see tens of thousands of men and women dressed in blue Mao hats and jackets, the workers' fond emulation of their hero. Instead, I saw men and women flashing by in all kinds of colors—yellows, greens, browns—and in khaki pants and Members Only jackets. I watched them weave in and out of the hazy pollution caused not only by factories but by the staggering number of automobiles on the road. There were so many cars I could have been standing at an intersection in Washington, D.C. It made my palms get sweaty to think about the day when the middle class rises up in China, a billion or so strong, all demanding, like their American counterparts, to have gas for their SUVs. A few hundred years ago, Napoleon said, "Let China sleep, for when she awakes, she will shake the world." Within a half century, many experts predict that China's economy could be double the size of the United States's.

Despite its great leap forward into the twenty-first century, China is a country of superstitions and festivals—tomb sweeping day to worship ancestors, water splashing festival to wash away the sorrows and demons of the old year, or ghost month in August when the spirits from hell walk the earth and people would be wise to avoid swimming, marriage, and travel. We entered Beijing during the full moon festival. The festival takes place on the fifteenth day of the eighth moon, and it's not uncommon during that time to find a Chinese man gazing at the moon, setting off fireworks, or eating moon cakes in a back-alley family gathering. It is also a traditional holiday time for lovers, and it was not uncommon to see hundreds of middle-aged couples dancing in parks to ballroom music or dozens of couples on the side of the road practicing tai chi, moving like starfish floating in a translucent bay. Every movement seemed slower than the laws of gravity would logically allow. The dancing in the park was a lyric poem of arms and legs. It seemed that way, that is, until Jo-Ellen dragged me into the crowd. Then it felt slightly less than lyrical, more like being trapped at a high school dance in the ninth grade at Mount St. Michael's High School. But Jo-Ellen soon found another partner, a Chinese man who asked her or she asked him. It was hard to tell what was happening when my full concentration was on escape. But I enjoyed watching her, the only blonde-haired, blue-eyed American in a sea of black-haired, dark-eyed Chinese couples, drifting along as if she belonged to the music and the Beijing dusk. Jo-Ellen rolled her eyes when I looked at her, as if to say, "What am I doing here? Come rescue me." But I was certain she didn't need any rescuing—she never does—and I remained an observer until the man politely bowed to her when the music stopped.

Later that night we exercised with senior citizens on what appeared to be children's playground equipment on a side street near apartment buildings. Much of the real life of Beijing went on at a distance away from the wide boulevards built by the Chinese Communist Party. Away from those boulevards, old men practiced calligraphy as if it were an act of worship, and people scraped for a living in the shadows of skyscrapers. Old and new shared a precarious balance in Beijing, the market economy in a tug of war with the communist philosophy. The ads on television sold cars and mouthwash with the same vigor that one saw them being sold on American television. But for all of its cars and building permits, Beijing, like much of urban China, was full of silences. Our guide in Beijing, his name reinvented for us as Parker, made some things clear from the start of our journey around the city. "Keep all questions for the bus," he said. "No questions in Tiananmen Square, please. You can ask me anything you want on the bus, but be careful what you say outside, especially in Tiananmen Square. Don't ask people questions. Anyone could be listening." Another guide on the bus told Jo-Ellen that he could not talk about the "accident of 1989." A third guide we questioned—in the narrow corridors of a second-rate hotel—explained, "You know more about Tiananmen Square and 1989 than I do. What could I tell you that you don't know already? You see more than I do."

In Tiananmen Square, I was responsible for a group of about fifty students and other adults. Jo-Ellen was one of that group. She got lost and came close to being arrested and creating an international incident. With a few of the students, I was gazing at Tiananmen itself, the gate of heavenly peace, at the southern entrance to the Forbidden City, when I realized that Jo-Ellen was nowhere to be seen. The crowd around me looked like a forest of dwarf trees in the Pine Barrens of New Jersey covering the wasteland of cement that constituted the square. I saw a lot of faces but not hers. Leaving the students with "stay put—I'll be back," I pushed into the crowd the way you shove into a thicket of high weeds. After a few minutes, I was getting anxious, recalling Alfred Hitchcock films in which husbands lost their wives or children in foreign lands, in which innocent men and women are accused of crimes they didn't commit, and it didn't help that when I called her name out loud, my voice was quavering like Jimmy Stewart's. Everywhere I went, the threatening eyes of Mao from the monstrous image in the square followed me.

I saw a few flashes of light brown hair that I rushed toward, convincing myself that it might be blonde, but it was always the same German woman winding her way through the crowd, taking surreptitious photographs of the ubiquitous Chinese military police presence. Every police officer looked alike to me. All in neatly pressed green uniforms that were slightly too big for their bony frames. The coat sleeves hung down past their knuckles, the pants crumpled around the shiny brown shoes, and the hats made them look like children playing at being men. Most of the police I saw in Tiananmen Square didn't look a day over eighteen years old. But every uniform had glinting brass buttons, as if some mother wouldn't let her boy out of the house without a spit shine. The youthfulness of the police didn't make me feel better but worse. As I got older, I equated age with wisdom and mercy and youth with a testosterone-fueled disregard for such things. To add to my paranoia, I had just finished reading and discussing Ha Jin's story "Saboteur" with one of my classes onboard the ship. The story details the plight of Mr. Chiu and his bride in their encounter with the Chinese police in a restaurant near a railway station as they are about to start home after their honeymoon. For no apparent cause, one of the police officers in the restaurant throws a bowl of tea toward Chiu and his wife, splashing and damaging their shoes. When Chiu protests, the police arrest him for being a saboteur, for disrupting the public order. From that point, Mr. Chiu's situation unravels. He is beaten, imprisoned, interrogated, insulted, and eventually forced to admit to a lie so that he can be released. The story is reminiscent of McCarthyism in America or, more aptly, of the way things work in totalitarian regimes all the time.

Mr Chiu is dour but he is law abiding. When he is released, Mr. Chiu, a product of Mao's destructive Cultural Revolution, makes good the lie of saboteur that the police forced on him, and he infects the innocent populace of the town with hepatitis, dramatizing Ha Jin's point that societies founded upon repression and violence create self-fulfilling prophecies. In such societies, lies become truth.

Although I realized this was not the best story to be thinking about as I searched for my lost wife in Tiananmen Square, that's the thing about remembering something you shouldn't. Once you do, there's no way to make it fade away by being logical or rational. The more you try to be rational, the more irrational you become. I searched for about five minutes, the kind of five minutes that seems to be hours, and when I saw her, the crowd was parting from her as if she were Moses and they were the Red Sea. She was bending over helping up a pale-faced woman who was trying to rise up from the ground. The woman was dusting off her clothes and saying, "A cheeky lot of nerve they have, don't you think?" Two of the teenage police officers I had spotted in my search of the Square were walking away with a shopping bag in their hands, the one Jo-Ellen later told me they had confiscated for some reason from the woman. Jo-Ellen had come upon the argument between the woman and the police and witnessed the tug-of-war between them that landed the woman on the ground. Jo-Ellen helped dust the woman off, telling her that what had happened was an outrage, while I imagined my wife in prison after the police returned to arrest the woman and anyone who had aided her. But before my rich fantasy life could become reality, we heard Parker, our guide, barking, "Follow Parker! Please follow Parker! Follow Paaa Kaa! Where is the professor?" We saw his yellow tour guide flag flapping over the heads of the crowd like a college banner, and we followed it, knowing we could never tell him about Jo-Ellen's encounter with the police for it could easily have been seen as an attempt at sabotage.

Following the reedlike and bespectacled Parker as if his little yellow flag could protect us from any danger, we again marched under Mao's stern, watchful eye across the square. The image of Mao in Tiananmen Square is colossal, Orwell's Big Brother on steroids, and the face appeared to observe every move of the individuals in the crowd. Appropriately enough, Tiananmen led to the Forbidden City, and we went in, if for no other reason than to escape Mao's enormous gaze.

The Forbidden City was built in the early fifteenth century by over 100,000 artisans and probably close to 1 million laborers. It is situated on over 170 acres, with seventeen palaces, a moat, and a ten-meter-high wall surrounding a structure reminiscent of a Chinese box, one square fitting neatly inside the next. Home to two dynasties—the Ming and the Qing— and twenty-four emperors over 500 years, the palace, like most monuments of the past, was built on the backs of the many poor people who suffered and died in its creation. Only in 1912, with the abdication of Pu Yi, the last emperor, did the palace lose its status as a domain forbidden to all but those who had the emperor's permission. In 1924, after Pu Yi was expelled, the government turned it into a museum.

The palace was a city, a self-contained miniature world, surely, large enough for the emperor and his retinue of slaves and advisers and three thousand concubines. A magnificent statement of one man's wealth and power, it also showed how the emperor was imprisoned by his own authority. Being a god comes with drawbacks. The emperor needed to ensure male heirs, thus the thousands of concubines. I can't imagine even in my wildest fantasy what kind of a Mormon complexity of family relationships and jealousies this must have created. One wife (or husband) is enough for most mere mortals. Too much for many. But the emperor had a few wives and a few thousand concubines, to boot. Because of all the wives, he had a few thousand eunuchs, as well.

Eunuchs have a long history throughout the world—in Greece and Rome and India. They were used for their lovely soprano voices in the Vatican choir until they were banned in 1878. They attended Indian princes under British rule. They served Egyptian pharaohs. But they had an especially significant role in the Chinese imperial story. With three thousand nubile women and only one emperor—even a godlike one—eunuchs were the allowed palace guards to make certain that any child born to a concubine was the emperor's heir. Pre–DNA testing, the eunuchs were the last line of defense, the only way to make sure the next son of heaven was not a fake. They had to keep a watchful eye on all those women with so much time on their hands and so little to do.

Some parents had their sons castrated because it was a possible avenue to advancement and job security. One emperor said that he trusted eunuchs because they were "creatures docile and loyal as gelded animals," and others assumed that never being able to have sons would eliminate a eunuch's sense of ambition and thus make him exempt from political intrigue. Of course, none of this was even close to the truth, and eunuchs were probably involved in more political intrigue than Rasputin and his cohorts ever were. Eunuchs often corrupted their charges so that they could control them when they came to the throne. But who can blame them, I suppose, after what they had to go through to get the job. It is probably unnecessary to offer a specific description of the surgery. Let's just say it was radical, and to make matters worse, the eunuch had to make sure that the severed parts, the pao, were hermetically sealed and displayed on a shelf. A eunuch aspiring for promotion needed to be reexamined by the chief eunuch and show his pao, or "precious." If he lost his pao (although it sounds like the kind of thing one would be careful with) or if they were stolen, the eunuch would have to rent a set from another eunuch.

As I thought about all of this walking through the Forbidden City, I clutched Jo-Ellen's hand, thankful to have only one wife. I remembered the day before complaining to her that I was tired of carrying our precious passports around all the time in the money belt that bulged at my waistline. Right then and there, standing in front of the emperor's throne, imagining a dozen eunuchs bowing before the emperor and at the same time eyeing their pao, I vowed never to complain about such things again.

The next day, in Badaling, I was able to shake thoughts of passports and other matters out of my mind as I contemplated the magnificent stone wall snaking out along the ridge line of the mountains as far as I could see, into a fog-shrouded world impossibly remote from Beijing. The Great Wall, 4,500 miles long, was another attempt, like the Forbidden City, to keep ideas, along with people, out. Begun two thousand years ago, it was actually many separate walls built by independent kingdoms to shut out invaders. It was built in stops and starts over those years by millions of workers, hundreds of thousands of them political prisoners, exiles, and conscripts. Some historians suggested it was more than legend that, besides earth and stone, the bodies of dead workers were used as part of the building materials. And many must have died carrying heavy stone blocks up the mountainsides on their backs in the baking sun. Over the years, the wall was forgotten and many miles of it disintegrated from exposure to the elements and neglect. What rescued it, of course, was not traditional Chinese xenophobia but its opposite, the love of the tourist dollar.

Badaling had probably more tourists climbing the Great Wall than a daunted Ming emperor could have envisioned in his worst nightmare of invasion centuries before. About fifty miles northwest of the heart of Beijing, the Badaling section of the Great Wall was restored in the late 1950s. The army of tourists that descended upon it after that made it necessary to build not added defenses but a cable car to keep them moving swiftly up to the inner ramparts, what amounts to a highway twenty-five feet above the ground that once had thousands of defenders staring toward the wild west. Now, everyone streamed in from the east, and it was the tourist who had to be careful. Every person walking up the hill toward the cable car or the steps leading to the wall had to pass through a gauntlet of screaming hawkers, selling everything from T-shirts to "authentic" Chinese jackets to gold-painted Mao cigarette lighters that played the national anthem as the flame changed from yellow to green. They called to us as if they had all been trained by the same sales manager.

"Hello. Hello. You buy from me. What your name?"

Jo-Ellen usually stopped to tell her name and say we would look at their wares on the way back down. That was a tactical mistake because on our way back, in our weakened condition a few hours later, every stall owner had the same cry.

"Jo, Jo. I remember you. You come buy from me. You promise. I remember you, Jo."

I ended up with two Mao lighters, a blue silk jacket, a Mao watch in which the green-jacketed leader waved a friendly hand as if he were signaling a cab, two T-shirts, a comb, and five postcards offering the same pictures of the wall that I had on my camera. But I have to admit, years later I still have the Mao watch. His hand still waves if you wind it every half hour or so, and the lighter changes flame from yellow to green and whines out the Chinese national anthem with an annoying consistency. The blue silk jacket I gave to a friend who I never heard from again.

The Great Wall was one of those structures, like Stonehenge, that you expect to be a disappointment because you have seen it so many times in the media—you assume it will be impossible to see afresh or genuinely. As Walker Percy said in his essay "The Loss of Creature," for the tourist, "the thing is lost through its packaging." But for some reason, once I was atop the wall and gazing out into the distance, seeing it stretch before me as if it circled the earth, I felt the way I did when I had seen Stonehenge years before—taken by surprise. It was as if I were seeing this amazing sight for the first time in my life. And that, I understood, was the only difference between being a tourist and a traveler. It was *seeing*. I wasn't sure what it took exactly—luck, some special concentration, or strenuous effort—to see things anew, but I sensed that struggle was what this trip was really about.

I was thinking about the question that night in Beijing as we walked through the city and saw everything in its congested and confused harmony. Everything was measured in slivers and inches—and pennies and fractions of a yuan. The cars and bicycles and people all navigated atoms of space on the roads, avoiding collisions by an exhalation of breath or a half second. That night in Beijing, we saw a different China from the one we had seen—children playing with hula hoops in the moonlit back alleys, families cooking in woks outside their front doors, more ballroom dancing in the parks and tai chi ballets under the streetlights. I didn't try to make sense of it all—the open, smiling faces contrasting with the urgent cries of "Dollar! Dollar!" from street vendors and the grasping hands pulling us in for a sale. I just held onto whatever form of "negative capability" I could muster and watched.

In the morning, as we flew from Beijing to Hong Kong, where we were to meet up with the ship, I peered out the window at the endless, epic landscape of China below and remembered a book my mother had bought for me when I was a boy. When I was in high school, she had given me a copy of *The Good Earth* by Pearl S. Buck, one of her favorite novels. For many years, that book gave me my only notion of China. Wang Lung, the main character, a simple farmer, had been my picture of the place. He was the land and its recent history, from the old China to its revolutionary present, and his story is a naturalistic tale in which his wife, O-lan, the moral center of the narrative, dies after many years of suffering and, ultimately, humiliation. Wang Lung works hard and rises in the world, only to fall and rise again, but the last scene of the book tells the far-reaching and ironic story of the country, a story in which tradition and honor and loyalty are lost. Wang Lung is an old man and he stands with his two sons on the land that he has given his life to: "And his two sons held him, one on either side, each holding his arm, and he held tight in his hand the warm loose earth. And they soothed him and they said over and over, the elder son and the second son, 'Rest assured, our father, rest assured. The land is not to be sold.' But over the old man's head they looked at each other and smiled."

Buck's portrait of China matched the one I had seen, a hard naturalistic world in which the odds were not good for tradition to survive the onslaught of commerce.

If any place on the planet was proof of the power of commerce, it was Hong Kong. It was the strange netherworld that Pico Iyer described in *The Global Soul* this way:

> the rare city that had been built up almost entirely by people from abroad, and so had become a kind of Platonic Everyplace, the city-state as transit lounge . . . Hong Kong felt like a hyperconvenient luxury hotel, a shopping mall-cum world trade center where there were no taxes, few real laws, and no government other than the freest of markets. English was spoken, even major credit cards were accepted and, just around the corner from me, there were 7-Elevens and a Circle K, open at 4 A.M. Entering Hong Kong could feel a little like going on-screen, into a world buzzing with options and graphics, itself a kind of rough diagram of the digital city of the future.

Iyer was right—the place seemed more like a music video on MTV than a city. Our ship docked alongside the labyrinthine shopping mall of Ocean Terminal, and even some students, skillful and experienced shoppers as they were, got lost in the maze of turns and couldn't readily find their way back.

We had only one day in Hong Kong, so we spent it becoming part of the culture, shopping, eating, and getting ten-dollar haircuts in an establishment where every stylist looked like Edward Scissorhands and cut hair with the same slightly unnerving and awe-inspiring speed and dexterity. Jo-Ellen's wavy blonde hair was now as short as mine and barely blew in the wind as we took the Star Ferry back to Kowloon, a name that refers to the nine dragons suggested by the peaks on the peninsula. On the ferry, just before we returned to the Ocean Terminal and its confusing corridors of upscale stores, we saw two men who appeared to be subsistence fishermen on a bridge in the shadow of one of those peaks, both using crab traps and white plastic buckets. In one hand each held a frayed rope attached to the bucket, and in the other hand each held a cell phone that sparkled like a newly minted coin in the sunlight. It wasn't surprising to see them, framed by skyscrapers towering above them and shacks below them near the water's edge. Some of the wealthiest and some of the poorest people in the world live in Hong Kong, in what is some of the densest real estate on the planet, millions of people stacked like CDs in forty-story buildings.

Like Shanghai, Hong Kong was once a small town on the edge of one of the world's finest deep-water harbors. The Portuguese had taken over nearby Macau as a trading center, but Hong Kong was not much more than a fishing village. By the mid-1800s, though, the opium trade had paved the streets with gold. For years, the British had balanced the tea trade deficit by selling opium to the addicted masses in China. By the early part of the nineteenth century, opium had become a significant source of income for British merchants. When the Chinese government, fed up with the debilitating effects of the drug on its people, declared opium illegal and confiscated 20,000 large chests of it, the first Opium War began. British military might forced the Treaty of Nanking in 1842, and Hong Kong, which means "fragrant harbor," was given to Britain "in perpetuity." Twenty years later, and after a second war about opium, Britain acquired Kowloon, the part of the mainland facing Hong Kong. Over the years of British domination, Hong Kong became the business capital of the Far East for a number of reasons. Initially, Chinese merchants moved there because they sensed British rule would mean free-wheeling trade. Laborers followed, and political and financial refugees as well. In 1984, however, after two years of difficult negotiations between the

British government and Chinese leaders, an agreement was made that Hong Kong would be given back to the People's Republic of China in 1997 with certain stipulations about human rights and democratic and economic freedoms in the territory for the next fifty years. Hong Kong became a "Special Administrative Region" of the PRC. Thousands lined up for British passports and emigrated, fearing what Communist Chinese rule would mean politically and economically, but millions stayed, perhaps because Hong Kong had always been a place to come to, not a place to leave.

On the evening of September 26, 2002, we sailed out of Hong Kong Harbor, the glowing city like a strobe light against the shadow of the mountains. At night, the city was as close to dreamlike as any I had ever seen, the skyline aflame with multicolored lights that burned into my memory like the afterimage of a camera's flash. In three days we would be in Vietnam, entering a past I had not lived but had dreamed of so often it felt more real than actual experience to me. A few moments before stepping on deck to watch the lights of the city disappear, I was reading another favorite book of my mother's, the *Tao de Ching*. One of the passages she had marked was verse 27, which began this way: "A good traveler has no fixed plans / and is not intent upon arriving." Finding her marked passage was like hearing her voice once again, a mother's advice between the lines. I tried hard to understand the underlined idea as I yearned to see Vietnam after thirty years of dreams and nightmares about the country. As the lights of Hong Kong Harbor faded to the black emptiness of the South China Sea, I read the concluding lines of that verse:

> What is a good man but a bad man's teacher?
> What is a bad man but a good man's job?
> If you don't understand this, you will get lost,
> however intelligent you are.
> It is the great secret.

Getting lost was all too easy, I realized, and I had a suspicion that Lao-tzu was reflecting on the necessary and complicated relationship between the imagination and action, between dreaming and duty. Traveling was a way of being in the world, my mother and he might be suggesting, not a way of getting to a place.

Vietnam

In Ho Chi Minh City, we ate the beating heart of a cobra, drank its warm, licorice blood, and learned that the *Tao* works better than traffic lights when you are trying to cross the street. Crossing any major street—and most small ones—in the former Saigon requires the skill of a kung fu master and the wisdom of a Tibetan lama. Only occasionally were there streetlights, and those worked only in a desultory way. When they did work, drivers treated them, at best, with a casual disregard. Pedestrians were compelled to trust the flow of traffic, to have faith that it would stream around them as they entered its mayhem. We were warned as we left the ship, "Never run, never dart out into an opening, always step out gently into the midst of cars and bikes and walk determinedly forward. Forget everything you ever learned or were taught as a child about crossing the streets in New York City or Boston or Atlanta. None of those rules apply. In Vietnam, the cars and motorbikes will float around you as if you were protected by magic. Just keep walking across the street at a steady pace and you will find yourself safe on the other side." I expected the advice to come from a Buddhist monk who called me "Little Grasshopper," but it came from Karen Burns, the field office coordinator on the ship, a woman as unlike David Carradine's Kwai Chang Caine in the television series *Kung Fu* as any person on the planet could be. Always smiling, with excess energy drifting off her like fuel exhaust, she was, by most accounts, "perky"—a word few would use to characterize Carradine. Once I saw the heart-stopping traffic in the city, I was glad that I had paid attention to her admonitions. I threw away my well-learned notions of looking both ways and then making a mad dash for the other side of the road. Instead, I trusted to an Eastern oneness with the universe and the vehicles that screamed toward and around us, slicing in front of and behind Jo-Ellen and myself, but always missing us, by inches, milliseconds. The motor-cycles, cars, and cyclos—a bicycle rickshaw common in Vietnam—drifted by as if I had just dreamed them up. No one knew exactly how anyone survived the chaos, but somehow it all worked.

From the South China Sea, we had sailed into the murky green waters of the Saigon River on the morning of September 30. By early light, we were heading into the center of Ho Chi Minh City, traveling on a bus from the ship, a thirty-minute trip from where we were docked. We had to share the road with more bicycles and motorbikes than I had ever seen in one place in my life, thousands and tens of thousands of them, it seemed, all crisscrossing one another without signaling, without having to sig-nal, without having even to look left or right. Young women in masks and long-sleeved gloves to protect them from sunlight and pollution rode motorcycles past alleyways in which herds of cats and dogs vied for space with roosters and people and carts of fish—and more dogs. As a Vietnam-ese man who spoke a perfectly accented and grammatical English learned from dealing with tourists on the streets of the city told me, "People in Vietnam are dog lovers, like Americans. Vietnamese are closer to their dogs, though. We like them for pets, but we like them to eat, also. Tastes like chicken, eh? Everything tastes like chicken, I guess. But dogs are a good luck chicken."

I didn't eat any dog in Vietnam, at least not that I was aware of at the time. On the whole, our food was delicious—seafood and fresh vegetables, spring rolls and handmade candies—and so inexpensive that we could contemplate living there like kings and queens on $5 a day. Everything seemed inexpensive—clothing, transportation, hotels, massages. But everything required negotiation, and students from our ship negotiated over 5,000 dong (40 cents in U.S. dollars at the time) as if it would make a significant inroad into their weekly allowance. A few students reput-edly belonged to what they called the $10,000 club, a group that strove to spend—for each individual—that much money in each port. By my calcu-lations, that would have meant finding a way to spend many millions of dong, but it was too high for me to count, so I paid for everything I bought in American dollar bills. In the Dong Khoi section of the city, we ate in a restaurant called Lemon Grass, with appetizer, soup, entrée, dessert, and beer for $4 a piece. At first glance, everywhere we went the people were smiling and friendly and beautiful. Even the beggars or kids on the street selling postcards or coconut milk appeared to be taken up by the energy of the city. Most of the people we saw had to be under thirty, but Graham Greene's intuition in *The Quiet American* seemed as true then as it had likely been fifty years before—"with the Vietnamese age drops suddenly like the sun—they are boys and then they are old men." The children, men, and women I saw were beautiful, sloe-eyed apparitions. Everyone else was stooped over with wear and age. I never saw anyone who might be considered middle-aged by American standards. People in Vietnam, as Greene suggested, leapt over those years as if they didn't exist.

I had bought a copy of *The Quiet American* from one of those women who had left her youth behind her a few seconds before. She looked at me with pleading eyes, her youth haunting them like a ghostly recollection. She pressed a stack of pirated books toward me outside the main post office, a lovely French building framed by cyclo drivers and adolescents selling postcard images of the countryside. It was a dizzying pleasure to read a pirated copy of Greene's novel in Saigon. The narrative is an investigation of the subtle relationship between innocence and experience. The American Pyle is seemingly naïve, a U.S. government official in Vietnam at a time before the American war fully started. Like Henry James before him, Greene ponders the question of innocence and the harm it may do in the world and considers that a person like Pyle may actually create more evil than a cynical, experienced man like the narrator, Fowler. There was something surreal about looking up from the pages of a novel that drew me into its story with the force of true experience and being in the very setting that the writer was describing. It was like waking up from a dream about a place to find myself in that very spot, and trying for a moment to distinguish between waking and sleeping life. I followed Pyle and Phuong into the Continental Hotel. I watched the same busy streets that they observed. The same waiters bought Jo-Ellen and me Tiger beer. Nothing had changed from the novel. I was inside it.

Stranger than reading Greene's novel in Vietnam was standing in that country thirty years after my own nightmares about being sent to fight there. Like many men of my generation, I had some survivor's guilt about escaping the war in the early 1970s. As for many of my friends, college gave me a deferment, and then the lottery (the only one I've ever won) freed me to live my life at home in the Bronx. During those years at Fordham University, I wondered what kind of a soldier I'd have made or if I would have been brave enough not to go. Years later, after reading Tim O'Brien's *The Things They Carried*, in which he described the moment when he decided to go to war, I knew his life could have been mine: "The day was cloudy. I passed through towns with familiar names, through pine forests and down to the prairie, and then to Vietnam, where I was a soldier, and then home again. I survived, but it's not a happy ending. I was a coward. I went to war."

In 1968, I followed every piece of news I could find on the Tet Offensive. My good friend Frank Fitzpatrick, more older brother than pal, had broken up with his girlfriend and, with the self-pitying sense of melancholy and Romanticism that only seventeen-year-old boys can muster after listening in a drunken stupor to the song "Soldier Boy" over and over again on the jukebox of a Bronx bar, he had gotten his parents' permission and joined the Marines. He was sent to Vietnam right before the North Vietnamese and Vietcong began the assaults of January to June in 1968. Each morning I read the papers, and each evening I watched the news accounts of the heavy artillery bombardment as if I were the one being shelled, not Frank. When he returned home after the battle of Khe Sanh—home for good before his tour of duty was complete—he had been transformed like some character in a twisted fairy tale. He had gone to war a confident, smiling boy, the companion who always knows how to talk to the girls, the one who always finds the right thing to say; and he returned a silent older man. When I looked into his eyes, they had a knowledge of something I could not fathom. It scared most of us to see that life could change that fast, that one day we too might be men who knew more than we wanted to know. When I went out for a few beers with Frank, I wanted my old friend back, but he was gone forever.

The next fall, with Jo-Ellen, I took a train from New York City to Toronto. The rolling hills of New York State had already lost their blush and chilled to a somber brown. The sky was an unending grey tunnel as the train shook its way up to Lake Ontario and traced its shoreline into a wintry Canada. Jo-Ellen and I went to the unimpressive storefront that served as the headquarters for Draft Resisters Coalition. The young men who worked there weren't rabid revolutionaries but, like me, ordinary nineteen-year-olds, and, like Frank Fitzpatrick, they had a look in their eyes that told me they had made a decision that would stick with them for life. Jo-Ellen and I returned to the United States after a few days talking to draft resisters and exploring Toronto. I made no decisions about what I should do, and I could easily imagine myself in two years, when I graduated from college, in the military and on a troop transport heading toward Vietnam. Most nights, as I closed my eyes to sleep, I saw myself in Canada or Southeast Asia, and when I dreamed, I felt the chill of death either way.

On July 1, 1970, the night of the lottery, I played basketball at Public School 8 near my apartment instead of sitting home and listening to the numbers announced on the radio. Many of my friends—surely more logical than I—stayed home to watch Representative Alexander Pirnie reach into a large glass bowl and pluck out a blue capsule, open it, and read with heartbreaking clarity for many the first date—September 14. It hadn't been long before that I had read Shirley Jackson's "The Lottery" in my high school English class, and death and chance now seemed as luridly connected in my life as they did in her story. I returned home after all the dates and numbers had been chosen. I called my friend Dennis Murphy to find out if he knew anything.

"June 18th?" he asked. "Damn, your number is 12."

He drifted off into silence. After all, what could he say? We exchanged a few mumbled curses about Nixon and Westmoreland, and I spent the rest of the night in my bed with my eyes wide open seeing in the darkness my bleak future, no matter what course I chose.

The next morning I picked up the *New York Times* and saw that my number was in the 300s and out of draft range unless the NVA decided to attack Minnesota. When I called Murphy again, he said, "Aw, shit, I was only kidding." I responded the only way I could, saying, "Fuck you," hanging up, and promptly forgiving his joke because I was a man who had been given a new life and deserved to be generous with everyone else in the world. But Murphy's joke was most likely the sort I could have expected if I had ended up in Vietnam, the kind that Tim O'Brien describes when he recounts a soldier named Azar strapping a Claymore antipersonnel mine to another soldier's orphan puppy and squeezing the firing device. O'Brien explains it this way: "The average age in our platoon, I'd guess, was nineteen or twenty, and as a consequence things often took on a curiously playful atmosphere, like a sporting event at some exotic reform school. The competition could be lethal, yet there was a childlike exuberance to it all, lots of pranks and horseplay. Like when Azar blew away Ted Lavender's puppy. 'What's everybody so upset about?' Azar said. 'I mean, Christ, I'm just a boy.'"

From that point on, the war in Vietnam became a moral and philosophical problem for me but not a desperate choice between life and death. Nevertheless, it haunted me because I had been lucky enough to have so easily escaped its horrors. As a young writer, I wrote more stories about Vietnam than I did about the Bronx, where I had lived my whole life. That country thousands of miles away held my imagination in a vise grip for years.

Now, all those years later, I was there by myself, having left Jo-Ellen and a friend to shop in the Dong Khoi section of town. I had thought hundreds of times about being there, idling along in the melting early October heat past Notre Dame Cathedral, a Romanesque church with iron spires that preside over the skyline in the government quarter. I was heading towards the War Remnants Museum, and time slipped away. I was nineteen years old again and in Vietnam. I was living the past I had been destined to live. Anyone could be my enemy. The woman in a rice hat coming up the street carrying two sacks of rice balanced on a pole resting on her shoulders. The fruit seller kneeling on the cracked sidewalk. The fortune teller, the schoolgirl, the slim man lounging on his Honda Dream as if it were a hammock. Death could be lurking anywhere. But, when I looked more closely, there were nothing but smiling or indifferent faces all around me, and the dream was of the past, not the present. I shook my head clear of that other time and came to the present, the grimy streets of Saigon on a noisy Saturday afternoon. I was not reminded of *Apocalypse Now* or *The Deer Hunter* but of Proust and the enigma of time. I became a time traveler, riding back into a past I was not required by fate to live, and, for those moments walking along the streets of Saigon, pressing forward into a future I had imagined so often it had become as real as a recurring dream.

Once known as the Museum of Chinese and American War Crimes, the name had been changed to the War Remnants Museum so it would not offend the Chinese and American tourists nor, I suppose, hinder the flow of their dollars. But like the museum in Hiroshima, it did not paint a flattering picture of the United States. In the yard, American artillery, bombs, and tanks were on display, a sculpture garden of killing technology that was not enough to defeat the spirit of a peasant farmer army. Inside the building, there was a guillotine used by the French to take care of Viet Minh "troublemakers," but most of the photographs depicted American atrocities—napalmed jungles, babies disfigured by Agent Orange, and the guiltless victims of My Lai. Standing there looking at a photograph of a charred corpse of a young Vietnamese woman, I realized that they were right—this was the American War. I had gotten the name wrong for the past thirty years.

With my literature class on the ship, I had been reading Tim O'Brien's *The Things They Carried,* but I had been reading the Vietnam writer Bao Ninh's *The Sorrow of War* at the same time. For me, O'Brien's collection of stories was the more lyrical and powerful, a work of literature that would stay with me forever, but Bao Ninh's novel offered something that O'Brien's could not—a picture of the war from the perspective of a North Vietnamese soldier. Similar to O'Brien's *The Things They Carried,* Bao Ninh's story was an autobiographical account of his experiences as a soldier. One of five hundred men who went to war with the Glorious Twenty-seventh Youth Brigade, Bao Ninh was one of ten to survive the years of conflict. Originally published in 1991 and banned shortly after for its antiwar sentiment and critical view of the Communist Vietnamese war machine, *The Sorrow of War* offers a dark and heartbreaking picture of the lasting effects of the American War on Vietnamese soldiers and citizens. As Bao Ninh says, "The sorrow of war inside a soldier's heart was in a strange way similar to the sorrow of love." Bao Ninh's story had this, among other things, in common with O'Brien's story—they were both about love as much as they were about the tragedy of war.

Both were about the lingering consequences of the brutality of battle, the humanizing nature of storytelling, and the changing shape of truth and memory.

In one passage, Bao Ninh describes his main character, Kien, as he is being tracked by an American patrol with a German shepherd:

> The dog was pulling at a strong leather leash which was held by a black soldier wearing a bullet-proof vest and steel helmet. Another black followed him, this one bare-chested except for a massive cartridge belt slung diagonally across his body. Following him a white American, also well-muscled and naked from the waist up. Then a fourth . . . and there were others, fanned out behind the fourth. It was difficult to tell just how many, but they were quick and light-footed in the jungle, and they moved relentlessly, like cunning wolves on a trail, in total silence.

For the first time, I had read an account of the terror a young North Vietnamese soldier felt in facing the strong, well-armed, and carefully trained American soldiers. O'Brien's story was mine, but Bao Ninh's was, too. The American War *was* the Vietnam War. They were both mine. What Bao Ninh said, he said to me as much as he did to his Vietnamese readers: "What remained was sorrow, the immense sorrow, the sorrow of having survived. The sorrow of war."

The next day in the Cu Chi tunnels on the outskirts of Saigon, the war seemed even closer at hand. Cu Chi was in a location known as the Iron Triangle during the Vietnam War. The tunnels, which stretched from near Saigon to the Cambodian border, helped the Vietcong control the rural area around the capital of South Vietnam. The Vietcong mounted attacks on Americans and ARVN troops from the underground passages—even within the confines of the U.S. military base at Dong Du—and disappeared into hidden trapdoors. In the district of Cu Chi, there were more than 250 kilometers of underground corridors snaking through the jungle. The shafts were often several dozens of feet deep and contained field hospitals, command centers, kitchens, and living areas. When we crawled down into the tunnels with about thirty students, it was hard to contemplate being there for an hour, let alone living there for weeks or months at a time. Most of the students came out of the tunnels with their eyes narrowed with anxiety. Many couldn't go in at all. The tunnels—even the enlarged and upgraded versions, widened and smoothed out with cement—had an aura of darkness and death to them. For many, just squeezing into the trapdoor and going under the ground produced a visceral fear. My students and I had read and discussed all of the stories in Tim O'Brien's *The Things They Carried,* but before we came to Cu Chi we spent a good deal of time talking about his account of American soldiers crawling down alone into the enemy's hiding place:

> They would sit down or kneel, not facing the hole, listening to the ground beneath them, imagining cobwebs and ghosts, whatever was down there—the tunnels squeezing in—how the flashlight seemed impossibly heavy in the hand and how it was tunnel vision in the very strictest sense, compression in all ways, even time, and how you had to wiggle in—ass and elbows—a swallowed-up feeling—and how you found yourself worrying about odd things: Will your flashlight go dead? Do rats carry rabies? If you screamed, how far would the sound carry? Would your buddies hear it? Would they have the courage to drag you out? In some respects, though not many, the waiting was worse than the tunnel itself. Imagination was the killer.

Imagination was the killer. We had no enemy to fear, but many students still could not crawl through the tunnels. I felt my own heart start to beat faster as we entered the close darkness. In our group, a girl screamed when a bat flew into the tunnel. Our group went from the twenty who entered the tunnel complex to the five with me who slithered through the narrowest section toward the anticipated light. It was easy to let your imagination run away with you—perhaps your breath would just stop coming, someone would suffer a heart attack in the line in front of you, the tunnel—refurbished or not—might collapse, the light could be lost forever. For me, though, and maybe for some of the twenty-year-olds by my side whose fathers had served in Vietnam, I imagined the past I could have lived with O'Brien.

Cu Chi eventually became a free-fire zone for Americans during the war. They had tried everything to defeat the Vietcong in their underground lairs. Tens of thousands of troops marched in, but they could not find the tunnels. The wooden trapdoors were camouflaged with vines and branches and often booby-trapped as well. When the Americans could not find the entrances, they bombed and bulldozed the territory surrounding Cu Chi, defoliating jungles and leveling villages. Ultimately, the U.S. military sent "tunnel rats" down into the holes, but the casualty rates were so high that instead they began sending dogs after the VC. So many dogs were maimed and killed that their handlers came to a point where they balked at using them for that purpose. Cu Chi then became a dumping ground for random artillery rounds and for extra bombs. American pilots dropped unused napalm on the area before returning to base after missions. At a time when the war had already been lost, American pilots carpet bombed Cu Chi, destroying most of the tunnels and just about everything aboveground as well. More than half of the VC fighters who lived in the tunnels died during the war. Thousands of villagers were killed, too. And if imagination was a killer for the American soldiers who had to contemplate entering the tunnels to face a hidden enemy, for those VC living beneath the earth for months on end, it must have been the same or worse.

On our last afternoon in Vietnam, Jo-Ellen and I paddled in a dugout through the tributaries of the Mekong Delta. The darkness of the tunnels was replaced by the sunlight flickering in and out of the shadows of tree limbs that hung over the river. Imagination was still the killer. It was impossible not to think of young Americans slogging through the rust-tinted waters, seeing a snake in every vine and an enemy rifle in each twist and bend of the river. For us, though, after a while the countryside seemed as peaceful and slow as a daydream. Our dugout floated along silently. We passed farmers walking beside their water buffaloes and glided alongside women bent in the fields like stalks of wheat in a soft, steady breeze. The land was a fertile rice belt, and the air smelled rich with sugar cane, fish, and fruit. A woman in a peasant hat with a bamboo pole over her stooped shoulders balanced two impossibly heavy-looking bags of rice as she walked across a monkey bridge, an arch-shaped footpath suspended across the canal. These were the people and the land that could not be burned away or bombed into oblivion—by the Chinese or the French or the Americans. Looking at them, one had to consider that war might be a form of arrogance and foolishness that only human beings were able to devise.

≋≋≋ By the time we arrived back in Ho Chi Minh City it was nightfall, and the town throbbed with sounds and lights. Jo-Ellen and I accompanied five students who wanted us to be with them to share their last Vietnam adventure—at the Tri Ky Restaurant on the corner of Nguyen and Lieu streets. They had been directed to the place by a cyclo driver—it was the only nearby establishment where a person could have a good snake dinner. Or at least that's what Mark Pan, the handsome, dark-eyed, twenty-year-old student from the state of Washington, was told. Mark would be the last young man on the ship whom I would expect to be fixated on the idea of eating the still-beating heart of a cobra. There were plenty onboard who seemed to have the amplified levels of testosterone that would have pushed them into such a quest. There were many who always seemed to find the seediest bar, the raunchiest night-club, the adventure most likely to conclude in stitches or a black eye or a reprimand from the executive dean. But Mark was not one of them. He had a gentle nature, quiet in and out of class, attentive in the communal Core Geography course offered every morning, polite at dances and pub nights and even during the ship's often-belligerent half-court basketball games. But, nevertheless, there he was, surrounded by four young women and his professor and his professor's wife in the Tri Ky as a man with a gloved right hand brought a cobra into the dining room. The people at the other tables barely seemed to notice as the waiter allowed the cobra to slither onto the floor, its flared hood making it look as if it were taking a last stand, raising a literal question mark about who was to be dinner for whom. The other diners might have been concentrating on the eclectic menu—armadillo, tortoise, bat, wild boar, porcupine, fox, eel, deertendon, or white small chicken. I wasn't sure what "deertendon" was, nor did I know how a chicken, even a "white small" one, fit into such exotic company. I left that analysis for others: I was focused on the cobra.

At our table we all stared. We were used to our dinner coming out on a plate, long dead, not raising its cold-blooded head toward us as if it had a few final remarks.

"Does it spit?" I wondered aloud.

"Cobras can spit venom pretty accurately up to about half their own length," Mark said calmly. He'd obviously done his homework. Everyone at out table went silent, calculating, I assumed, how far this snake, which appeared to be about eight feet long, could spit if it took a mind to having one final moment of revenge. By my estimation, we were six feet away from its dangerous mouth.

"All cobras are venomous, but they're not poisonous," Mark continued. "They have deadly venom in their sacs, but the rest of the snake is perfectly edible."

He got a wistful look in his eyes, as if he regretted what he was about to do. He turned to Jo-Ellen, who was looking at the scene as if she had been pulled into an episode of *The Twilight Zone,* and he recited a few more things he had learned about snakes: "For the Hindus, the cobra is a manifestation of Shiva, the god of destruction and rebirth. For the Buddhist, it was the cobra who shielded Buddha from the sun as he meditated."

"And for us," the bright-eyed young woman with red hair who sat directly across from Mark at the table said, "it's dinner, I guess."

As she was speaking, the waiter held the snake with his gloved hand as another waiter cut off its head and deftly slit it open, popping out its beating heart and plunking it into a shot glass half-filled with blood and some kind of dark wine. Mark swallowed the beating heart with an awkward grin. The expression on his face was not one of ecstasy. It was not the picture of a man who had been granted a new sexual potency or extraordinary courage. It was just the face of a kid who began a gesture that was ill-advised but once begun couldn't be reversed without choking on the decision and spitting his scruples all over the table. As for the rest of us, we drank the blood of the snake (or made believe we were drinking it by putting the glass to our lips)—compelled by team spirit or adventure or a sense of pity for Mark or the snake. The blood tasted like licorice wine. The snake meat itself, mixed as it was with ginger and spices, tasted (as our Vietnamese friend had said about dog) like chicken.

Laws in Vietnam controlling the sale of snakes for food had made such restaurants scarce, but the belief that eating snakes offered aphrodisiac, medicinal, and spiritual benefits kept some of them in business,

I suppose, no matter how expensive they were compared to the typical fare of the land. And, perhaps, there was something else that kept them in business: the desire of American tourists, scared breathless by the abstraction of history and the concreteness of realities such as the claustrophobic Cu Chi tunnels, who wanted to prove to themselves that they were capable of looking into the dark eyes of the cobra as if they were staring into the face of the past. Or maybe such places will always remain open because people need some help in conjuring stories that will join them together—in some strange communion with one another, sharing the blood of what they most fear. As Tim O'Brien said, "That's what stories are for. Stories are for joining the past to the future. Stories are for those late hours in the night when you can't remember how you got from where you were to where you are. Stories are for eternity, when memory is erased, when there is nothing to remember except the story."

Malaysia

The next day we sailed for Malaysia. For most of us, it was just a stopover, a vacation interlude, on our way to India. So much discussion onboard the ship and in Core Geography had centered upon the emotional and physical strain of experiencing India that Malaysia became a rest stop, a place to gain strength before we encountered a world unlike any we had ever seen. For most of the students, Malaysia was just one big beach and although from my perspective, the students usually appeared extremely relaxed and, on any given day or night, more than fulfilling the ordinary human fun quota, they geared up for Malaysia the way undergraduates typically prepared for spring break. Most of their time was spent on the Web, searching for rental cabins or hotel rooms on one of the islands near Penang, where the ship would dock. They scanned the Internet for spas and massage parlors, for scuba diving and scooter rentals, with the same intensity Ahab's crew in *Moby-Dick* searched the horizon for whales. The students discussed how they would pair off, which clusters would head to Lankawi and who might be up for a trip across the border into Thailand. It was against Semester at Sea rules for students or faculty to leave the country we were docked in unless it was a trip sponsored by SAS. Of course, that didn't stop some from making emigration plans any more than it restrained a young woman in Vancouver from taping a bag of marijuana to her inner thigh or a young man in Japan from storing a bottle filled with vodka in his crotch. Most of the students had seen Leonardo DiCaprio in *The Beach*, and the island it was set on, Phi Phi Leh, was not far from us. You could read it in the students' faces as they talked about the movie: Leo's not any better than we are. If Leo could break the rules, many of them figured, why couldn't they find an island paradise, at least for a few days before classes resumed onboard the ship.

Before the students hit the beaches in their search for Leo's paradise, though, we had to get safely through the Strait of Malacca, the narrow body of water that separated Sumatra from Malaysia and opened into the Andaman Sea and the Bay of Bengal. We were warned to watch closely for speedboats carrying pirates armed with long knives and rifles. In recent months, we were told, pirates had boarded tankers and other vessels in the area, robbed and kidnapped people, stolen goods and even ships themselves, casting the crew into lifeboats and sailing off into the night. When Captain Ryan spoke to the ship's company about the Strait of Malacca, he left any trace of humor out of his Irish lilt.

"There were six attacks recorded this past month," he announced. "And the suggestion is that the attacks are getting more and more violent these days. Many of these pirate boats carry AK-47s and some use rocket-propelled grenades. There are stories of gun battles fought onboard tanker ships in these waters. This is not some romantic Errol Flynn movie." Captain Ryan looked out at the gathered crowd, mostly students. "You do know who Errol Flynn is, don't you? Oh, no matter, discard whatever image you have of Bluebeard or Long John Silver or Johnny Depp. These men are the kind of people you'd avoid if you saw them walking down one of the streets of your city. They kidnap, rape, rob, and murder. There's nothing romantic about them at all. In the past ten years there have been more than 3,500 pirate attacks. Three hundred and forty crew and passengers have been killed."

Some ships are equipped with sonic blasters, he explained, which emit loud, debilitating noises. All have fire hoses. Some may even have armed guards. But, according to Captain Ryan, our best weapon was watchfulness and whatever speed the ship could muster to get out of harm's way. So, for the next three nights, students and faculty volunteered for pirate watch, carrying flashlights and eyeing the night sea for any suspicious vessels. Some took it more seriously than others. We got through the Strait of Malacca unscathed, and the only strange noise recorded by one of the volunteer watchmen in the dark night came from a couple discovered in a tethered lifeboat that rocked and moaned enthusiastically to their lovemaking.

In Penang, Malaysia, we came into the one of the centers of the Muslim world. Before the fourteenth century, Indian and Arab traders carried

Islam along with spices to the Indonesian islands and the Malaysian peninsula. Now Islam was the official state religion. There was no such thing as separation of church and state. In terms of the constitution of Malaysia, to be a genuine Malay, one must be a Muslim. Someone who was not a Muslim could not, legally, be a Malay. Each Malaysian citizen held an identity card that defined the carrier as Christian, Hindu, Buddhist, or Muslim.

Our students needed no identifying cards to indicate that they were foreigners. What they needed was some advice on how not to stand out too aggressively as spoiled, hedonistic Westerners. For the environment they were about to enter, their skirts were too short, their blouses too tight and cut too low, their lipstick too bright, their voices too loud, their heads uncovered. Many of the young women on the ship had every intention, it appeared, to step onto Malaysian soil in the same tank tops, exposing belly rings and shoulder tattoos, that they had worn in China and Vietnam. The young men intended to traipse off in shorts, baseball caps, and muscle shirts and expected to blend into the Malaysian culture. The staff advised some restraint in dress, noting what was considered respectful among Muslims. There was one other piece of advice: not to buy drugs. Possession could result in a death penalty.

I could not say for sure how carefully the students listened to the staff's warnings, but I watched the morning that we docked in Penang as the young men walked down the gangway in cut-off shorts and torn T-shirts, and the young women strolled down in bathing suit tops or halters, their windswept hair twisting against glittering earrings.

Our entry into Muslim territory was made more tense by the fact that President Bush and the American government had begun to beat the drum for war in Iraq, a drumbeat that would last our entire voyage, a harbinger of the conflict that would begin in the spring of 2003. For many onboard the ship and in Muslim countries, it appeared to be the beginning of a battle between the Christian and Islamic worlds.

It seemed particularly odd for some of us, then, to be vacationing in a Muslim country as President Bush alluded to the axis of evil and implied the beginning of a new Crusade. As the United States headed inexorably into war, we wended our way through markets loaded with durians (a popular fruit but so vile-smelling that they were banned from Singapore's buses and airlines). We hiked along streets crowded with women covered in baju kurings (a tunic that pulls over the head) and men dressed in traditional Malay wraparound skirts. So, while the Bush administration struggled to convince the public that Iraq had weapons of mass destruction and a hand in the terrorist attacks of 9/11, hundreds of us—citizens of the SS *Universe Explorer*—ate satay, a celebrated local dish of grilled meat seasoned with tumeric and coconut milk, and headed into a land that seemed, for the moment at least, far, far from politics and strife at home.

Most people from the ship boarded ferries or hydrofoils to Lankawi or one of the hundred islands dotting the northwest coast of Malaysia. Jo-Ellen and I traveled with two adult passengers and a female student in a cab that took us to one of the main beaches on the island. Our driver said he would be our tour man for the day, and although we all knew accepting such an offer had its dangers, we agreed on a price and put ourselves in his hands.

"Come," he said, "we'll see the tomb of Mashuri. It is safe now."

At the tomb, he told us the story of a Malay princess who was unjustly accused of adultery and condemned to death. As much as she tried to convince people that she had gotten pregnant from drinking from Tasik Dayan Bunting, a nearby lake, they would not believe her. She had the same problem that Jesus's mother had to face, I suppose. But Mashuri was more revengeful than Mary, and she put a curse on seven generations of residents of Lankawi. Our driver assured us that we were among the eighth generation now. I didn't try to do the multiplication. With taxi drivers and religion, faith is the only answer.

On the way to the beach resorts, our driver stopped at the entrance to a wooded trail. He pointed. "Waterfall. You see."

The trail led back a mile or two to a waterfall that could have been plucked from a painting by Cezanne. We would have stayed there for hours if Jo-Ellen had not been attacked by a pack of monkeys who seemed upset over the inequities of evolution. They might have been attracted to a plastic bag she was carrying that had a few cracker crumbs in it. Or she may have been the first flailing blonde they had ever encountered on the Main Street of their jungle. Whatever caused them to swarm around her, she let out a muffled scream and swatted at them with a copy of the book she was reading—Jhumpa Lahiri's *Interpreter of Maladies*. But it took a few well-placed stones that I tossed at them to turn their attention from her. Then it took a broken tree limb to get them to stay away until we could head back down the path to our driver. It was another one of those coincidences that would not pass the test for fiction, certainly, that the climactic section of the titular story of Lahiri's collection was about an attack by a group of monkeys: "Mr. Kapasi [the tour guide] took his branch and shooed them away, hissing at the ones that remained, stomping his feet to scare them. The animals retreated slowly, with measured gait, obedient but unintimidated."

Jo-Ellen's monkeys hovered along the slope of the hill—unconvinced, it seemed, of my evolutionary authority or the accuracy of my rock throwing. They followed us all the way back to where our driver sat waiting for us. He leaped up when he saw them and, like Lahiri's Mr. Kapasi, charged them with a stick of his own. They scattered and disappeared as soon as they saw him coming. He waved our thanks away, looked over at Jo-Ellen, and said, "Sama, Sama," what I assumed was the Malaysian equivalent of the Spanish "de nada" or the English "no problem." But the way he looked at Jo-Ellen, her blue eyes still wide in fright, he could have been saying *I love you* or *Leave this man for me and I will find paradise with you and always protect you from monkeys*. But despite the infatuation I read in his eyes, the monkeys brought a different message. It was as if they had showed up to remind us not to be too taken with our place in the hierarchy of things. They were a reminder that there was no hiding from strife in paradise. Frankly, they made it clear, there was no paradise.

At first sight, the white sand beaches along the north shore of Lankawi came pretty close, though. The road leading to the beach was dotted with water buffaloes and mouse deer (an animal the size of a cat with the face of a rabbit). We caught a glimpse of a few blue-ringed pheasant and a group of long-tailed macaques. But when we got to the beach, it was not the unpopulated paradise we had hoped to discover. It was crowded with SAS students who had not found Leonardo DiCaprio's island. For ten dollars a night, you could rent a nice room a few yards from the water. For another few dollars, you could have a good meal. The problem was that the students had taken all the luxury suites, leaving us in a makeshift hut on the edge of the jungle with a view of them sipping frozen drinks from their hammocks. That night, unable to get to sleep in a wooden-plank bed, I read the Malaysian writer Shirley Geok-lin Lim's story "Mr. Tang's Girls" and knew when I finished it that dream and reality were darkly entangled in this land just as they were in my own, that even in the Muslim world, tradition and change found themselves in a hallucinatory struggle.

A few days later, as we lined up with students to reboard the ship, one of the young men from my writing class came up to me to ask my advice. His name was Steven, and he was as handsome as Billy Budd, if not quite as innocent. But what had happened to him had made him stammer as Billy Budd had.

"I, well, I wonder, what do you think I should do about . . . about . . . something that happened, a weird thing, uh, an accident that happened to me on Lankawi."

I was expecting something about a traffic accident or an unfortunate love affair with a Malaysian girl, one of Mr. Tang's daughters, perhaps. I had seen quite a few students coming back to the ship with lovelorn expressions or crutches and stitches thus far on the trip. I had also been in the student union to see condoms tossed out like confetti at a New Year's Eve party. I had heard the doctor bemoan the fact that they were running out of the "day-after" pill because couples did not want to use condoms because it inhibited their spontaneity. I had heard the doctor argue, "It inhibits AIDS and venereal disease as well." But Steven's question was not about a girl. It was about a midnight stroll along a moonlit beach he had taken the night before. Walking by himself along the water line, barefoot, daydreaming about paradise, he stepped on something that stuck in his right heel. At first, he thought it was a sharp shell or even a jellyfish. When he bent down to see what it was, he saw a needle attached to a syringe.

I didn't have much to say to him. I don't think he expected me to give him any advice he hadn't already given himself—"Go to Dr. Jo right away, but don't worry, I'm sure there's nothing to be concerned about." Of course, I was thinking the opposite. There was a lot to be worried about. He was probably trying to tell himself the same things I was hoping for him—a syringe lying around in salt water had most likely lost any toxic material or the odds were slim that the syringe came from some Malaysian junkie with AIDS. But there were probably no tests that Dr. Jo could do that would answer any of those questions immediately. *And he didn't have the syringe.* He had thrown it into the night and dashed back to his hotel room.

So what Steven was left with were questions and doubts—and it seemed to me that his situation represented us all on the ship, hearing the distant thunder for a war we could not fully understand. We all had our questions as we traveled the world in the shadow of 9/11, wondering what lay along the darkened beaches ahead or what awaited us when we landed in India.

India

Nothing can get a person ready for India. I had dreamed of the country for days before we arrived in Chennai, ragged visions of crowded streets, rivers of filth, and the calloused hands of beggars reaching toward me, tearing at my clothing. In my dreams, hundreds of millions of people flooded the pinched streets until there was no air left to breathe.

When we stepped onto the soil of India, I found that my dream had become real. I was wide awake in my own nightmare—the beautiful dark faces of Indian women and ancient sadness in the babies' eyes everywhere I turned my head. When we docked in Chennai, the biggest city on the east coast, the country had recently topped the 1 billion mark in population on a landmass roughly one-third of the size of the United States. Chennai, known as Madras until its name was officially changed in 1997, was founded by the East India Company in the early seventeenth century. Before the British came, there were Portuguese and Armenian traders. And the British settled there, from all accounts, not for the natural harbor but because the price of cotton was favorable in that area along the coast. It did not take the British long to build forts and churches and palatial residences to dwarf the locals' huts. By the eighteenth century, it had become a city of wide avenues and thatch-roofed slums. That is what it appeared to be in the twenty-first century.

The city was noisy and dirty, and anything primly British seemed a distant memory in 2002. The heat, even in October, was tropical. We were close enough to the equator to make me feel I needed a shower after I was off the ship for five minutes. But the water in the harbor looked like a sewer, and the water that pulsed out of the faucet on the ship was the color of tar. After an hour on the streets of Chennai, Jo-Ellen's white T-shirt was damp, and my skin felt coated with soot. I had to contemplate what it might feel like a week later if I did not have the mettle to take a shower. I knew I'd have to toughen up—after all, millions of people bathed in the microbe-infested, feces-laced Ganges every day.

Onboard the ship the day before we reached India, my nonfiction writing class had discussed an essay by P. J. O'Rourke titled "Weird Karma." None of us had ever been to India, and O'Rourke put some of our fears into comic perspective. Those of us who were not George Harrison or Mia Farrow, who were not mystical by inclination, and were not necessarily ready for transcendental meditation, felt a kinship with O'Rourke—not having "the kind of bliss you'd care to tailgate." O'Rourke had gone on an excursion across India sponsored by the makers of Land Rover and had ended up with the kind of illumination many of us feared we might discover: "a reverse enlightenment. . . . I now don't understand the entire nature of existence."

What I discovered—and many of the students did as well—was that O'Rourke was right. India had a way of confusing, disorienting, and unnerving. Driving on a road in India was just what O'Rourke said it was—"Think of it as doing sixty through a supermarket parking lot and the school playground." The population density may have been considerably less in India than the Netherlands, but somehow the stunning poverty made the number of people seem twice as many as places like Japan or the Netherlands. The convoluted bureaucracy one saw at every turn in the road in India, along with the sacred cows blocking every intersection, the piles of unholy garbage, the muddy lanes, the shoeless beggars, the homeless children, the stray cats, the scurrying rats, made the country seem to be a tangle of inconsistencies. It was a democracy but spiced with such corruption and payoffs of minor officials, such broken infrastructure and cluttered paperwork, that it made one wonder if democracy worked when there were so many and so many of them slept in dirty puddles in the road. O'Rourke called it the "smartest country in the stupidest way" and in noting all the many newspapers that could be found at a typical Indian newsstand, he also pointed out that it was easy enough to "think you're in a country of Einsteins. . . . Then you look up from your newspaper and see a man walking along wearing a bucket upside down over his head." Trying to make sense of it all in India made a person dizzy.

Spirituality and superstition stood in awkward relation to one another just as the Taj Mahal cast its opulent shadow over some of the most abject poverty in the world.

Being in India was like experiencing years in a second, an assault on all the senses—more cars and trishaws and people, more smoke and pollution, more noise, more of everything you've ever seen or heard or smelled at one time and in one place. Mainly, it is the poverty that gets to most visitors. In 2002, one out of every three people in the country lived below the poverty line, and I'm certain their poverty line was below the imagination of most Americans. Eighty percent of the population in 2002 made less than $2 a day. Forty percent made less than a dollar a day. Estimates were that the population would double in thirty-five years, making it by far the most populated country on the planet.

As Jo-Ellen and I rode into the business center of Chennai in a trishaw, rocketing through inches of space, bouncing along the potholed roadway, another trishaw passed us with two of my writing students—Alex and Steve from Emerson College. They were two of the comedians onboard the ship, both experts in improvisation. I expected to see them one day on *Saturday Night Live* or pictured on the wall of the U.S. Post Office. They stuck their heads out of the left side of the rusted vehicle and contorted their faces, yelling "weird karma" into the roar of the engines as they blew past us in a burst of smoke and rattling metal. One of them appeared to be wearing a turban and the other had on a lungi, the equivalent of a sari for men. We watched them streak ahead of us, past shacks held together by old newspapers and Hindu temples with thousands of gods carved into the walls. There are thirty-three thousand gods in the Hindu pantheon. As confusing as the three gods in one of the Holy Trinity was to me growing up in the Catholic Church, thirty-three thousand gods to worship seemed excessive, even in a country of more than 1 billion.

But in India it was just as easy to be amazed and inspired as it was to be confounded. For most Indians, life is an endless cycle of birth and death and rebirth, a transmigration of the soul, a reincarnation into a higher or lower forms, a balance sheet of the inevitability of karma and the moral responsibility of dharma. The faces of the people I saw were lined with a bright intelligence or a hopeless apathy. Children on the street, in rags and bare feet, had eyes as weary and lost as soldiers who had spent too many months in battle. But there were trishaw drivers or storekeepers who smiled radiantly as if life were offering them all that anyone could expect. In India, eighteen different official languages, including English, were spoken. The country had millions of well-educated people, but it also had an astounding illiteracy rate—only 52 percent were literate (and only 37 percent of women were). Many high-tech businesses had relocated to places like Chennai but mainly to take advantage of the highly educated people who had no choice but to work for low wages.

In my view, India was a chaotically democratic nation in the grip of ancient ways, a society shackled by an illegal but quietly accepted caste system, a nation of equals in which hundreds of millions were designated Dalits, or untouchables. It was another one of those inconsistencies in India that I could not fully comprehend. Hinduism seems to profess universal brotherhood, but for thousands of years the caste system had been rigidly in place. Not until 1949, with the new constitution, was the caste system outlawed. Before that, the four major castes were locked into place in Indian society, and castes are determined by birth. There is no way to change one's caste, and the group a person was born into controlled everything in life—job, spouse, living circumstances. Caste was a naturalistic trap. The only escape was reincarnation. At the top of the Indian caste system are the Brahmins, the priests and scholars. Then come the Kshatriyas, the warriors or rulers. The Vaishayas are merchants and farmers. The lowest caste consists of the Shudras, laborers and servants. In the caste system there are also the outcasts, those beyond the pale of ordinary society, those who had to make sure that the reach of their shadows did not contaminate upper-caste members of society. These untouchables handle dead bodies and human waste. It seemed another example to me of religion working hand in dirty hand with those in political power to keep the masses subjugated. As long as the Hindu cycle of birth–death–reincarnation kept the hope of a better life in the next life alive, the powerful could remain in control. As long as the lower castes believed that living a life of quiet acceptance would result in their being reborn into a higher caste, the status quo stayed the same.

Ghandi called them the *harijan*, or "children of God." Traditionally, in Hindu life and culture, they were churas or bhragas, scavengers. The modern untouchables shed the Hindu terminology and used the word *Dalit* because it meant "oppressed" or "crushed." The word suggested a new political view of those who have been traditionally cast out from Indian society. It had a political connotation and not a religious one. It did not designate a certain kind of job or a birthright but pointed to a discriminatory policy in a supposedly democratic society. But tradition and history—as we know in America—runs deeper than law. Laws do not change people's hearts. Sometimes they don't even alter their actions. In Indian society, even though some Dalits had managed great success in politics and business, most were still virtually untouchable, laboring with death and excrement as those around them stepped with hurried indifference past their tainted shadows.

Most of the students and faculty onboard the SS *Universe Explorer* assumed that an encounter with India would make them more open-hearted, but many students, in particular, felt guilty because their experiences seemed to make them more insensitive. One young man from the University of Colorado said to me, "I can't get the strange smell out of my nose. I can't even say what it is—cow shit mixed with curry or motor oil and rotten vegetables. But there's so much poverty and so much sadness, it's hard to look at it all. What can anyone do about all these hands pulling at us for help? I feel like I'm watching these kids drown right in front of me and I can't do one real thing to save even one of them. I don't know where to look—so I do what everybody does here—I just stare into the distance and don't make eye contact with anyone near me."

I understood how he felt. On our second day in Chennai, Jo-Ellen and I walked from the ship to a post office a few garbage-strewn streets away. We were followed by a half-dozen of the most persistent beggars we had ever met. By the time we reached the post office, I felt a wall rising around my heart. I felt ashamed that I yearned for the peace and silence of the ship. On our way back, we saw an accident. It was the first one we had seen in India, but, given the mangled state of the traffic in the city and the lack of any discernible rules of the road, I'm sure it was one of many that day and every day of the year. A small black car struck a man and a young girl on a motor scooter. The young girl lay unmoving in the road, blood pooling at her head. She appeared to be dead. The man knelt at her side, bent over, rocking slowly back and forth as if he were whispering some secret into the girl's ear, speaking some words that would wake her from a fairy-tale sleep. The car paused and then entered the stream of traffic that flowed around the man and girl. Our trishaw sped into the traffic, and I turned my head to watch the cars and motorbikes gush around the man and girl as if they were boulders in a fast-rushing river.

The next day we were ready to get out of the city. With a bus full of students, we skirted the shacks and debris. Women in brightly colored saris scratched in piles of rock, and dogs sniffed at mountains of trash, warily eyeing their competition—goats, water buffaloes, cats, and emaciated men and women. Men urinated in the streets, and cows stood like sacred statues blocking the roadways. The Dalit Liberation Education Trust Center was a few hours south of Chennai in a rural India we had not yet seen and, when we were in Chennai, could not have imagined. The school, the Dalit Center for Education, was run by Henry, a soft-spoken man with a shock of white hair who occasionally let bitterness creep into his sing-song sentences. "Brahmins accept our blood when they are sick," he said to me as we looked out at the Palar River that bordered the school grounds and opened into the windswept waters of the Bay of Bengal. "But there are still 250 million Dalits, and those in power want to keep it—so they adhere to the ancient myths that suit them. The old exploitation keeps them safe and secure in having someone below them. There is always someone to step on if the ground gets too dirty for their feet." He picked up a stone from the sandy ground and flung it into the riffling river. The fishing skiffs stood out like silhouettes against the red-tiled roofs and the whitewashed walls of the cement school buildings.

But Henry could not stay bitter for long, it seemed, and his face broke into a broad, polished grin when a column of young women in white saris passed us as if they were butterflies fluttering against a grey background. They turned toward us, all shy smiles and bindis, red dots in the centers of their foreheads, earrings glittering in the sun. "They are nursing students," he said to me. "They will change the world." I wasn't sure if he was saying this to convince me or himself. It was possible to step outside of one's "jati," the caste into which one is born, but it was unlikely at best, and he knew that better than I did. It was a dream, something akin to the American notion of "anyone can grow up to be president." We continued down the dirt road to the Delta Training Center. Photographs of Martin Luther King dotted the walls, but there were none of Ghandi. That seemed remarkable to me, but the reason was simple. Ghandi felt that all untouchables should be treated humanely but that the caste system needed to remain in place and Indians needed to find value in the work they were *destined* to perform. In Indian Hinduism, fate was caste and could not be separated from politics. The Hindus, like the early American Calvinists, twisted the strands of religion and politics and economics until they were knotted beyond untangling.

With a group of faculty and students on the ship, I was reading Arundhati Roy's novel *The God of Small Things,* and each moment on land one passage or another from the book broke into my consciousness like a footnote to my experience. Walking along the river's edge with Henry, I was reminded of a line near the end of her story. Roy mentioned "human nature's pursuit of ascendancy, Structure, Order, Complete monopoly. It was human history masquerading as God's purpose." This seemed as apt a description of the caste system as I had heard anywhere. The people I saw in the Dalit village, bending their way out of the tiny openings to their thatch-roofed huts, had the same inquisitive doe eyes that I saw in the upper classes in Chennai. The women holding babies against their saris and the shoeless, shirtless men could have been from any caste. I could see nothing in their faces that told me these were "untouchables." Nothing to say that these people would be required to sweep away their footprints from the earth, hide their shadows from their "betters." The confluence of the history of India and the story I was seeing in the Dalit village raised a question I could not answer. In Roy's images, it was "a question mark that drifted through the pages of a book and never settled at the end of a sentence." Her own novel, *The God of Small Things,* told the story of India from the point of view of two children, twins, Estha and Rahel. In their experience in the late 1960s is the dark chronicle of Indian caste and segregation. It is the story of a miscast love affair between Ammu, a pickle factory owner's daughter and the mother of the children, and Velutha, an untouchable handyman. It is an account of history and lies and the consequences everyone must pay for both. In 1997, a lawsuit was brought against the novel in India, claiming it was obscene and likely to corrupt the minds of its readers. The opposition was not, I would guess, to the explicitness of some of the sex scenes but rather to the depiction of the affair between the upper-class factory owner's daughter and the untouchable handyman.

Visiting the Dalit village and the Delta Education Center for two days was like taking a journey back in time and entering a story not unlike Roy's. There was no electricity or running water in the village, no indoor plumbing or playgrounds. The water for the village was drawn from a common well. The houses had roofs made of palm leaves woven into the same sort of fragile strength that appeared to hold their whole world together. Each house had a dirt floor, and the oval doorways could not have been more than four feet high. It was typical for a family of six or seven to live in a one-room home slightly larger than our cramped cabin onboard the ship. Cows, dogs, cats, goats, children, and old men roamed the village paths with us as we walked from hut to hut, smiling women marking us with red and yellow oils.

"Why?" I asked someone as we watched an old hunchbacked woman apply the oils to Jo-Ellen's cheeks and forehead.

"So that she doesn't look too beautiful," the man replied. "You don't want the evil spirits to see her and envy her. It is better to hide her beauty a little. It will protect her."

We were part of a parade, people from the village lining the path as if we were dignitaries from another planet. The beautiful jeweled eyes of the young women floated against skin as dark as night. Their smiles lit our way. One old woman, her skin as wrinkled and worn as an elephant's, reached out to touch Jo-Ellen's elbow as she passed by but quickly pulled her fingers back before they made contact. When Jo-Ellen hugged her, the woman's eyes filled with tears. At first, I wasn't sure what had happened. But then it dawned on me that the woman was crying because someone outside of her caste was touching her. It was as simple as it seemed: she had never been touched by an outsider, by a pale-skinned member of another caste.

Hope and a timid brand of joy whispered through the village and the education center, but they were both sad places, populated by undernourished children, fourteen-year-olds who could have been frail eight-year-olds, and hollow-cheeked women who had already turned old at thirty-five. But in a way that was impossible to understand in the context of American wealth and opportunity and hope, there was a sense of peace there that I did not see in the city. Despair was not carved into the villagers' faces. The people in Chennai seemed despondently alone in the crowded city, but the villagers did not. It made me think about my own country. What Americans viewed as a tragedy that must be rectified, these rural Indians seemed to accept as a simple consequence of living. These women accepted the inevitability of slipping from breathtaking beauty to stooped old age in a breath itself. What my own culture fought with creams and surgery and every ounce of energy and spare dollar, these people acknowledged as ineluctable.

I wondered as we drove in our air-conditioned bus down the dirt road away from the village, the dust and humidity swirling behind us, if I was just romanticizing a poverty and fate I could not absorb. But as we touched the periphery of Chennai and saw once again people living in concrete water pipes, women and children curled into fetal positions along the muddy back alleys, untethered cows and rawboned dogs, and the ancient, glittering eyes of the battalions of beggars, I knew that romanticizing such a world was wrong but that understanding it might be impossible.

〰〰〰 The next morning before Jo-Ellen and I marched through the wilting heat and pollution of the streets of Chennai to take our final glimpse of India before we sailed toward Kenya, I had breakfast with a student from the University of California at Berkeley. Jason was in my nonfiction writing class, and he was by far one of the best writers on the ship—and he knew it. When I first met him, on the second day of our voyage as we sailed to Japan, he struck me as a young man who had a passion for learning. He sat down with me at an outside table on the stern deck and late into the moonlit night discussed writers like John Irving and Michael Chabon and Kurt Vonnegut. I remember coming back to the room and telling Jo-Ellen that if there were enough students like Jason who were as genuinely interested in literature and writing, this would be a great experience for me as a teacher. I found out later that Jason was more taken with himself than he was with any piece of literature, and the attractive humility I saw on that second day was not a part of his personality often on display in the classroom when he discussed his peers' work. Then he had a condescending manner, an inclination that came near the line of plain meanness at times.

But on our last day in India, I was still feeling like a teacher who had discovered a modest and genuine young man who was curious about every aspect of the world. I had already found out that for many on the ship every experience on the journey was filtered through a strange competitive lens. In every port, there was a rivalry among students and faculty alike. *My trip to Tokyo was fascinating. Mine was amazing. Mine was magical. The people of China are, I don't know, incredible. My time there was M-A-G-I-C-A-L.* There were some people who never seemed to go anywhere that didn't turn out to be magical. Sometimes coming back to the ship after a half-dozen days in a port felt like eavesdropping on a group of people reciting a compendium of movie blurbs plucked from American newspapers. The competition seemed more intense for students. It became a matter of who could have the more forceful (read *more dangerous*) encounter with the new world. If one student went to a loud bar, the next had to find a more raucous bar. The next had to end up in a bar fight. The object—a valid one—was to shed the drab robes of tourism and become a traveler who enters the world more exposed and involved. But sometimes the quest had the aura of a reality television show about it, making it hard to tell where the stage ended and the pavement began.

Jason was a child of the twenty-first century, for sure, a citizen in the age of self-consciousness. A few days before, he told me, he had entered Jaipur with the goal clearly in his mind of stepping away from the "very safe, very clean, very sterile" tour that took him from restaurants serving palak paneer and guides offering elephant rides up to the Red Fort. He was going to make sure that photo ops of the Taj Mahal and glimpses of barefoot children from behind the grimy bus windows would not be his exposure to India. He was determined to head out on his own and to bring back an adventure. He also had an entrepreneurial instinct, and he planned to buy items that he could sell for a huge profit on eBay. Perhaps he got more than he bargained for—maybe India always gives more than a person expects.

He told his tour guide that he wanted to rest and would stay in the hotel while they went sightseeing and had dinner. But as soon as the bus left the hotel parking lot, Jason got in a cab and headed for the bazaar in the heart of the city. There he met a chubby, clean-shaven Indian man in tailored slacks and a purple silk shirt who spoke in a perfect accentless English. Within a few minutes, Jason was whisked to the man's family-owned jewelry store, a four-story white stucco building surrounded by crumbling tenements. Jason was taken to the showroom at the far end of a maze of burgundy carpets and dazzling white walls. There the man, Anup, and his brother, Dayan, placed a black velvet pillow on the glass desktop in a private back room and poured diamonds and rubies and sapphires onto it.

They served Jason a few Kingfisher beers and brought out more gems than he had ever seen in his life. He picked out a reasonably priced pair of gold earrings with lavender stones for his girlfriend and a few other pieces to sell on eBay and gave one of the brothers his credit card, address, telephone number, and passport number. Normally, they didn't sell retail, they said. According to the brothers, the family exported gems, wholesale. By the time the transaction occurred, it was after 7 P.M. That was when they introduced Jason to an older man, their uncle, whom he described to me as looking like a caricature of a movie villain—white hair, leathery skin, one eye black as opal and the other a clouded, all-seeing glass that seemed to look right through him. It was the uncle, with five or six employees standing in a half-circle behind Jason, who explained that exporting gems out of India meant a 600 percent tax for him. But he had a way of avoiding such taxes and that's where Jason *was* going to assist his company.

"No worry, though," he told Jason. "A tourist like you can make a lot of money and there's no trouble at all. You'll be my courier. You just have to pay a little insurance and you'll make money when you deliver the gems."

It was clear that Jason did not have a choice. He was coerced into sign-ing a credit card slip for 94,000 rupees (a little more than $2,000 U.S.) then handed a black Sharpie marker and told to address two envelopes—one to

Cape Town, South Africa, and the other to Los Angeles, California. Next to his name on the envelopes, they demanded that he write his passport number. He was to pick the envelopes up in South Africa and Los Angeles when the ship docked, get the packages to someone who would contact him, and then send the money (minus the $6,000 per envelope he was to keep for himself) back to the gem dealer.

"How will I get it to you?" Jason asked.

"No need to worry," the uncle told him, smiling. "We have your address and information. We'll find you. I have many friends in South Africa and the United States. I do not think you will fail me. We'll find you."

With that threat echoing in his mind, Jason took my advice and others'—dispute the charge on your credit card and tell the authorities. He also called Anup and told him he had spoken to the U.S. Embassy and if his company did not release him from the duties they had coerced him into, he would bring charges against them.

There was a moment of silence on the other end of the line. Then Anup said, "My uncle will be very disappointed." The line went dead. All Jason heard careening through the silence was the voice of the uncle warning, *No need to worry. We will find you.*

I got to know Jason much better as the months passed. I saw him playing cat-and-mouse games with his classmates in writing workshops. I heard the teasing tone he used with them that bordered on cruelty. He was competitive and could, at times, be cold-blooded. He had brought back a good story from India. Better than most of the others. It was probably true, although I'd never be absolutely certain. If it were true, though, he would hear those words—*no need to worry*—for a long time to come. If India offered any lesson, it seemed to me, it was that the world would find us, whether we wanted it to or not. What India suggested was the impossible gap between our dreams of the world and the way it actually was. A person could get lost in that gap, a deep black hole, filled with questions and no answers.

At sunset on Friday, October 18, 2002, Jo-Ellen and I bounced along in a trishaw through the sultry evening congestion in

Chennai toward the ship. We had spent the afternoon in a Hindu temple. The ninety-two-year-old May and her friend Betty, the woman who came aboard to be her companion after Barry's death, and Jo-Ellen had strolled barefoot like schoolgirls down the gritty street leading to the temple as if there were no hidden dangers in the invisible microorganisms that swam in the discernible filth. They had more faith in the world than I did—although they cleaned their feet afterward, I noticed. Or India had taught them something I couldn't quite accept yet—that there was no way to enter the world but on its own terms. Maybe Jason's jewel smuggler was right: *no need to worry*, or at any rate what good did it do?

As our vehicle rattled over the cracked road, slipping in and out of spaces too small for atomic particles, I watched our driver. Seeing him negotiate the traffic was like watching a savant work an algebra problem beyond my reach. In my lap was the copy of Arundhati Roy's *The God of Small Things* that I was close to finishing. The driver, eyeing it, told me something I already knew.

"India is not a country that can afford the intellectual," he said, missing by a hairsbreadth a motor scooter with a man, his wife, a baby, and a young boy all squeezed together. "India is too concerned with its stomach."

I nodded, but he didn't turn his head to see. He was like a character in Roy's novel. He knew, like most Indians, that "there was nowhere for them to go. They had nothing. No future. So they stuck to small things." In India, small things were like stones—they could be something to build on, I suppose, or something that crushed the spirit flat.

Kenya

On a safari in Kenya, I learned that lions have sex every twenty minutes for four or five days in a row during mating season. Hyena scat is pure white from all the bones they eat. The Masai cut out the bottom front teeth of boys and girls for the sake of beauty. A rhino can be faced on the plains in broad daylight at a distance of ten feet. I admit that as Jo-Ellen and I walked up to the rhino, I thought about the character in Hemingway's "The Short Happy Life of Francis Macomber" and wondered if, like him, I'd "bolt like a rabbit." In the Hemingway story, Macomber had faced a lion on the open plain, heard the "blood-choked coughing" and saw a swishing rush in the high grass. The next thing he knew "he was running wildly, in panic in the open, running toward the stream." Thinking of Macomber, I gazed at the thick-skinned rhinoceros. Its name comes appropriately from two Greek words that combined mean "horn-nosed." In the case of this rhino, there were two horns, a big one that stood where the nose should be and a smaller one directly behind it. Its skin looked like armor, and it must have been close to a ton of sinew, a death machine a few arms' lengths away from us. Jo-Ellen held my hand. I squeezed back, thankful she was nothing at all like Margot, the jealous wife in Hemingway's story who killed her husband because he found a way to become brave.

"Is it looking at us?" Jo-Ellen asked me.

I explained in a calculated whisper that rhinos have acute hearing and a precise sense of smell but extremely poor eyesight. I didn't tell her that rhinos were considered to be one of the deadliest creatures to man on the face of the earth. I just hoped we were not upwind and kept my mouth shut. I never felt the need to bolt as Francis Macomber had. Perhaps I'm not a coward—or maybe the lanky and solemn Masai warrior with an

71

elephant gun who stood a few paces from our group by some scrub brush kept me from becoming Macomber.

The day before, in Mombasa, we had taken our seats in a small propeller plane to go on a safari on the Masai Mara, about one thousand square miles of the Serengeti Plain that covers northern Tanzania and the southwest corner of Kenya. The Masai Mara National Reserve is a sunwashed stretch of open grasslands. The shaded, tree-lined Mara River cuts through the dry land like an artery pulsing life to the heart of a wild beast. Our plane looked old and, once in the air, creaked and wheezed in ways that made my hands sweat and my own heart beat a little faster than usual. A few days before we had gotten to Kenya, I had reread Ernest Hemingway's *Green Hills of Africa* and Isak Dinesen's *Out of Africa*. As the plane slid on currents of air between the mountain ranges to the north and the south, I tried with only partial success to let my mind float on the poetry of their observations about the dark, bloody beauty of the country. I couldn't get Denys Finch-Hatton's plane accident out of my mind, especially as our own plane fluttered like some balsa wood toy in the blasts of wind. Finch-Hatton had been Isak Dinesen's lover and the supposed model for the safari guide Robert Wilson in "The Short Happy Life of Francis Macomber." As the plane wobbled a few thousand feet above the ground, I came within a second of turning to say something to Jo-Ellen who sat next to me. But Wilson's ghost rose up from Hemingway's story and stared harshly into my eyes: "Doesn't do to talk too much about all this. Talk the whole thing away." I heard him admonishing me, *Worst it can do is kill you*. I said to myself, *Worst? That's pretty bad. Talking it all away might actually be a good thing*. However, by the time I was concluding this schizophrenic Hemingwayesque conversation with myself, the plane bounced down onto a rutted field that appeared no more like a runway than any other part of the rolling countryside. It wasn't until I felt the reassuring thump and bump of our landing that I realized I had been holding my breath for a while. Exhaling, I looked out the dust-caked plane window at the Kenya that Hemingway and Dinesen had helped me imagine over the years.

In his writings on Africa, Hemingway spoke a great deal of other writers—Turgeniev, Tolstoy, Flaubert, and Twain—and the animals he killed. Most likely, Hemingway linked these writers and his African prey together because they were just that—all prey, all to be killed so that Papa proved he was the best. In terms of the place, Dinesen's writings and her connection to Kenya were more to my taste. Her descriptions of the area surrounding her coffee plantation in the Ngong Hills of Kenya were a sketchbook of copper skies and wide-branching mimosas with spiky thorns. I carried her descriptions with me each morning as we went out on to the Mara: "The chief feature of the landscape, and of your life in it, was the air. Looking back on a sojourn in the African highlands, you are struck by your feeling of having lived for a time up in the air. . . . In the middle of the day the air was alive over the land, like a flame burning, it scintillated, waved and shone like running water." Dinesen was right. It was like being on another planet. The air seemed a presence as distinctive as the flat-topped acacia tree or the bat-eared fox. In the morning the air was cool and dry, in the afternoon like a slow-burning torch, and in the evening warm, a gloved hand resting on your throat. At times the air blew softly across the open spaces, and at others it was still as a knife blade sitting in the sunlight. You didn't just breathe the air, you stood alongside it as if it were a companion.

Karen Blixen, who wrote under the pseudonym of Isak Dinesen, knew Kenya well. From 1914, when she married her cousin Baron Bror von Blixen, until 1931, when the Great Depression forced her to abandon her coffee plantation, she lived there in a place she loved as much as any on earth. In 1925, she divorced Blixen and began a long and stormy affair with Denys Finch-Hatton, the famous African hunter. In 1931, around the same time her business interests were deteriorating, Finch-Hatton died in a plane crash, and she returned to live permanently to the home of her birth, Denmark. Kenya had become her heart's home, though, and she knew, like the Kikuyu tribesmen she admired, that there was something about the environment that had the elemental beauty and truth of the stone age, the power of the primeval. Dinesen sensed what another, later, writer from Kenya, James Ngugi, understood: "the whole country had a stillness almost like the stillness of death."

The word *safari* comes from the Swahili meaning *journey*, and it is difficult to imagine a better place than the Masai Mara to make a pilgrimage from the world of men to the world of animals as Dinesen once made. For us the war in Iraq was coming closer, the political speeches were getting louder, the saber rattling more ominous. Turning from the shouts and subtle whispers of human motives and language to the simpler, somehow less devious world of animal savagery seemed comforting. The Masai Mara had the honesty and fairness and truth that the wilderness always has.

Man is a domestic animal and devious in his cruelty. But wild animals kill for less complicated motives than humans do—most often because of simple hunger. As Twain said, "Man is the only animal that blushes, or needs to." There is a morality in basic survival, a simple, uncontrived ethics to it. Human history is a tale of moving away from what is wild in us, farther and farther away from anything connected to the simple truths of living and dying. Dinesen's years in Kenya taught her that we have moved far from the things that could balance our natures. "No domestic animal can be as still as a wild animal," she writes in *Out of Africa*. "The civilized people have lost the aptitude of stillness, and must take lessons in silence from the wild before they are accepted by it. The art of moving gently, without suddenness, is the first to be studied by the hunter, and more so by the hunter with the camera."

I could not exactly say that we moved gently across the land as there were six of us riding in an open-air Land Rover across the knobby landscape. Sitting or standing in the truck felt like taking a ride on a bucking horse. The six of us—the diminutive Dr. Jo, her husband Hal and young son Cody, Jo-Ellen, myself, and our Masai driver-guide Sammy—spent four days together, gathering before sunrise, again in mid-afternoon, and around sundown to buck along the cratered roads and onto the plains to get a close view of the animals. Sammy always seemed to know where the lions or elephants would be. There were a half-dozen other guides and vehicles and they kept each other apprised of where the animals were, but Sammy never seemed to need their advice. He just drove and we ended up a few feet from a pride of lions. On the wheat-colored savannah, it was almost impossible to see the sandy brown lions until we were right on top of them. In the first group we saw, there were five lions. The male had a golden mane and a lazy, slant-eyed look that suggested he was not concerned at all by our presence, even though we were only about six feet from where he reclined in the shade of a bush. Sprawled some yards away was the female lion, smaller by a foot or two and two hundred pounds than the male, which looked to be over eight feet long and 400 pounds. The spotted cubs cuffed one another at her side and rolled in the matted yellow grass. Like so many males in the undeveloped world, the male lion appeared to have a good life in comparison to his female counterpart. It was the female's job to hunt and to rear the young. The male had to act only to defend the territory of the pride against intruders. Until that time, he seemed to be off duty, and his main job was to look regal, which he did with an indifferent grace, an insouciant expression that said he would eat me without any pangs of conscience if I stepped out of the Land Rover.

I did step out of the Land Rover a few times over those four days but never when I was in the vicinity of lions or cheetahs. Sammy showed Jo-Ellen and me a world we could not have seen as long as we remained bound by the economic constraints of the American middle class. But luck had gotten us to Kenya, and there we viewed the symmetry of the wilderness, a world where humankind was not much more than an interloper or observer. Sammy got us within a few yards of gazelles, giraffes, elands, zebras, warthogs, and wildebeests. He corrected us on the terms—it was a *troop* of baboons, a *school* of hippos, a *herd* of elephants, a *clan* of hyenas, a *colony* of mangoose. We skirted acacia trees and bounded across the pathless plains searching for side-striped jackals, skunk-like civets, vile-tempered honey badgers, and, by far the ugliest creature I had ever encountered, the hairy bushpig.

At one point, we stopped to watch two lions stalking a group of antelope. They moved stealthily through the high grass. Another time, we paused to see a family of lions gnawing at the raw, red flesh of a recently killed topi. What we saw was the Darwinian order of things, everything governed by need and sinew, nothing more. Every creature had its place, except, it seemed, us in our ticking metal beast. We seemed extraneous, but not all humans on the Mara were irrelevant. The Masai were as much a part of the environment as the velvet monkey or oryx.

And yet the Masai stood out against the land, for as Dinesen described it, "The colors were dry and burnt, like the colors in pottery." Against this pale world, the Masai stood like a red flame in the breeze. It's not an uncommon sight on the silent, deadly Mara to see a red-robed Masai tribesman walking, spear in hand, like a bloody apparition across the horizon. Dinesen knew that it was nothing for the Masai to take "a walk of any length, even in country like this." That is, country where lions and elephants roam at will. Any trek across such ground is fraught with dangers. Walking across the open plains is something I could as readily imagine doing as I could envision myself striding naked at midnight down the back alleys of south central Los Angeles. The Masai herdsmen walked their ground, though, like Roman foot soldiers, alone and in groups, armed usually with nothing more than spears. Their reputation as fierce warriors was probably laced with hyperbole and cinematic mythmaking, but they were a proud and brave people whose history was inextricably tied to this country.

Around the eighteenth century, the Maa-speaking people, always seminomadic, moved south into the Serengeti and the Mara and east to Ngong, near Dinesen's plantation. By the mid–nineteenth century, with colonial rule and expansion, the Masai were, essentially, put on a reservation, but Masailand covers about 100,000 square miles, roughly twice the size of the state of New York but with a population under 1 million. So there is plenty of open space for the Masai to build their small round houses made of sticks and cow dung. Entire villages, enclosed by thorn-stitched fences, can be left behind as the Masai search for water and fresh pastures. Masai tradition disdains agriculture and land ownership. The Masai society centers upon their cattle. They are cattle herders, wandering across the land, leaving behind one village to raise a new one. As one Masai warrior in a village we visited told me, "All land is ours. All cattle in the world belong to us." Their wealth hinges on how many cattle a family owns. It is a patriarchal society. Women can marry only once in a lifetime, but men can marry as many wives as they have the cattle to buy. As with female lions, Masai women carry an unequal burden, it seems. The men protect the household and watch over the cattle, but the women build the houses, make the meals, and take care of the children.

To Jo-Ellen and me this seemed a separate world, so different from what we were used to in the United States that it could as well have been another planet, a moonscape with otherworldly creatures—ant bears and dik-diks and oribis—and strange and charismatic inhabitants who roamed the dangerous ground armed with little more than sharp sticks to defend themselves against the most ferocious animals on earth. Like the animals on the Mara, the Masai were an integral part of the environment, and their rites and ceremonies were tied to the land, as well.

When a young man becomes a warrior at about fourteen years of age, he undergoes a public circumcision ceremony and soon after is required to build a livestock camp, or warrior village, and live in it on his own for a number of years. During the circumcision operation, boys are required to remain perfectly still and not utter a sound. If they do, their family is shamed. No anesthetic is used. Boys are allowed to bathe in ice-cold water to numb themselves before they are cut. Girls undergo clitoridectomies in a more private ritual, and it is common practice to pull the lower front teeth of young children. Ears are pierced and disked. Our driver, Sammy, explained all this in a mournful tone, his dark, wide eyes staring out of the Land Rover toward two elephants mating by a cluster of trees in the distance.

Jo-Ellen pushed down the brim of her beige FDNY baseball cap and followed his gaze.

"Did you ever think of leaving here?" she asked.

"No, miss," he said. "This is my home. This is where I was meant to be."

In the days to come, both Jo-Ellen and I wondered what was to become of the Masai people as the modern world encroached on them. As early as the 1930s, Isak Dinesen sensed the threat to them. "From the farm, the tragic fate of the disappearing Masai tribe on the other side of the river could be followed from year to year. They were fighters who had stopped fighting, a dying lion with his claws clipped, a castrated nation. Their spears had been taken from them, their big dashing shields even, and in the Great Reserve the lions followed their herds of cattle." It was hard to tell how much the spears and shields were now ceremonial totems held primarily for the tourists. Some of the villages had been opened to the public so that travel groups could troop in and queue up before tables of Masai women selling trinkets and beads for a few dollars. With the video cameras running and digital cameras whirring, lines of Masai women sang. The warriors leapt high in the air in their traditional dance. The children gathered shyly in a circle. The Masai had held their place in the world of wild animals, but the threat from human civilization could prove far more daunting.

Jo-Ellen and I lived a privileged existence on the Mara. The deluxe tent that was our home for four days in the Mara Mara Safari Club was one Ernest and Mary Hemingway would have envied. It had a wooden foundation and deck that overlooked the bend of a branch of the Mara River. The water was the same dirty brown color as the dozens of hippos who sat motionless in it. The tent had a luxurious king-size bed with a mosquito net, a toilet and shower, and a dressing room with a writing table. The meals were as close to fine dining as we had seen for months, and we ate lunch by a club swimming pool. I almost expected someone to address me as *bwana* as I strolled the grounds.

By the lamp that hung over the bed and shimmered against the mosquito netting, I read stories that kept me up listening to the hippos grunting and all the other unfamiliar sounds that surrounded our tent. The hyrax screeched as if it were a machine winding up and then screamed like a woman being torn apart by a pack of wild dogs. A bush baby, bug-eyed and clinging with its human-like hands to a tree branch, would add to the chorus—a plaintive cry, an infant's wailing. The first night I read James Ngugi's *Weep Not, Child*, a novel about a young man's coming of age in Kenya during the deadly Mau Mau uprising in the early 1950s, a rebellion against British colonial control that left thousands of Africans dead or displaced. The story of the rebellion in the world press left the image in Western minds of blood-thirsty Africans murdering their kinsmen and European settlers with machetes. But it also led to Kenya's freedom and the country's first independent president, Jomo Kenyatta.

The next night I read Mark Ross's essay about one of his experiences as a safari guide in Uganda, the country directly to the west of Kenya. Reading Ross's story, the flickering lamplight creating ominous shadows on the dark green tent wall, I heard every distant lion roar as if it were a few feet away. Every rustling in the grass made me turn my head. Reading "The Last Safari" amidst the sounds and silences of the African wilderness was like reading Truman Capote's *In Cold Blood* in a room on a hillside farm turned into a bed and breakfast in Holcomb, Kansas. On the first day of March 1999, Ross had been lying in his tent on the edge of the Bwindi Impenetrable Forest, not all that far from where Jo-Ellen and I were on the Masai Mara Reserve. His clients were soft-spoken, middle-aged computer software executives who were looking forward (as we were) to a few days of safe adventure. Instead a dozen of his clients and other campers were kidnapped by Ugandan rebels and forced to march toward the Congo border. In a calm tone that made one think of the controlled, unflinching voice of Robert Wilson in Hemingway's "The Short Happy Life of Francis Macomber," Ross explained the horrific few days as "a terrorist bid for publicity that would damage and maybe even destroy gorilla tourism that was the mainstay of Uganda's economy." Six people were murdered, at least one was raped, all of the others were terrorized in one way or another, and then the rebels disappeared like ghosts into the jungle.

Throughout the ordeal Ross remained cool-headed, composed, always calculating how to get his clients safely away from the terrorists. Once again, as Tim O'Brien had written in *The Things They Carried*, imagination could be a killer. Throughout the nightmare, Ross controlled his fears, not letting his imagination take him anywhere that would be destructive. But once it was over, he realized that Africa, the place he once loved more than any other in the world, now seemed to have a bloody curse on it. "I know no cure for the horror and grief we all feel," he says, "for the wars that split and ravage our land, for what happened in Africa."

It was not the sounds of wild animals a few yards from our tent that fired my imagination. It was the memory of the bombing of the U.S. Embassy in Nairobi in 1998, it was the specter of 9/11, it was my country's unwavering march toward war in Iraq that made my mind hear terrorists' gunshots in every dry branch that snapped and see rebel soldiers in every moving silhouette against our flimsy tent walls. Men with guns patrolled our camp day and night. Usually they were red-robed Masai warriors with carefully braided hair and colorful beads around their necks. We were informed they were there on the lookout for wild animals getting into the campsite, but something told me different, that they were there because of Mark Ross's safari. They were there because we all suspected that Ross might be right: there was no cure for horror and grief, for the wars that split and ravaged our land, for what waited for us if our luck ran wrong.

⚞⚞⚞ But our luck and the weather held up, and our flight back to Mombasa was smooth after a rickety takeoff. As we sat on the dirt field waiting to depart, the pilot came out of the cockpit and asked a few people to change seats—just to balance the weight, he said. Fat girls moved one way and skinny guys another, sidling past each other as they crossed the aisle. I couldn't turn my neck because I had thrown it out bouncing along the plains in the Land Rover, but I heard some mumbled complaint behind me and made a silent prayer that some chubby person didn't hold political correctness above our lifting off. But I wasn't all that encouraged by the scientific and professional quality of the procedure anyway. The wings seemed to flutter as we rose above the plains and the mountains in the distance. Fat and skinny, we left the wilderness behind.

As we approached Mombasa, it looked like a place in battle with itself, a city on the edge of the wilderness, torn by poverty and politics into pieces of a puzzle that would not quite fit together. The name *Mombasa* in Swahili means "island of war," and that suggested its history as a trading town on the Indian Ocean, Kenya's only large seaport. Its direct line to India made it a traders' dream, and in the early sixteenth century it was sacked by the ever-ambitious Portuguese. Over the years, the Portuguese attacked the city a number of times, leaving dead bodies and Fort Jesus as their legacy. The Dutch and the English made inroads, but Arab traders had the final say, and now Islam held most of the heart of Mombasa. As Jo-Ellen and I walked around the crumbling Old Town, a mix of architecture that suggested its many colonizers, we saw al-Qaeda graffiti on the chipped and scarred walls. On one wall, with the paint peeling from the cement, we saw in large red letters:

Message to the World
For How Long
Faith is the Answer
Muslims

On another wall, next to an intricately carved wooden door, was a statement painted in black paint:

Islam is the ANSWER
Osama bin Laden

I wasn't sure what either of the pieces of graffiti was saying precisely, or if the Osama bin Laden was a signature or a prophecy of the true answer. I was not certain if the first piece of graffiti we stumbled upon was implying that Islam offered the answer or that Muslims would not wait much longer for equity. Both scribblings could be read as threats, though. Behind nearby latticework we heard the rhythmical song of a man's voice in prayer. The streets were dotted with piles of dirt and debris, pieces of stone and wood, shards of metal and glass. Amid the litter, young boys played soccer in sandals and bare feet, and head-scarved girls huddled together whispering, pointing at us and laughing. As she always did, Jo-Ellen reached out to them, smiling, offering candy or her hand, trying her best to speak with them. In return, she often got a skittish grin or hands grasping hers, touching her blouse or reaching to feel her pale skin and blonde hair. It was as close as we could come, it seemed, to erasing the red and black paint on the decaying walls.

Outside the Old Town, the central city of Mombasa highlighted the statistics for Kenya in general. The life expectancy was forty-seven for men and forty-nine for women. There was one doctor for every 6,000 people, and the average salary was less than it was in India. It took only a day in Mombasa for me to be nostalgic for the hard-edged clarity and terrible beauty of the wild Masai Reserve. Mombasa was crowded and dirty. People rode on Matatus, the euphemism for public transportation in the city. In essence, they were crowded minibuses, unimaginably overloaded with people. They shuttled around the city, blaring music from one garbage-scattered street corner to another. In the densely packed city, it was difficult to find the open faces or diffident smiles of the Masai people.

The night before we left port to sail toward South Africa—a Pinkerton threat notice about a possible terrorist attack on our ship echoing in my mind—Jo-Ellen and I called our youngest son who was in college in Virginia. We huddled by the pay phone in the lonely port area. Talking with

him, I was reminded of one of the ironies of our around-the-world journey—that we were observing parts of the world that might have seemed
as far away as other planets a few years ago, but in our immersion in them
now we often lost touch with what was happening in our own homeland.
Our son told me of the sniper attacks on the highway in Virginia where we
lived. He told me of the series of unsolved and seemingly indiscriminate
murders, of the fear that was crippling the East Coast of the United States,
reminding me, if I had forgotten, that the world always lies in wait, that
terror was real for those who go on safari or for those who stay at home.

South Africa

A day before we arrived in South Africa, Jocelyn, one of the young woman Jo-Ellen and I "adopted" as a daughter on the ship, was caught smoking marijuana in her cabin with a faculty member's son. Caught in the act and given the ship's zero tolerance for drugs, both were to be sent home when the ship docked. Besides being our "adopted daughter," Jocelyn was in one of my writing classes. She was not doing well because she missed a few classes and failed to hand in assignments on deadline. But she always made it to the "family dinners" when Jo-Ellen and I ordered an ice cream cake for the group. She always had a good excuse for not making it to class or not having a paper done. I had an intuition that she was something of a con artist, but after raising three sons, Jo-Ellen and I refused to believe that our little princess did not fit the fairy tale. And, besides, generally I'd rather err on the side of trust until the facts prove otherwise. After Jocelyn's drug bust, Jo-Ellen and I felt sorry for her (more for the faculty member who had to put her son on a flight back to the United States), but I had to admit a sense of relief that I did not have to confront Jocelyn again about a late paper or a missed class as we ate ice cream cake. I probably should have suspected that Jocelyn required stricter parenting skills than we were prepared to offer when she announced at dinner one evening, "It's my twenty-first birthday tomorrow. Mom and Dad, how about taking me to the faculty lounge for a cold one? I'd like to get my funk on!"

When we laughed, she made it clear that she was serious. Since we couldn't send her to her room, we escaped to our own and had a cold one ourselves as we contemplated the mysteries of parenthood. There were far bigger mysteries awaiting us in South Africa.

In Cape Town, I had lunch with a round-faced, fair-haired eleven-year-old boy who carried a pistol tucked under his shirt when he wasn't playing soccer with his chums. The very air around us crackled with an anticipation of violence. Cape Town, where our ship docked on the crystalline morning of November 8 after a turbulent seven-day journey past Tanzania and through the Mozambique Channel, was one of the most stunning ports I had ever seen, Table Mountain holding the eye like a monument and the rugged seacoast a breathtaking swerve of white-flecked water and dark blue sky. Mountains framed Table Bay, rising above sea and buildings in almost a dismissive manner. The rock formations twisted and turned from the harbor of Cape Town to Cape Point in the south, suggesting the raging geological story that went back millions of years. Amid all the physical beauty of the landscape, though, in a country that offered evidence of the beginnings of humankind, there was a palpable terror in every corner, a postapartheid chasm between the races that was as distinct as the line between the people who lived in twenty-room mansions protected by twelve-foot-high walls and barbed wire and those who existed in thousands of tin-roofed cardboard shacks in the many townships.

On those days of high seas along the coastline of East Africa, in my literature class we prepared for South Africa in our glass-walled room on the fourth deck. The classroom, some sort of disco lounge in one of the ship's past lives, was one of the oddest venues I've ever had as a teacher. As I taught, every way I turned I faced my own image. Most days I felt lost in a funhouse filled with mirrors, more Vic Damone than Mr. Chips. I did my best to avoid seeing my image, afraid that like Narcissus, seeing too much of myself might not be a good thing—and not because of my beauty. Being a college instructor is generally a safe occupation, but it has its dangers. You stand in front of a classroom, in front of dozens of people who stare respectfully, sometimes even affectionately, at you for hours on end. It's easy enough to fool yourself into thinking that what you see in their eyes is real. *I may be this smart. What I have to say is that important.* Floor-to-ceiling mirrors on all the walls don't help. They only add to the possibility of delusions of grandeur. The novel we were studying, however, shattered any romantic illusions about the importance of professors and their special wisdom.

In the week that we headed toward South Africa, we discussed John Maxwell Coetzee's disturbing and unyielding novel *Disgrace*. It had recently won the Booker Prize, and Coetzee was the only writer to have achieved that feat twice. Nigel Penn, a history professor at the University of Cape Town, acted as our interport lecturer and outlined the historical context of the novel. He introduced us to another novelist, a former colleague of J. M. Coetzee's at the University of Cape Town, Andre Brink, and his book *The Rights of Desire*, a novel that took its title from a line spoken by David Lurie, the main character in *Disgrace*. Both novels focused on sexual relationships between older men and younger women. Both delineated the oppressive violence in Cape Town and the surrounding areas. Both stories captured the stark sadness of South Africa, the burdens of history, and the torment, brutality, and humiliation in a land in which tyranny had found itself transformed into anarchy. According to Penn, statistically, the average woman in South Africa could expect to be raped twice in her lifetime. Of course, this does not mean that every woman was raped twice, but that many thousands of women were raped multiple times. In my mirrored class of forty-seven students, thirty-five were young women, and Penn's remark sent a shudder through the air-conditioned atmosphere. In our class discussion of *Disgrace*, there was no consensus as to whether Coetzee saw even an intimation of hope for South Africa. At one point in *Disgrace*, David Lurie considers the grim reality of the country: "One gets used to things getting harder; one ceases to be surprised that what used to be as hard as hard can be grows harder yet."

My students were entranced by *Disgrace*. Watching their pensive expressions in class, I saw a group of individuals who were spectators at a complex and terrible scene that held their narrowing eyes with its awful mystery. *Disgrace* was that kind of book, and South Africa, we were to discover, was that kind of country. The novel tracks the fall of Lurie, an instructor of Romantic poetry at a technical college in South Africa. Lurie seems a scion of Camus's Meursault, drained of genuine passion or hope. He is fifty-two, twice divorced, a frequenter of prostitutes, and has become, in his view of things, a drone teaching the listless young. Once a professor of the classics, he is now an adjunct professor of communications since his university was "rationalized." Lurie lives in what he considers to be the South African wasteland until he notices one of his students, Melanie Isaacs, and seduces her. Melanie, like the black prostitute Soraya he sees every Thursday, is "the dark one," and Coetzee may be suggesting an interracial relationship to compound the other inequities of age and situation. It may make Lurie's disgrace when it becomes public even more pronounced in South African society.

The novel is not only about Lurie's humiliation but his daughter Lucy's rape and transformation as well. It is a parable about the nature of justice and punishment and forgiveness and redemption in a country in which the strands of race and history are raveled beyond untangling. *What will make up for the wrongs of the past in South Africa?* Coetzee asks in *Disgrace*. And the answer he presents is not an encouraging one—or at least it was not an easy one for my students to accept. Toward the end of the story, Lucy tells her father how she feels about her new situation: "Perhaps that is what I must learn to accept. To start at ground level. With nothing. Not with nothing but. With nothing. No cards, no weapons, no property, no rights, no dignity . . . like a dog." And that's where David ends up at the conclusion of the novel, caring for dying dogs, or rather giving up dogs to death, like some participant in an ancient sacrificial ritual. It seems he has taken his daughter's final advice: "I am determined to be a good mother. A good mother and a good person. You should try to be a good person too." After my students got to Cape Town and traveled around South Africa for a few days, Lucy's advice did not seem an adequate political solution to the problems they saw. But maybe her advice is as good as one can find amid the deep-rooted inequities and boiling hatreds of the country.

For many students, South African culture and history were impossible to hold clearly in view. The novel *Disgrace* and Coetzee's life in South Africa represented their confusion. They couldn't make sense of Lucy's unwillingness to bring her rapists to justice. Many of them could not understand David Lurie's redemption by starting at ground level. Even Coetzee's life as a South African they found disorienting. He was born in Cape Town in 1940, a descendent of seventeenth-century Dutch settlers, the first European colonizers to come there. Rivalries between Dutch settlers and native tribes soon turned into hostility and wars in the eighteenth and nineteenth centuries. In the 1820s, the British arrived with more guns and military might than the Dutch and took charge. This led, in the late nineteenth century and the early twentieth century, to the Boer Wars. The word *Boer* literally meant "farmer" but referred to the Afrikaaners who resisted British rule in South Africa. Those wars left the country with thousands of dead British soldiers, Dutch farmers, and African natives. The power had shifted from the Dutch to the British, but for the native Africans it made little difference. It was just another white face, another accent, in charge of their destinies. Until the late twentieth century, whites, although in the vast minority, were the supreme power. Apartheid, an Afrikaaner word that means "separateness," adhered to the "one drop" rule, the same notion that haunted American race distinctions into the mid–twentieth century. From 1948 until its official abolition in 1994, apartheid categorized the people of South Africa into blacks, whites, Indians, and coloreds. This is the strange mix that Coetzee described and my students found difficult to understand. Whites were whites but Afrikaaners were white but somehow different. Blacks were black, but not coloreds who were mixed in some, often indiscernible, way.

In the late fall of 2002, when we arrived in South Africa, natives and Europeans and coloreds and Afrikaaners were all mixed and jumbled into a place twice the size of Texas. By the established categories, the population was about 4 percent Asian, 10 percent colored, 16 percent white, and 70 percent black. Despite the fact that Nelson Mandela had been released from a twenty-seven-year imprisonment in 1990, the country was still infamous for its segregation, for many years' worth of repressive legislation—for the Population Registration Act, for the Mixed Marriages and Suppression of Communications Act, for the Separate Amenities Act—and for, in 1976, the Soweto Uprising, in which Bantu students protested the Afrikaans Medium Decree that forced all black schools to employ Afrikaans and English in a 50-50 mix in instruction. The strands of history and politics were twisted in ways that we—as foreigners stepping onto this shore—could not readily figure out. Not even Nelson Mandela or Desmund Tutu with their saintly smiles and calm tones had been all that successful in untangling the baffling complications.

Archbishop Tutu came to our ship and spoke to our group a few hours before we set foot on South African soil. His spirit shone from his soft brown eyes, magnified by the lenses of his wire-rimmed glasses. In the glare of the lights of the student union, his crop of white hair could have been a halo. "Welcome to a crazy country," he said. Then he smiled and broke into a resounding laugh. "Most people may have thought that this country was going to be destroyed by racial conflict. You look around this world here and you could almost want to give up. But Mandela was in prison for twenty-seven years and he didn't give up. You might go to Robben Island, I don't know. You'll see where he was. But he didn't come out of that experience full of hatred. Each of us has an extraordinary capacity for evil. None of us can ever predict what we might do in given circumstances." He paused, his doleful eyes brightening in the lights, his voice rising into the respectful quiet in the room. "But this is not the end of the story. Nor is it the most exhilarating part of the story for human beings. We are made for goodness." His smile widened. "We are made for laughter. For love. For gentleness. For transcendence." He smiled at the applauding crowd of students and teachers. "The world can be changed. Will you help me? Will you? And you? And you? And you?"

With Tutu's words echoing in my mind, words not all that different from Coetzee's in *Disgrace*—"A good person. Not a bad resolution to make, in dark times"—Jo-Ellen and I clattered down the gangway and onto the Victoria and Alfred Waterfront. One of my literature students, a copy of *Disgrace* in her hand, followed us down the walkway, holding the book up to shade her bright green eyes from the sun-drenched windswept harbor.

"Professor P," Kat said, nudging me from behind and waving the novel like a warning, "I don't think I'll ever understand Lucy."

I shrugged by way of commiserating with her. I wasn't sure I understood that kind of forgiveness either. Jo-Ellen, Kat, and I stood blinking into the sunlight, the Victoria and Alfred Waterfront shops gleaming in front of us like upscale monuments to capitalism, as if we were in Naples, Florida, instead of within sight of Robben Island, one of the most notorious prisons in the world.

"A friend of my sister went to Stanford and knew Amy Biehl, you know, the girl who was killed in one of the townships in 1993," Kat said. "Amy was just trying to help the people there, just giving some people a ride home in her car, and they smashed her car windows, and hit her in the head with a brick. A screaming mob of boys dragged her out of her car and beat her and kicked her and stabbed her to death. That was horrifying and I don't understand how they could do that or how frightening that must have been for her, but I was even more confused by Amy's parents. Her father shook hands with the convicted murderers and forgave them. They were set free. Two of them work for the Biehls now. Forgiveness without justice, I don't know, it just seems wrong somehow to me."

I thought about the people I loved and wondered if it would be possible for me to forgive a rape or murder. The possibility of such forgiveness was at the core of the Truth and Reconciliation Commission in South Africa, founded by men such as Desmund Tutu in 1995. I remembered Tutu's wise and generous eyes when he spoke to us on the ship. He had a calm wisdom about him, a saint's gentleness. Maybe the Biehls were saints too. Perhaps it would take saintliness to change the heart of South Africa. Maybe all saintliness meant was starting with nothing.

All I said to Kat, though, was, "Be careful out there." I looked at her and noticed for the first time that she reminded me of newspaper photos I had seen of the freckle-faced Amy with dirty blonde hair to her shoulders.

"Maybe by the time we've had a chance to see the country," I said, "some things will make a bit more sense."

It wasn't very good advice. I knew that, but I knew I didn't have any answers. Teachers are a lot like writers in that respect. They just have a lot of questions. I came close to saying something like this to Kat, to quoting something Nadine Gordimer had written about the writer's vocation in her introduction to *Selected Stories*. "Writers need solitude," she wrote, "and seek alienation of every kind every day of their working lives . . . excessive preoccupation and identification with the lives of others, and at the same time a monstrous detachment. . . . The tension between standing apart and being fully involved; that is what makes a writer. That is where we begin. . . . This is the moral, the human justification for what we do." But I wasn't sure if Kat had ever thought of being a writer, and that would have made such a statement the sort of particular truth that would have held little value for her unless she realized that it was the traveler's truth as well—being apart and involved, having an excessive preoccupation with the lives of others and at the same time a monstrous detachment. Writers may not be saintly enough to forgive, but they must be able to empathize. And empathy is a territory on the border—always—of forgiveness. Kat had once told me that she wanted to become an English professor. She loved the dusty security of libraries, she said. So I could have advised her to spend more time studying books on South African literature and history, but I was worried that she would end up like the main character in Andre Brinks's *The Rights of Desire*, saying, "That might be my epitaph one day. He died chasing a footnote."

Jo-Ellen and I watched Kat head toward the fancy restaurants and shops of the Waterfront Mall, and we boarded a van loaded with bicycles to tour the Stellenbosch winelands in the foothills of the mountains west of Cape Town. The view from our bus was similar to Paul Theroux's description of the city in *Dark Safari*: "The cold gusting wind and the frothing sea, with the sunny dazzle on Table Mountain's vertiginous bulk looming behind it, made Cape Town seem the brightest and least corrupt city I had ever seen. That was its appearance, not its reality." I understood, as any writer must, that the gap between appearance and reality was what made a story. Without some conflict between the two there was harmony, what just about everybody but writers sought.

There wasn't much disharmony in the bike trip, though, unless you count Jo-Ellen's saying after half a dozen miles on dirt roads through the stunning mountain passes of the Jonkershoeck Nature Reserve, "Wasn't this supposed to be a wine tasting expedition?"

I said I thought it was, but I assumed the wine tasting came *after* the twenty-six-mile ride, not *during* it.

"You mean we ride the whole twenty-six miles without a drink of wine?" Jo-Ellen asked. "Well, I'll ride in the van until we get there then."

That's exactly what she did. I tried to make her feel guilty a few hours later by sweating profusely all over the picnic table at the winery where we had roasted chicken and grilled vegetables and glass after glass of local wine. But she seemed too busy eating and drinking to notice me. On the way back to the ship that evening, I was too drunk to recall why she should feel guilty anyway.

The next day we were supposed to hike up Table Mountain, but the winds were gusting dangerously and the cable car, which we were scheduled to take for part of the hike, was inoperable. Table Mountain loomed more than 3,500 feet over the city of Cape Town, flanked by Devil's Peak to the east and Lion's Head to the west. Devil's Peak was almost as high as Table Mountain and equally exposed to the winds. For that reason, we hiked up the aptly named Lion's Head, which was just a little over 2,000 feet to the top and more protected from the elements. From a distance, the granite peak looked exactly like a majestic lion's head with its shoulders draped in a regal, grassy green cloak. About a dozen of us hiked up the circuitous, rock-strewn path, occasionally needing to claw our way up a cliff to get to the top of the mountain. One student, a young woman named Leslie, came on the trip, we found out three hours into the hike, because she was deathly afraid of heights and wanted to break that fear at all costs. We helped her up the face of the cliff to the peak of Lion's Head, and she stood there in the howling wind, tears in her eyes, and said, "Next time, I'll climb this on my own. Now I know I can do it on my own. Maybe I'll try Table Mountain."

The next day we heard a rumor that a few students had gotten lost on Table Mountain. I never found out if Leslie had been one of them, but they were lost for a few hours before another hiker showed them the way back. When I first heard they were lost, my mind flashed to Brinks's *The Rights of Desire*. Toward the end of the novel, the main character, Ruben Oliver, after "catching up on the week's quota of murders, attacks, hijackings, rapes, robberies, miseries," goes on a hike with his beautiful young tenant, Tessa. On the mountain path, a group of men attack and rob them. They hold a knife to Ruben's throat. As they are about to rape the young woman, a group of hikers scares the men away. *The Rights of Desire* attempts to be a complement to Coetzee's *Disgrace* as a portrait of contemporary South Africa. Brinks's novel is an elaboration, perhaps, on the meaning and consequences of desire. Like David Lurie, Ruben, a librarian lost in dreams and footnotes, finds a way to let go of desire and discovers a way to live in the anarchy of needs and longings that make up life in contemporary South Africa.

The next day we hesitated before going to the one of the townships. Originally, the townships were like camps for migrant workers, set up temporarily as a means to get cheap black labor during the day but keep the workers out of sight after dusk settled. We were not sure up until the very afternoon we departed whether we would go to Langa or Bonteheuwel or even Gugulthu, where Amy Biehl had been brutally murdered. We ended up going to the Crossroads Township, an unending sea of plywood shacks that looked at first glance like an awful parody of an American suburb in Virginia Beach or Indianapolis. The houses, though, were the size of sheds for lawn mowers in those places and the locks on the doors were more flimsy than kids in the United States used on their bikes. The houses were a patchwork quilt of sheet metal, fragments of glass, and sections of fabric. Our bus had to ride slowly to avoid getting hooked on the spider web of electric wires that looped and hung like Spanish moss from the electric poles on main roads leading into the township. The low-hanging stolen electricity appeared ready to spark and sizzle off the metal top of our vehicle.

We were only a short ride from the glittering and wealthy waterfront, but it seemed another planet. It was how Paul Theroux later described it, a place of "heightened contradictions." As he said in *Dark Star Safari,* "No sooner had I decided the place was harmonious and tranquil than I discovered the crime statistics—carjackings, rapes, murders, and farm invasions ending in the disemboweling of the farmers. Some of the most distressed and dangerous squatter settlements of my entire trip I saw in South Africa, and among the handsomest districts I had seen in my life—Constantia comes to mind, with its mansions and gardens—I also saw in this republic of miseries and splendors."

In our few hours in the Crossroads Township, we went to a school where students taught us how to play traditional African flutes and drums, we ate in a local restaurant that served papaya stuffed with rice, sweet potatoes mixed with cheese, and deep-fried dough, and we spent a few hours in a shebeen, a bar where the men sat slumped in corners drinking bottles of Castle lager. Women and children gathered outside the shebeen to sing with us. Many of the young girls asked us if we knew Whitney Houston or Oprah, as if as Americans we might run in the same circles on occasion. The preadolescent boys, all wearing wool skull caps and wide white smiles, danced around in a circle, and some of our female students joined them. The younger boys stood back, shy toothless grins peeking from their faces. I remember one woman in particular. She had close-cropped hair and chipped front teeth. Her grey sweater was tattered from age. She was most likely in her early forties, but she could have been seventy—her eyes were that old. As she sang and danced a South African song, she swayed to the music and manufactured what she seemed to think was a smile, but her eyes suggested such a deep sadness and hopelessness that nothing her lips did could suggest anything but defeat. Besides, she had been drinking heavily. That was clear from the way her body listed in the dark ocean that the evening had become. Her eyelids began to droop from the alcohol and she started to slur her words. She looked into Jo-Ellen's eyes as we were about to board the bus and said, "I will remember you. Remember me. Remember me, please."

As we drove past the palm trees and office buildings in the center of Cape Town, along the immaculate streets toward the harbor and our ship, I wondered how long she would remember us or we her. I tried hard in the flickering shadows of the bus light to see the faces of the students who had gone with us to the township—the diminutive young woman with short brown hair who had danced with the young boys in the streets, the adult passenger who had made such a valiant and inept attempt to play a kwela, something like an Irish pennywhistle, and the young men who had kicked the soccer ball around a dust-choked yard with a group of teenagers who howled with delight. I tried to recall the face of the woman who had spoken to Jo-Ellen, to fix her image and those of all the students who had come with us in my mind so that I would not forget. Remembering seemed the only decent thing to do.

The next day at Robben Island was all about remembering as well. Nelson Mandela's cell in the prison was 6 x 6 feet, and he had spent eighteen of his twenty-seven years of imprisonment in that space, smaller than many walk-in closets in suburban ranches in the United States. The island reminded me of Alcatraz, stuck as it was like a second thought in the icy ocean. Alcatraz, though, felt more connected to the city of San Francisco than Robben Island, named originally by the Dutch settlers for its seal population, did to Cape Town. The island stood about seven miles north of the city, a rocky, flat expanse with a history of suffering that ended in 1991 when the last prisoners were released. Instead of letting it go back to the seals, the government made it a museum, a way of remembering the stories of political prisoners like Mandela who were condemned to serve out life sentences within view of Table Mountain and the noble coastline of their home in South Africa.

Our guide was a former prisoner on the island and now lived in the village there, near his former cell. Remembering did not seem to have made him bitter. From what I could sense, it freed him to live in the present. He stood before us in the concrete cell block, a round-faced man in a neatly pressed tan shirt, wearing a baseball cap and gold wire-rimmed glasses that stood out against his dark brown skin and faint moustache. "I spent twenty years in this building," he said without a note of resentment that I could detect. "I was sent here in 1967. This was my prison. Now it is my home. I remember the past so that I do not have to relive it, so that no one has to relive it."

History haunts South Africa, though. Faulkner's lines from *Requiem for a Nun* echo throughout this country: "The past is never dead. It's not even past." On our last day in Cape Town, Jo-Ellen and I, Carolyn Dudek, a professor on the ship, and Eduardo, one of our students, gathered with a South African businessman, an Afrikaaner, near one of the docks. Jo-Ellen's cousin knew the man and had arranged for us to meet. Graciously, he had planned to take us on a drive along the northeast coastline and anywhere else we wanted to go. But he had not expected us to bring Carolyn and a student. His wife did not want to be "crammed" in their car, so he drove her home to their contemporary house sitting on a cliff overlooking the ocean. She was a carefully dressed, perfectly manicured woman, beautiful and bedecked in gold jewelry. In the car, on the way to her house, she swiveled her head from the front passenger's seat to speak with Jo-Ellen in the back of the car.

"What have you seen so far?"

"You have an incredible country," Jo-Ellen answered. "We saw the wine region and hiked up Lion's Head. We went to Robben Island yesterday and to one of the townships the day before. It was very sad, but. . . . "

"Why would you go there?" the woman interrupted, raising her polished nails and tapping them sharply against the window. "What's the point in seeing all that? It would be like me going to the slums in New York City if I went there on vacation."

I knew that Jo-Ellen probably wanted to say that we weren't *on vacation*. We hoped to be travelers of a different sort, but Catholic school training kept her silent. And that was surely wise, for the woman's question suggested her defensiveness and not much good would come of challenging it as we accepted her husband's hospitality.

After we dropped her off in a house that looked over all that was beautiful in Cape Town, we drove on along the coiling road that hugged the side of the mountain. After a time, her husband and our guide, Adam, asked us if we would like to go to lunch at a typical Cape Town establishment. When we said yes, he took out his cell phone and dialed someone. "Meet us there in ten minutes," he said.

The restaurant was probably not typical for the majority of South Africans in the area. It was an outdoor café in a small town about ten miles from Adam's house. His friend, Monique, met us a few minutes later, bursting into the restaurant like a throwback to a 1950s Jayne Mansfield or Marilyn Monroe film, all hips and cleavage and wide-eyed sighs. Her son trailed her, a chubby eleven-year-old with a concealed weapon. At first, Monique bantered back and forth with Adam in a manner that made me wonder if it had been his idea and not his wife's to leave her at home. Like South Africa, Adam and Monique appeared to have a hidden history. Within a few minutes, though, Monique took an interest in me. Jo-Ellen didn't seem happy about it, but I felt mildly gratified until Monique made herself clear.

"Why are we eating here," she asked me, resting her gold-cluttered hand on my right leg, "when we could be eating on your yacht?" She bent toward me, the diamond necklace falling precipitously into her cleavage, reflecting the sunlight and blinding me for an instant.

"The ship, you mean?" I asked.

Jo-Ellen smiled, getting a clear sense of the picture and my true charms.

"It's not Mike's yacht," she said in what sounded to me like a self-satisfied tone. "There are 600 students onboard. Mike's just one of the professors." Jo-Ellen put a bit too much weight on the word *just*, as if she were really saying *justice* and meaning the poetic kind.

After that, Monique never glanced at me again. She returned all her attention to Adam or to the abundance of sunshine or to the service in the restaurant. She complained that the sun was getting in her eyes. To the table she announced, "I didn't get this skin sitting out in the burning sun!"

Our student, Eduardo, had gone to the men's room a few minutes before, and as she was complaining about the ineffectual umbrella, he was walking back to our group. Monique squinted up at him.

"You," she said imperiously. "Get me another umbrella. One that works!" Eduardo was from Chile, and his olive skin was just dark enough for Monique to assume he was there to serve her.

When we explained that Eduardo was our student, that he had been sitting with us at the table for the past twenty minutes and knew no more than she did about the umbrellas in the place, she said, "Oh, how was I to know? Where was he sitting?" Then she turned to the young waitress who had come back to our table and said, "Perhaps you could hold this broken one over me while I have my lunch?" But before the waitress could respond—and I was anxious to see what that response would be—Monique's cell phone rang. When she answered it, the waitress took the opportunity to disappear.

"Yes. Yes. I understand. Well, I'm having a drink right now. I can't do anything about it, can I? That's what I hire you for, isn't it? Call the police. And please don't bother me again during lunch time."

She took a sip of her drink. Her house was being robbed, she told us. "That was my security company. It's nothing."

"My God, shouldn't you go home?" Jo-Ellen asked.

"Why?" Monique responded. "It's the fifth time this month. I don't disturb my lunch for such things."

Monique, we found out as the afternoon wore on, did not let much disturb her equilibrium. She proudly announced she had never done a stitch of laundry, never cooked a meal, never cleaned her house, and never intended to do any such thing. Her former husband owned thirty thousand acres in the country and had enough leftover cash to keep her hands away from dishwater.

"That's what maids are for," she said. "I'd never leave South Africa. Why would I? Where else could a woman get such cheap help? Where else are things so beautiful and so inexpensive?"

She turned and smiled at her cherubic-faced son, who sat next to her, his ruddy cheeks and blond hair caked with potato chips, and his shirt billowing out at the waist from too many rich meals in the past. Or was it simply the pistol protruding from his pants? I couldn't be certain. But when I noticed him reaching toward his waistline to loosen his belt or to check his weapon, I hoped the waitress would remember to bring him the right dessert.

On our way back to the ship, we met Jocelyn outside a music store. She was carrying an armload of CDs.

"Hey, Mom and Dad, what's up? I just got my own place. I'm moving to South Africa. Why go home? All I need is my music and somewhere to play it. I can live like a queen here."

All I could think was *like Monique*. But Jocelyn had one final surprise for us and for herself as well. The next morning the ship's departure was delayed slightly because a stowaway—Jocelyn—was found hiding in a storeroom. She was put off the ship again, and this time disappeared into the heart of the city, a young woman as unfathomable as the inscrutable country, and she may be there still.

Brazil

We sailed away from the Cape of Good Hope and into the Atlantic on the evening of November 11 on our ten-day voyage to Salvador, Brazil. It was approximately 1,500 miles and rough seas for the first few days. Around the Cape itself, the seas were particularly high. That stood to reason: the first European to round the Cape in 1488, the Portuguese navigator Bartholomeu Dias, had honestly named it the "Cape of Storms." King John II of Portugal had a politician's ear for the soft sell, though, and changed the name to the Cape of Good Hope. I knew the story of Dias and should have paid attention to it, but instead I ended up with cracked ribs. One of the students who played basketball in the intramural student-faculty league on the ship learned a bit of Afrikaans on shore and posted a sign— "Rough weather or not we pass the Kaap die Goeie Hoop today. That sounds like a challenge to me. See you at noon." The wind was blowing and the seas were high, but we played anyway. By 1 P.M. I had ice on my ribs and begged Jo-Ellen (who thought I should have outgrown basketball years before) not to make me laugh, even if she felt I deserved to suffer for my sins.

The trip across the Atlantic gave me a chance to breathe shallowly and rest up. In my literature class, we read Jorge Amado's witty and ribald *Dona Flor and Her Two Husbands*. The students loved it. For me, well, it was painfully funny. Amado's subtitle called the long, meandering story "a moral and amorous tale." It was certainly both, but like any good narrative, the moral came embedded in the amour. The novel recounted the story of the beautiful Flor's two loves—Vadhino, her irresponsible but charismatic first husband, and Teodoro, her reliable but dull and predictable second spouse. The novel was set in the city of Salvador de Bahia de Todos os Santos, where Amado had spent the last years of his life. His house there was made into a museum shortly after he died in August 2001, a little over one year before we arrived in Salvador and a few days shy of his seventy-ninth birthday.

Like the culture of Brazil, perhaps, Amado's novel has a split consciousness that somehow found a unity of expression. The first part of the novel is essentially a flashback after Flor's first husband dies during a raucous but, for him, typical bit of Sunday partying during Carnival. When Vadhino dies, the gamblers and women of Bahia go into mourning. Children, as well, feel the loss of him. For all practical purposes, Vadhino is a child, as Rip Van Winkle in Washington Irving's story was. "When he was with children, Vadhino was one of them, as though he were their age, and his patience was unlimited." Children "preferred being with him to any kind of game, calling out his name, running after him." Flor, too, is heartbroken by his death, even though he treated her shabbily most of the time, gambling away her money, cheating on her, and generally taking her for granted. After Vadhino's death, Flor devotes herself to the cooking classes she teaches, sublimating her sexual desire in recipes. But cooking does not hold her hidden emotions at bay—"Asphyxiated was Dona Flor, too, roweled by desire." She spends her days demonstrating cooking techniques to housewives, but she is "outwardly, calm water; inwardly, a raging fire." After a few years of widowhood, Flor marries a man who is the polar opposite of her first husband. Dr. Teodoro is a pharmacist, a successful and respected man in the community. Where Vadhino was a man of passion, Teodoro is a man of order. Vadhino was dissipated. Teodoro is a "superb forty-year-old specimen." Vadhino did everything on impulse. For Teodoro, all things must be scheduled precisely—even lovemaking with Flor is scheduled for Wednesdays and Saturdays only.

About three years after his death, Vadhino reappears to Flor, willed back to life by her, a naked presence in her bedroom. Lovable con man that he is, he cajoles and maneuvers until he is back in her bed and her life. In the magical-realist context of the novel and Brazilian culture, Vadhino's returning and making love to Flor seems perfectly reasonable, almost more real and true than his death. Vadhino's motto—a very Brazilian one it seems—is that a person who doesn't pursue luck doesn't deserve it. Luck, for Amado, is like magic, and in magic one finds marvels. One of the characters late in the novel says, "Happiness leaves no history. A happy life is not the subject for a novel." This echoes Tolstoy's wisdom in *Anna Karenina*, but, ultimately, it belies the happy truth of Amado's novel—that Flor finds the perfect man by merging two together, and although this scenario might not say positive things about men, it suggests the strength of women and their imaginations. In Flor's story, one man has a lust for life and the other a meticulous sense of morality. She ends up with a respectable husband and sexual fulfillment, even if it does take two men to accomplish that feat. What Flor finds is probably close to what most would consider the perfect artistic sensibility—a balance of passion and discipline. The final scene of the novel offers a picture of contentment— "That clear, rain-washed Sunday morning, with Dona Flor strolling along, happy with her life, satisfied with her two lovers." And if the somber realist has trouble putting his faith in the veracity of the story, Amado says, "And with this we come to the end of the tale of Dona Flor and her two husbands, set forth in all its details and mysteries, as clear and dark as life itself. All this took place; let him who will believe. It took place in Bahia, where these and other acts of magic occur without startling anybody."

Officially, Brazil is a Catholic country. Right now, it claims the largest Catholic population of any country in the world, but other forms of superstition and magic pulse through the land. There are many Afro-Brazilian cults and mystical sects. Candomble, an African word pointing to a dance in honor of the gods, is probably the most famous. It was brought to Brazil from Africa by the Nago, Yoruba, and Jeje peoples. Candomble rituals are practiced in a *caso de santo* (house of a saint) and directed by a *pai* or *mae de santo* (literally a father or mother of a saint), a priest or priestess who speaks the Yoruba language. In Candomble beliefs, each person has a god (an *orixa*) who follows him from birth, protecting him from harm. A person's orixa is identified by a mae or pai by throwing shells onto the ground and determining from their positions a person's fate and relationship with the supernatural powers. In this world, Vadhino's coming back to life might be commonplace indeed.

In the Candomble ceremonies, Exu is a messenger between the gods and human beings, offering advice on everything from love affairs to money matters. It is Exu who warns against thieves and gives protection from them. When we arrived in Salvador on a balmy afternoon in late November, I could have used Exu's help. Jo-Ellen was off with a friend on a shopping excursion, and I decided to look for the shade of Jorge Amado or at least his house. Maybe, like Vadhino, he would appear to me if I willed his presence.

I found his house in the Pelhourino section of old Salvador, led there by a scam artist. I knew he was one—I could tell by the ferocity of his smile and the way the words edged from his lips with a calculated nonchalance. But that was fine with me. He reminded me of how I pictured Vadhino, an engaging swindler. I was ready to meet one of Amado's creations in the flesh.

"You come with me, eh?" he said, brushing back a shock of curly brown hair from his dark forehead. It sounded like a question, but it wasn't. "I am a friend."

He saw the book in my hand. "I love Amado," he said. "I love America. I can show you more than anyone in Salvador."

We had been warned by embassy officials who came on the ship before we disembarked that half the population in Salvador was looking to pick our pockets. The SAS ship that had come the year before had been targeted by every thief for miles around. Hundreds of students had lost cameras, watches, wallets, passports, all slid silently and skillfully from their wrists and backpacks and pockets by hands they never saw or felt. According to one report, every single person onboard the ship had something taken.

"Don't bring a digital camera off the ship," we were warned. "Get a disposable camera. Don't wear a watch, even a cheap one. Keep your money and passport in a money belt."

I had no watch on my person, no camera strapped to my shoulder, and my money was tucked away where only someone who had a very close relationship with me could find it. So, other than life and limb, I didn't have too much to lose by going off with a middle-aged man named Lucio onto the sloping stone-lined streets of Salvador.

As we walked along, Lucio took an evaluative look at every woman under seventy that crossed our path. Occasionally, he said "bela" as a pretty young woman in tight jeans strutted past us. He smiled widely, his large yellow teeth glinting in appreciation. There was a carnival atmosphere in the old section of the city, on the streets of Pelhourino, a word that means "whipping post." The place is aptly named, for it was there that the slaves were whipped and sold in the eighteenth and nineteenth centuries. Even on a Wednesday afternoon in November, the people jiggled to samba music in the middle of the cobblestone squares, men danced to African drum beats on street corners, and dark-skinned beauties tossed their long black hair and smiled seductively as young men whistled. It was easy enough to imagine a Flor or Valdhino dancing unselfconsciously on one of the plazas in the twilight. Salvador, like Rio de Janeiro, has a reputation as a wild-hearted town, with all the lures and dangers associated with such places. With the music, laughter, and beautiful men and women taking their *passeios* along the streets, Vadhino's statement in *Dona Flor and Her Two Husbands*—"God is fat"—seemed perfectly true. When I told Lucio the line from the novel, he said, "Yes, yes, that is correct. People say that God loves Carnival. How could He not?" In Brazil, rumor had it that even God was a hedonist.

At Amado's house and museum, which was closed for renovation, Lucio looked sad, as if he had failed to raise a gregarious ghost.

"Amado lived in the Hotel Pelhourino anyway," he said, shrugging. "Not here." He pointed across the street to the brass plaque that adorned the wall of the hotel.

But even if Lucio had not gotten me much closer to Amado, he had done me a good service in helping me find my way around the town. It was an easy place to get lost. There was the lower city and the upper old town, linked by a lacerda, an elevator, and the Plano Iclinado Goncalves, a cable car. Each were crowded and a fine location to lose a wallet for anyone foolish enough to carry one. But riding the lacerdo or the plano inclinado was safer than walking through the winding labyrinth of streets that led from the lower city to the upper one. Street names, like traffic regulations, changed at the discretion of the pedestrian or driver. One could get a half dozen sets of directions to the same street address because each person had a different name for the same place—so Praca Novembro could be Terreiro de Jesus or Rua Francisco Muniz Barreto might be Rua das Laranjeiras.

"Ah, it is too bad," Lucio said, gazing mournfully at the Fundacao Casa de Jorge Amado. "I knew Amado. Like him, I am a writer. If you give me ten American dollars I will send you a copy of my novel, just published last month. It is the story of an American seeking Jorge Amado right after Carnival. It is a mystery book. I cannot tell you what happens."

Lucio's story had the right sort of reflexiveness for it to be an Amado creation. Of course it was a lie, but a good story and quickly devised and funny, nonetheless, and I gave him $3, all I had in my pocket. After all, I was not going to reach into my underwear in the middle of the crowded and darkening plaza.

Brazil is more than Salvador, of course. It is a big country, bigger than the continental United States without Alaska. It has a little more than half the population of the United States, though, with its vast unpopulated regions, mainly in the rainforest. The poverty that stained the cities and the outskirts makes most American poverty seem inconsequential. People live in little more than large boxes in favelas, or shanty towns, and the average income was $6,000 a year. But Brazil was one of the richest countries in the world in terms of natural resources, much of them in the lush Amazon region. The third world collided with the first in Brazil. It had some high-tech industries—electronics, aerospace, and automobile—and rampant poverty, crime, and disease, as well. The fairytale rich lived within sight of the nightmarishly poor. And this paradox was part of the history of Brazil.

When the Portuguese arrived in the early sixteenth century, some say blown off course on the way to India, they "discovered" a diverse Indian population that had not developed an advanced, consolidated society like the Mayans had created in present-day Mexico and parts of Central America. The first Portuguese sailors stayed in Brazil only long enough to build a cross and say Mass. They did not see much there to hold their attention as they sought the gold and spices of the Far East. Initially, the red dye they could extract from brazilwood was the only commodity worth taking from the environment. Within a few years, the name of the colony was changed from Terra de Vera Cruz to Brazil, a sign many Portuguese took to suggest the godlessness of the place.

It did not take too many years for the Portuguese colonists to figure out that the land and the climate were perfect for growing sugar cane. The European sweet tooth made this an immensely profitable market as long as the Portuguese could find cheap labor. They did—by enslaving the Indian population and by importing slaves from Africa. The plantation system made for huge profits for the few white settlers and a hard life and early death for the black and Indian population. Brazil stayed sparsely populated until the discovery of gold in the eighteenth century brought hundreds of thousands of white settlers with eyes dazzled by the thought of quick riches.

After the gold boom died, coffee became king. After the sugar market declined, coffee was the perfect crop to replace it. Growing coffee beans, another labor-intensive activity, was well suited to the plantation system. The end of slavery in 1888 did not help the coffee plantations, but the poverty of the general population kept a cheap labor market alive. The early twentieth century saw the rise of the rubber industry, as automobiles spread across the civilized world. For a time, the rubber tree was the new Amazonian gold. But the jealously guarded seeds of the rubber tree were smuggled out of Brazil in 1876 and sent to Kew Gardens in England and from there to Southeast Asia. Within a few decades, Brazil no longer had a corner on the rubber trade.

The nineteenth century in Brazil was the story of slave revolts and rebellions by the poor. In the early part of the century, under the son of the king of Portugal, Brazil declared its independence, and Pedro, the ambitious prince, declared himself emperor. The empire lasted until a military coup toppled the government in 1889. Since then, Brazil has been a land of unfulfilled promise, rife with political unrest, economic inflation, and environmental destruction. The last great boom in Brazil could be focused on the resources found in the Amazonian rainforest. The Amazon, by volume, is the world's largest river, and Amazonian basin is home to the biggest rainforest on the planet. It is probably the most species-rich piece of land in the world. Nowhere on earth can one find more diversity of plant life than in the Amazon basin, but greed and deforestation are proving disastrous. More and more land has been cleared to farm soybeans and other crops. Cattle farms and highways scar the virgin forests.

Highways brought and continued to bring more settlers. What was nearly 4 million square kilometers of untouched forest in 1970 was barely 3 million kilometers in 2002. Many scientists say that the Amazon rainforest serves as the lungs of the planet, and if they are threatened, so is every corner of the earth.

Brazil's future might be much like its past: a struggle between ensconced interests and outside forces, between the needs of the poor and the desires of the privileged. In many ways, this was Salvador's story, once the capital of the country and one of the richest cities in the New World and now as bifurcated into rich and poor as the elevator between the two parts of the city suggested.

On our last day in Salvador, Jo-Ellen and I sailed in a private boat with students and faculty across the Bay of All Saints to the island of Itaparica. We had lunch, drank a few beers, and watched the dark-skinned young men prance up and down the beach flexing their muscles as they passed young women lying on the sand. The water was calm and warm. Our boat had anchored about 200 yards offshore, and we came to the beach in skiffs. With the sun setting, the skiffs came back to pick us up. Two or three students decided to swim back to the boat, and I joined them. I did not realize that I had left my Teva sandals on until I swam out about fifty yards and the wind began to pick up. Then the waves started to rise. The crew had raised the boat anchor, and the more intensely I tried to get to my destination the farther away it appeared to drift. My sandals felt like weights. I swallowed a few mouthfuls of salt water. I've been a strong swimmer since I was a child. At twelve years old I had swum across a two-mile-wide lake in Maine. I had never had a moment in the water where I felt panicked—until this one. The waves seemed to push me away from the boat. I swam harder. Breathing became more difficult, and the waves broke over my head. I tried to wave to the boat, to signal them to wait, but raising my arms invited the water into my mouth. Panic creates adrenaline, but it also encourages more panic. I kicked my leaden legs more strenuously through the rough seas and moved my arms as vigorously as I could.

When the nervous energy drained from my muscles, I turned on my back and did the backstroke. Seconds turned into minutes, and the boat never seemed to get closer. I started to work harder, pushing thoughts of Billie, the drowned oiler in Stephen Crane's "The Open Boat," from my mind. I already had the Tevas to weigh me down. Literary allusions wouldn't help. After a few minutes of feeling as if I were in the frenzied motionlessness of a nightmare, I reached the rope ladder of the boat. It was like waking from a disturbing sleep and, weak-limbed, I hauled myself onto the deck. Not Jo-Ellen or anyone onboard had noticed my struggling in the water. The memory of it was mine alone, and a few moments after I sat onboard the boat, now sailing toward the emerging lights of Salvador, the whole experience seemed as private and imagined as a dream.

That night we strolled around the Pelhourino section of the city, along cobblestone streets that snaked downhill from the wide plazas and narrowed until they looked like alleyways between the colorful seventeenth-century houses and baroque churches. Somewhere along the way, Jo-Ellen went one way and I the other, and we could not find one another. I was not too worried, though, because Pelhourino was the safest place in the area to lose a loved one. Pelhourino, like the French Quarter in New Orleans, was the most shielded place in a dangerous city. Police dotted the landscape, protecting the tourists and, most likely more important to them, the tourist dollar and the industry it fueled. The *capitoes d'areia* (captains of the sand), the juveniles who snatched anything not bolted down, were swept back to the beaches and the lower city by the ubiquitous police presence.

I found Jo-Ellen after an hour of meandering up and down the streets of the old city. She was standing next to another ubiquitous feature of the Pelhourino section, Lucio. They were leaning against a bench on the edge of a crowd that was watching a capoeira demonstration, what appeared to be a master and his pupils. It was a balletic mixture of acrobatic dancing and martial arts. I came up silently behind them, close enough to hear what Lucio was saying to her.

"Capoeira is the dance of the slaves. Resistance to slavery took many forms in my country, and capoeira was one of them. At first, it was a way for slaves to fight their masters. When any practice of it was banned, they disguised it in a dance. Then, even the dance was forbidden and had to be done in secret. Now it is a great sport, as you can see. It is graceful and beautiful. *Bonito como voce, senhora.*"

I cleared my throat before she could answer—or ask for a translation. I could see where Lucio was headed, a direction that Vadhino would have appreciated. Jo-Ellen just smiled innocently, and we headed back to the elevator that would take us to the lower part of the city and from there a few short blocks to our ship in the harbor. Ahead of us, two students from my literature class ambled along as if they had all the time in the world to get back to the ship. In reality, they had only one hour. One young man turned to the other and said, "This place is fat. Maybe we should just let the ship sail without us."

When I thought about what he had said, I couldn't be sure if it was *fat* or *phat*, whether he was a disciple of Vadhino or a media-saturated American teenager. I knew it was time to leave, though. As we passed them and we waved in greeting, I was on one side of Jo-Ellen and Lucio on the other, like Vadhino and Teodoro with Dona Flor. When we got to the lacerda, I slipped him all the money I had in both pockets. It was worth the price to get rid of my doppelganger. As we headed down to the lower city in the crush of bodies in the elevator, I looked at Jo-Ellen's lovely face and thought I didn't want to share her with anyone. I could manage the responsibility of being two men. All it took was luck. I had that. My near-drowning had just been a baptism, of sorts, a reminder that time was an undeserved gift. Knowing that, I sensed that miracles, as Jorge Amado demonstrated, followed naturally.

Cuba

Cuba had many of the fading colors and breathtaking decay of Brazil. Of course it is an island, smaller than the state of Pennsylvania and with approximately the same number of people. Therefore, it is a place that can be encompassed in a way Brazil cannot. It seemed small enough for me to find the ghost of Ernest Hemingway, maybe even the living presence of Fidel. But I was prepared to be disillusioned. If years of reading Hemingway had taught me anything, it had dramatized that man should expect defeat. And I was well aware that Cuba had a capacity for manufacturing illusions. At least Castro did. He had been doing just that for years. Right now, he was trying to make a crumbling infrastructure appear to have the contours of paradise. Illusions go a long way back in Cuba, though, I suppose. When Christopher Columbus came to the north shore of the island at the Bay of Barlay in 1492, he thought he had found the Far East, perhaps Japan.

From what I knew of Cuban politics and history, Castro faced reality in much the same way that Columbus did. Both of them are significant men in history, sharing the qualities of passion, leadership, and unyielding dreams. And Castro, like Columbus, saw what he wanted to see. In his account of his travels in Cuba in the 1990s, *Waiting for Fidel*, Christopher Hunt says, "Despite cutbacks, the state continued to provide hospitals (without medicine), schools (without books), and a subsistence diet (without meat). Cubans knew theirs was the only country in the world where a person could do nothing, absolutely nothing, and not starve to death. Blanketed by security, many were afraid of the real world." Hunt goes on to point out one of the contradictions in the soul of the society: "Cubans deified Che because he fought for the principle that people should rule themselves." Instead, of course, the Cuban people ended up with an iron-fisted dictator who seemed invulnerable to death and incapable of getting tired as he gave one of his renowned three-hour speeches, and a country in which everyone was afraid to criticize the government except in hurried, hushed tones.

One of the reasons that Cuba placed such importance on its revolutionary heroes—Jose Marti or Che Guevara or Fidel Castro—might be because its people had never really tasted freedom. It was only about a decade after Columbus misidentified Cuba that Diego Velazquez landed there with three hundred men and began the conquest for Spain. He was looking for gold, but what he found were blood and slaves and, later, a launching point for colonizing expeditions to the continent. Like Brazil and America, Cuba is soaked in the blood of Indians and slaves. And like Brazil, Cuba became a thriving landscape for sugar plantations and then coffee growers, making it a stratified society where the separations between the rich and the indigent seemed unbridgeable. Cubans wanted independence, though, and the movement in that direction became inexorable. In 1886, two years before Brazil abolished slavery, Cuba passed a decree prohibiting the slave trade on the island. It was not long after, in 1895, that the war for independence, led by the Cuban Revolutionary Party leader Jose Marti, started. Once the United States intervened after the sinking of the *Maine* in 1898, the Spanish government ended its sovereignty over the island. Ostensibly, Cuba had its freedom, but America had a foothold in the country and an invisible hand in its administration.

In 1933, a military coup led to the takeover by Fulgencio Batista, who ruled as a dictator for the next quarter of a century. A Cuban lawyer— Fidel Castro—and an Argentinian doctor—Che Guevara—ended Batista's brutal reign of power in January 1959. Castro, along with his Council of Ministers, declared new laws for the country. American-owned companies were nationalized, large plantations were broken up, and the land was redistributed among the poor workers. Next came the United States embargo, the Cuban missile crisis, the Bay of Pigs fiasco, and nearly half a century of cold war and icy relations between the two countries. Communism, inept administration, and the stranglehold of the U.S. embargo made Cuba what it is today—a country where education was free but the educated could find no work commensurate with their training, where no one was homeless but homes were dilapidated, where no one had to pay for medical attention but the medicine needed to save a life was most likely not available. The Cuba I saw was a bizarre world, caught in some strange time warp. The cars dated to the 1940s and 1950s as if clocks had stood still or I had gone in a time machine back to the Bronx of my childhood. As Cuba drifted into the twenty-first century like a ship becalmed in the past, Castro was still the emperor with no clothes, standing before his people as if everything was as it should be. What those people saw, though, was a leader who had made their hard lives much harder. What they saw was the paint peeling off the buildings and the foundations crumbling, the shelves in the grocery stores empty, and the American dollar the only currency that had any value. The best means of transportation on the island was hitchhiking, and that everyone seemed to do. As Dave Eggers wrote, "Hitchhiking is what makes Cuba move. . . . The roads are littered with people." And they are all hitchhikers.

Despite all of the economic and political problems Cuba faced, Havana was a spellbinding place, a spoiled beauty of a city. If the city were a woman, it would be Gloria Swanson in *Sunset Boulevard:* like her, lost in the past but mysterious and elegant in its despair and disrepair. It displayed its Caribbean colors—pinks and faded golds and blues and greens—like once-magnificent garments that were now tatters. After a rainstorm, it was a city of muddy lanes. Puddles made a wet puzzle of every side street. On a sunny day, it was a slow-moving metropolis of dusty roads and cracked cement. Lines of schoolchildren in white shirts, blue ties, and red shorts wended their way along every avenue, past seventeenth- and eighteenth-century Spanish buildings pockmarked with bullet holes from the late 1950s and signs on the walls that announced REVOLUCION—another anachronism in a country swarming with them. Colorful laundry, washed to a ragged translucence, hung from rusted balconies. Underfed, sleepy-eyed dogs lay on every sidewalk in any available triangle of shade. Groups of men and women arranged themselves in lazy queues near the ration stations. Only the German shepherd police dogs appeared to be well fed and content.

Havana was a city of still-life portraits. Near the Calle Murualla, a group of young boys played a baseball game. Two-thirds of them did not have gloves. The gloves they had looked as if they had been stolen from Ty Cobb—my father had the same sort of glove from his boyhood in the 1920s, small as a hand glove and worn smooth from use. Their bat was a carved 2 x 4, splintered and chipped. One boy bent forward at shortstop in one shoe and frayed jean shorts, a grimy blue shirt, and a magnificent smile. The next street over, another group of boys played soccer with a miniature basketball. In the adjacent square, four boys climbed a two-story scaffolding as if it were a jungle gym; above their heads the sheets of laundry billowed out in the soft breeze like sails on a ship they would never take. They tossed pebbles on a rooster who eyed them critically from below. Tethered by its leg to the bars of a window, the rooster could only dodge their missiles. It had no escape.

As in the other countries we had visited, it was the children in Cuba—the children around the world—who broke our hearts. So many of them were miniature businessmen and women, selling coconut milk or post-cards—or worse—and growing up before they were little more than babies. In Havana, despite all the poverty—which Castro blamed exclusively on the American embargo—children did not seem exploited as we had seen in other parts of the world. They had time to play, even if they did not have the equipment that most American children took for granted.

🌊🌊🌊 On our second evening in Havana, I lost Jo-Ellen again. These disappearances were becoming a motif in my life, and I was not sure if she was trying to tell me something. This time she drifted away with Carolyn Dudek, our friend from the ship, and I roamed the darkened streets of the city in search of her. Even in the night and on streets without lights, Havana seemed safe. Castro's strong arm reached into every shadow, and tourists had little to worry about. That's the benefit, I suppose, of totalitarian societies—they make for safe tourist spots.

After a half hour of circling the same blocks, I decided to head toward Hemingway's favorite bar—El Floridita—where legend had it that he drank sixteen Papa Dobles (a double-shot frozen daiquiri invented for him there) in one sitting. The place probably looked much the same as it had when Hemingway was there in the 1950s—black and red décor, crowded bar, and cluttered walls. One thing had changed: there was a chain around the stool that Hemingway supposedly sat upon, a holy relic that drew the tourists in the door. I had a mojito, but I decided my friend Mike Frey in the Catskill Mountains in New York made a better one, and I headed out again in search of my oft-vanishing wife.

A few yards from El Floridita, a middle-aged woman with a red bandanna on her head and a wet cigar between her lips asked me if I wanted to exchange a few American dollars for a package of cigarettes. I was reminded of Josefino de Diego's story "Internal Monologue on a Corner in Havana," in which a woman sells her rationed cigarettes to supplement her eighty-peso-a-month pension. With that story in mind, I gave her a dollar and told her to keep the cigarettes, thinking for a second I wouldn't mind one but remembering that I had given up smoking twenty-five years before and wondering if the strange Cuban night was getting to me. I stopped at another bar (I had never given up drinking) and ordered a Cuba libre, a mix of ice, rum, coke, and lime, even though I had the first lines of Christopher Hunt's admonition from *Waiting for Fidel* ringing in my ears: "Rum spells trouble. Cuba had taught me that much." A mojito and a Cuba libre were certainly not what I needed in searching for a lost woman. But I reasoned *how could it hurt* as I headed toward the Parque de la Fraternidad on some alcohol-induced instinct.

As I neared the Capitolio, a woman floated out of the shadows of a building. She grabbed my arm, "Me quieres?" I remembered enough high school Spanish to understand what she was asking, and even before I saw her torn dress and her missing front teeth and the glowing green eyes of the cat at her feet, I tried to explain that I was looking for my wife and her friend. "Dos mujers, mira dos," I stuttered, unable to find the word for wife. She didn't understand me. Or she did, but kept her sales pitch going anyway. She pulled harder on my elbow and looked into my eyes, "Esperante dos, si, si. Venga con mi." Then I remembered the word for wife and like an incantation repeated "esposa, esposa, esposa" as I raced off down the street.

When I found Jo-Ellen, she was enjoying a margarita with Carolyn in the bar of a hotel. I tried to explain to her that there were women out there who wanted to teach me Spanish and other things, but she just smiled, patted my hand, and said, "Isn't it too late to become fluent in another language?"

The next afternoon some university students hand selected by Castro acted as our guides aboard a bus that took us to Finca Vigia (Lookout Farm), the sprawling house Hemingway bought in 1940 for $18,500 in San Francisco de Paula, nine miles from Havana. Years before, I had been to Hemingway's house in Key West and seen dozens of cats roaming the grounds. In Finca Vigia, Hemingway and Martha Gellhorn, his third wife, reportedly had fifty-seven cats. I started to have a better understanding of why he committed suicide.

The Cuban students knew virtually nothing about Hemingway, had obviously not read his books, and got most of the facts about his life and writing wrong. As tactfully as possible, I made corrections and additions to what they had to say to our bus filled with students.

"Yes, that's true," I said, "Hemingway did love Cuba, but he wrote *A Farewell to Arms* in Key West, long before he moved to the island. Hemingway did have sons, but three, not two. Four wives, not three. He didn't win the Nobel Prize for his great book on Cuba, *The Old Man and the Sea*. Individuals win the Nobel Prize for the body of their work, but that novel certainly helped sway the judges."

It became clear that the students were there to proselytize for Castro's government, not to act as guides informing us about Hemingway in Cuba. They had quite a bit to say about the unfairness of the American embargo, the efficacy of the Cuban education system, and the equality of medical treatment. Most of what they said came out in a pitch that was slightly too high. Their words rushed out as if they had all gone to the same training session.

When we got to the Hemingway house, now an odd kind of museum one could find only in Cuba, the place supposedly stood just as Hemingway had left it shortly after Castro's takeover. However, it was hard to get close enough to tell much about the house, for tourists were not allowed to enter the building. We were allowed to peer into the windows at the Robert Domingo paintings and the pairs of Hemingway's shoes and the well-worn copies of the books he owned—*Houdini, The Art of Cooking,* and *Big Game Hunting.* I took a photograph, although we were not supposed to, but the glare from the sunlight on the pane gave me a picture of the glass and an image of the face of one of my students, Evan Majors, staring with a bold, ghostly grin as if the young Hemingway were inside looking out at the world.

The store on the property sold postcards with images of Che on them and books about him and the revolution. There were no photographs of Hemingway and none of his books—not one. The closest thing to a piece of Hemingway memorabilia in the store was a photograph of Gregorio Fuentes, the supposed prototype for Santiago in *The Old Man and the Sea*. Fuentes had died a few months before our visit. Hemingway had met him in 1930 when the boat they were on was storm-tossed in the Dry Tortugas. In 1938, Hemingway hired him to be his first mate aboard his fishing boat, the *Pilar*. But Fuentes was most likely not the model for the quietly heroic Santiago. He transformed himself into a tourist attraction, charging visitors for photographs and tales of his relationship with Papa. The more logical source for the character of Santiago was Carlos Gutierrez, Hemingway's original first mate for the *Pilar*. Gutierrez was born in Cuba in 1883, which would have made him (unlike Fuentes, who was Hemingway's age) an old man when the book was written. In addition, according to most accounts, it was Gutierrez who told Hemingway the story of the old fisherman who was dragged out to sea for days by the great marlin he had caught. The old fisherman, exhausted after battling with sharks and losing most of his fish, was rescued by fellow fishermen. Hemingway took Gutierrez's powerful story of the indifference of the sea and refashioned it into a parable of man's stoical courage and calm resolution. What Santiago wishes to show to his magnificent adversary in the sea is what Hemingway dramatizes for the reader: "I will show him what a man can do and what a man endures. . . . a man is not made for defeat . . . A man can be destroyed but not defeated."

Hemingway loved Cuba, and he admired the simple dignity of its people, represented for him in the sun-scarred face of Santiago and his dreams of lions and baseball heroes. Right outside the Finca Vigia, in the slum that surrounds the property, there were a dozen such faces. Their dreams, though, may have been harder edged than Santiago's. As our bus was making a turn onto the main road, we saw a fight between a man in his twenties and an old man who looked enough like the photograph I had seen of Fuentes to have been his wide-eared, sun-wrinkled twin. The old man was trying to charge the young man, but four men restrained him. After a brief struggle, he broke free, went to a shed near an adjacent playground, and came limping back with a rifle cradled in his arms. Our bus turned the corner as the crowd converged on the two men, the story— along with Hemingway and Fuentes and Gutierrez—disappearing into the limits of our imaginations.

We did not have to imagine Castro, though. We got to see more of him than we had expected or, finally, felt we deserved. We met him at the Cuban Parliament, seven hundred of us filling the hall. Cuban students sat in the seats above us, with banners proclaiming the need to stop the march toward war draped over the balconies. The ceremony started promptly at 6 P.M. The van that took us to the Parliament had a police escort, sirens blaring. We passed ambulances and emergency vehicles as if they were standing still. We had to be going 90 mph on the city streets, but Castro wanted us there on time, I suppose. His speech—over three hours long—was a masterly stage performance. After the three hours, most of us in the audience were done in, but he appeared ready to go for another three-hour stretch. You had to admire his skillfulness and his Santiago-like endurance. We were sitting in comfortable seats, and I was exhausted. In his mid-seventies and presumably affected by a variety of health problems, Castro stood erect in front of a microphone with no podium to lean against and talked and talked and talked. If he hadn't had the trademark beard, his dark grey suit and purple tie would have made him look like a well-heeled Miami banker. His eyes were clear and his voice never wavered once. As a matter of fact, he often raised the pitch to a near-hysterical political railing that suggested at least his lungs were working fine.

Castro's fundamental principle of speechmaking, besides simply talking his audience into submission, was his confident failure to answer any question from the audience. Any significant question that was asked he sidestepped, danced around, and then turned into a platform to speak for thirty minutes on the subject he had planned to talk about all along. The first question, which was about the relationship between the Cuban government and Jews who lived in the country, brought forth a forty-five-minute circumlocution about the Inquisition, the corruption of the popes, sex in the modern world, Adam and Eve, and snowballs. After forty-three minutes, he did return to the Jews and the Cuban Revolution, but he never answered the question. But why would that surprise anyone? I'm not sure many remembered the question at that point.

After a while the questions deteriorated, perhaps because everyone had given up hope of getting a straight answer or maybe because the students had swallowed more than their share of Cuba libres before the meeting. So the questions went like this:

"Fidel, will you sign my passport?" Which he did to the great glee and shouts of approval from the many of the students.

"Fidel, can I give you a hug?" Which he allowed, as the faculty shrunk in their seats, afraid that we too might have to hug him or that some Cuban equivalent of *Candid Camera* was lurking in the wings.

Or the one that made some of us wonder if we would get out of there alive. "Fidel, did you and the Cuban government help the Mafia kill John F. Kennedy?" The question allowed Castro to launch a long story about the American government's many attempts to kill him with poisoned cigars or assassins.

I waved my hand with a decorous fury, but he never called on me. I thought I had a trick question: "Fidel, if you had *only one sentence,* how would you say you wanted history to remember you?" It was the *one sentence* part that I thought might stump him. Perhaps he looked into my sleepy eyes and sensed a trap. Or maybe the place had hidden cameras and he saw the note Jo-Ellen had passed to me in the last dreary half hour, like a bored schoolgirl in high school geometry class: *Now I know what killed Che. After listening to a few of these speeches, he would have longed for death. Do you think Castro drove Hemingway to mojitos, too?*

At the party after Castro's speech, we were offered rice and plates of horse meat (dressed up to look like ordinary barbecue) and more Cuba libres. We ate selectively and drank prodigiously. The Cuban students in the dining hall stuffed the meat into plastic bags and wrapped it in their jackets. Long before the end of the evening, the food was gone. All that was left was the never-ending rum. A group of us sat on the terrace outside the building, the bottle glowing like a talisman in the moonlight, and listened to the president of the student association tell us some things we did not know: "Elian Gonzalez was kidnapped by the American Mafia. It was all a plot to make Cuba look like a bad place." I wasn't sure if he actually believed what he said, but he looked around as if he were checking to see who was paying attention to his theory. All I could hear was an echo of the words in Christopher Hunt's book: "Cuba looks calm. But they watch. . . . They listen. . . . This is a very tense society." All the Cuban students I saw leaving with their pockets bulging with soggy horse meat appeared to look both ways before they shuffled out to hitch a ride.

That night we sailed out of Havana harbor, leaving behind the lukewarm breezes, the bright-eyed schoolchildren in their starched uniforms, the antique cars, the slow-paced life of the Caribbean, the fading old buildings that looked like aging movies stars, and we headed back to the United States—only ninety miles away. And if I thought I had some things figured out about the world, college students, and the United States we were returning to, Steve and Alex, the two students from my writing class who had shown themselves to be improvisational comic geniuses during the voyage, provided me with a reality check. Jo-Ellen and I were saying goodbye to some colleagues in the faculty lounge when Alex and Steve stepped across the threshold and said, "Psst! Dr. P, we have something for you."

I walked across the room.

"We have a card that we made for a select few on the ship. We loved your class. It was the best."

I thanked them. I was pleased to know someone appreciated the courses I taught. They left the room, and I unsealed the envelope and opened the card.

"Jo-Ellen, come here for a moment, okay?"

I showed her. The card told me how much they had gained from the creative writing class, and inside the card was a photograph of Steve and Alex. That was fine, and ordinarily I would have kept it to do just that—remember them. But the photograph showed them standing in a cabin dorm room, towels draped casually over their skinny shoulders.

Otherwise, they were stark naked and staring with wry smiles into the lens of the camera.

They were funny guys, and clearly this was a joke. *It is a joke, right?* I said to Jo-Ellen. But then I tore the photo into little pieces before I exited the faculty lounge, because that night we were to pack our bags, and the last thing I wanted was for some curious customs official to ask me why I had a photograph of two naked students in my stuff. I wouldn't have known how to answer. I had learned some things about dodging questions from Castro, but I hadn't learned enough. My only response could have been *Even after a voyage around the world with them, students are still a mystery to me. I really like them, you know, but not that much.*

2004

AN INTERLUDE

Pilgrimage in Spain

In 2004, as America was mired in the war in Iraq, I wondered once again about the nature and consequences of travel. The jeopardy seemed real enough, but what about the pleasures? All those planes, trains, and cobblestone paths? The bags to be pulled, the backpacks to be lugged, the cramped hotel rooms, the indifferent hotel clerks? But I considered that it might not be simple pleasure we sought—at least not those of us who never got to travel in first-class airline seats or relax in four-star hotel rooms. Maybe it wasn't pleasure but knowledge we searched for, the kind of understanding that could only be discovered by leaving home.

Some people yearn for genuine danger, to be in the shadow of Mount Everest or in the farthest reaches of the Amazon jungle, but most of us who travel looking for some form of revelation want the deepest experience we can manage in reasonable safety. Most of us would be happy if we could only discard our tourist status for a time and actually encounter people and landscapes with our own hearts and eyes. True encounters rarely occur in elegant restaurants and high-priced hotels where people are well-paid actors. Generally, there the world is deflected, not met. All most of us really want is to find something authentic in the world and ourselves.

I'm not certain what compelled Jo-Ellen and me to take the pilgrimage route to Santiago de Campostella—that our friends from the ship in 2002, Bill and Sherry May, had done it or some latent Catholic instinct to find redemption in suffering? But the adventure offered the modest threats and potential enlightenment that we wanted. There was the chance of heatstroke, sprained ankles, torrential rains, snarling dogs, or dusty roads without a place to stay. But no serious dangers, unless the risks of the Basque country and becoming hostages of the ETA were more than just my overactive imagination. But even the possibility of minor hardships makes travel seem real in ways that are defeated by air-conditioned tour buses and generic hotel lobbies. The opportunities in travel open up against sweat and sore muscles. A certain kind of travel allows a person to face the world at ground level, to meet strangers not as waiters or cab drivers but as fellow journeyers in the world.

At first, Jo-Ellen was nervous about the long hike, worried that her legs might not be up to fifteen miles a day on tough terrain. She was a realist. On the other hand, I rode a bicycle to work, played basketball and tennis, and had the arrogance of a middle-aged man who remembers too vividly for his own good what it felt like to be twenty-one years old. I was so unconcerned that I put the hefty new translation of *Don Quixote* by Edith Grossman in my already overloaded backpack. *Not to worry, I can handle it.* Jo-Ellen looked at me the way I imagine Sancho Panza looked at the Knight of the Sorrowful Countenance when he declared authoritatively that windmills were actually giants. So, although I did not realize it at the moment of departure, the two of us headed out like knight errant and skeptical friend looking for some undefined adventure and blessings along the way.

Somehow it seemed that every trip we took out of the United States was destined to follow in the wake of some devastating violence. On March 11, 2004, a few weeks after we purchased our airline tickets to Europe, terrorists bombed many of the rush-hour trains in Madrid, killing close to two hundred people and injuring thousands. We were scheduled to arrive in Spain in July of that year, when the feast day of St. James fell on a Sunday, a prime time for pilgrims to arrive at the cathedral in Santiago. A few months before, I had been prepared to lead a study abroad trip to northern Spain, but the bombing in Madrid had caused a panic among the students and their parents and the enrollment numbers dropped from eleven to four in a gasp, too small a group for the university to subsidize.

The exchange rate for the U.S. dollar against the pound and the euro was terrible, the threat of violence hung in the air like old smoke, and there were at least a dozen reasons to stay home, but Jo-Ellen and I decided to take off alone, making our way to Spain through two of our favorite cities in the world, London and Paris. We drove from Norfolk, Virginia, to New

York City, where we had grown up, met, and fallen in love. We drove on the East Side Drive past our memories of the Bronx and into the splendid impossibility of Manhattan, buildings elbowing each other into the grey sky, away from the surreal actuality of people and cars and light and sound. It seemed to us as if we were starting at the beginning place, perhaps where we must always start, in the deepest reaches of our past.

The few hours we spent in Chumley's Bar before heading to our motel on the edge of one of the runways at Kennedy Airport seemed right, as well. I had never been to Chumley's before, although I'd heard tales of the place and walked past 86 Bedford Street in Greenwich Village many times in my youth not knowing that Norman Mailer or Arthur Miller might have been sipping lager at the bar. So many writers—John Steinbeck, Ring Lardner, A. J. Liebling, Upton Sinclair, Willa Cather, Eugene O'Neill—had spent afternoons and evenings there when it had been a speakeasy. Staying true to those days when it went incognito as an off-limits bar, it had no sign announcing what it was—pub or enchanted castle or just another door leading to an exorbitantly priced rental on a narrow street in the Village. Stepping into the place was like reversing direction in *The Wizard of Oz*, crossing the line from color to black and white. The place was crowded with patrons and ghosts. Dust jackets and photographs of writers lined every wall. All the worn wooden booths were taken. There was just enough space at the bar for Jo-Ellen and me to belly up and order two beers.

The man standing next to me, who looked suspiciously like Dylan Thomas, the same untamed hair and drunkenness that I associated with the poet, at any rate, eyed the copy of *The Road to Santiago: The Pilgrim's Practical Guide* that stuck out of my jacket pocket.

"You're a bit off course, I think, mate."

"Just grabbing a beer before we head to the airport," I replied. "We have a good idea where we're heading, thanks."

"Are you saints or religious folk or something?" he asked. But before I could answer, he turned to the young woman on the other side of him and said, "You're not a saint, I hope, my dear."

His question to us was a good one, though. What were we doing on the road to Santiago, or at least heading toward that road? The motives that led hundreds of thousands of people in the Middle Ages to embark on a pilgrimage were religious, of course. They gave up the comforts and relative safety of home to engage in a journey fraught with robbers and storms and other dangers. Some of them lost their money. Some, their lives. They went to save their souls, I guess. Out of respect for the pilgrims' quest, people along the way offered food, shelter, and assistance. I had been raised a Catholic and had gone through Jesuit training at Fordham University and the University of San Francisco before I finally, at age twenty-five, slipped away for my PhD at the secular Pennsylvania State University, where, if any god existed, it was football. I could not consider myself religious in the narrow sense of the term. I tended not to ask too many questions about God or the afterlife. Jo-Ellen was more prone to bringing up such questions, and I admired her for it. I just didn't have any good answers.

But all that religious training had left its mark and followed me to Penn State, where I wrote my dissertation on one of the most Catholic of modern American novelists, Walker Percy. Like Flannery O'Connor, Percy believed in the power and possibility of grace in the world, and I was open to the proposition myself even if I didn't see enough of it in action. So, like a good fallen Catholic, I was ready to see what the world had to offer in terms of shelter and assistance and if there were any miracles left, perhaps, on the pilgrimage path. But I had fallen far enough to have three more beers at Chumley's before I tested the road.

We flew out the next morning, arriving in London in the evening light, the clouds breaking long enough for us to see the quilted landscape of England as we descended, a land that looked pieced and trimmed as if it were a series of couplets arranged by Alexander Pope for our entertainment. Of course, I may still have been feeling the effects of the beers at Chumley's, the lack of sleep on the plane, and the hours reading the first half of Cervantes' novel. The whole scene resembled another Quixotic illusion. All I can say for certain was that the countryside outside Heathrow Airport looked British enough for Robert Donat and Margaret Ashcroft to be strolling along, arm in arm, eating fish and chips.

We shouldered our bags onto the express train to Paddington Station, squeezed into an underground car that took us to Lancaster Station, and walked the quarter of a mile down Bayswater Road to the Columbia

Hotel. The Columbia, a second-rate beauty, originally five large Victorian townhouses and after World War II an American officers' club, is known affectionately (or not) as the "rock and roll hotel." I've been there a number of times and never seen Mick Jagger or Eric Clapton, but I've been in the sitting room on a weekday evening for some wild-hearted fiddle playing and had to step gingerly around piles of amplifiers and guitars in the lobby in the early morning. The Columbia has a sturdy sort of grandeur from the outside. The rooms were another matter entirely—dowdy, wallpapered by someone's spinster aunt, and generally unappealing. But the hotel sat across the road from Hyde Park, a short walk to the Albert Memorial, and close to the center of London.

Its real attraction for me was its proximity to Halepi, a few streets away. It's the best Greek restaurant I have found outside of Greece. It's embarrassing to admit, I suppose, but I like going to London and staying at the Columbia because I love going to Halepi, seeing the friendly faces of the owner and his sons, listening to the boisterous customers, being part of the whole bustling scene. I feel the sort of affection for the Greek salad and moussaka there that Don Quixote reserved for Dulcinea, but even he would not have traveled three thousand miles on such a whimsical quest. No, the food is great, but it's the sense I have there of being in a place where people know me even though I'm an absolute stranger (except for my yearly visits) that attracts me. Whenever I go into the restaurant, I feel as if I'm back in my old neighborhood—and I haven't felt like that since I was a teenager eating at Dominick's on Arthur Avenue in the Bronx.

I didn't feel too guilty about spending all our time in London in Hyde Park or at Halepi's. We had only a day and a half, and in years past we had seen everything from the Tower and Shakespeare's Globe to Parliament and Westminster Cathedral. Besides, spending as much time in Halepi's as we did allowed us to stumble upon one of the secrets of the British government. On our last night in the restaurant, we saw Tony Blair having a cozy, conjugal sort of dinner with a young Japanese woman. He left in a black limousine, she followed in another. Jo-Ellen was convinced I still had jet lag, but I know what I saw, even if she could not see it when I pointed it out to her. If it wasn't Tony Blair, then it was someone who looked exactly like him and most likely had the same name.

The taste of olives and scallions from Halepi and the sound of the raucous cheering produced by the news that the Greek team had made it to the World Cup finals in soccer were enough fuel to get us going the next morning to catch the train from London to Dover. The train wheezed and coughed along the tracks past the black-faced sheep that dotted the hills, stopping at towns with such British names they made me thirst for a spot of tea—Pluckley, Folkstone, Westenhanger.

The hovercraft from Dover to Calais had its share of Englishmen of a different variety, swilling beer and puking on the carpeted floors. In Calais, we boarded the train to Paris and rolled along the orderly French countryside, miles of green fields and shapely farms, clusters of trees and bucolic villages, all laid out like a painting by Millet. The Gare du Nord in Paris was another landscape altogether, graffiti and grifters galore. But outside the station was Paris nevertheless. Is there a more beautiful city? What makes Paris heartachingly lovely is subjective (although its beauty is beyond debate, I think). Adam Gopnik may have answered the question as well as it can be answered in *Paris to the Moon* when he writes: "What truly makes Paris beautiful is the intermingling of the monumental and the personal, the abstract and the footsore particular, it and you. A city of vast impersonal set pieces of architecture, it is also a city of small and intricate, improvised experience. . . . The passage from big to little is what makes Paris beautiful, and you have to be prepared for the small—to live, to trudge, to have your head down in melancholy and then lift it up, sideways—to get it."

One of my favorite spots in Paris is the courtyard of Shakespeare and Company at 37 rue de la Bucherie. There, in the reflection of the stained-glass light of the south windows of Notre Dame Cathedral, stands the little store, crowded with books and people and history, the airless rooms connected by pinched, winding staircases. It is the Paris of small spaces and enchantments set against the backdrop, as Gopnik says, of monumental wonders. A few yards from the store is the Seine, at a glance filthy but as strangely attractive as a ravishing streetwalker. Over the years I have spent many an afternoon browsing the dusty shelves or having tea and cookies at one of George Whitman's, the owner's, Sunday gatherings of would-be poets. The place attracts an eccentric mix of young and old who have a melancholy look in their eyes, as if they might have recently misplaced a winning lottery ticket. Paris is a city of parks and cafes but of the Louvre and Sacre-Coeur and the Pantheon, as well. But places like Shakespeare and Company are its soul, I think, for they represent a sadness that pervades the atmosphere. It has always seemed to me a city for unrequited love rather than love.

It drizzled most of the time we were in Paris, but I felt an odd exhilaration anyway because the rain-dazzled streets were less packed with tourists and because the city had, as it always seemed to have, the capacity to make me feel as if I belonged there. It offered a wonderful sense of anonymity. On our first day there, Jo-Ellen rested and I walked the streets by myself. Walking alone alongside the Seine, I was aware of every electron around me, but I was invisible, a spy in an unsuspecting land, a man without a country, just a citizen of Paris. That's the way the city made me feel, in the world but separate from it at the same time.

The next day, when the rain stopped and the sun broke through the clouds, Jo-Ellen and I went to the Luxembourg Gardens and sat for a while like Parisians listening to the cooing of pigeons and the rhythmic pock of a nearby tennis match. It was Sunday morning, and for a time we had the park to ourselves. When the people started to arrive, it didn't get crowded—a few runners, then a gentleman who looked like Peter Sellers playing Inspector Clouseau walked past us with his arms knotted behind his back, a mother pushing a baby carriage, a gendarme in a freshly pressed uniform. By 9:30, when lovers and families began to arrive, we left for Mass at St. Germain des Prés, a church of dull gold and chipped cement that forced my gaze heavenward in the same way it may have Hemingway's nearly a century before.

After Mass was over, it was lunchtime, and someone suggested a restaurant we might like. There was no sign, and it was such a small café that we passed it five times before we finally got someone to point it out to us. Parisians called it Tintin's because the owner loved the character from the series of children's travel-adventure books by the cartoonist Herge. Images of the daring Tintin and his faithful dog Snowy dotted the walls. Appropriately enough, the restaurant offered some adventure of its own. The specialty of the house—and the few tables were crowded with people, young and old, waiting for the fare—was horse tartar. Surprisingly, the raw horse meat looked strangely wonderful, mixed as it was with onion and a dressing of raw egg. I ordered turkey, though, and Jo-Ellen ordered chicken, but they both looked like overcooked steak. I ate mine anyway while the owner, a robust, red-cheeked man in his sixties, flirted with Jo-Ellen, offering her free drinks, some Parisian version of white lightning that made your eyes widen and burn as you held it close to your lips. The noise in the restaurant drifted to us through a thick haze, for every single person in the place seemed to be smoking two cigarettes at a time.

I had the urge to try the horse meat before we left, but at that moment Jo-Ellen was still playing the rational Sancho Panza and said, "Think of Rocinante." I went to the men's room, and when I returned to the table, my Sancho was under the spell of the place: Jo-Ellen held a lit cigarette in one hand, a full glass of white lightning in the other, and the owner was heading toward us with a plate of raw chopped meat. I encouraged a hurried exit. If we hadn't, Jo-Ellen might be there still, smoking, drinking moonshine, and eating horse. When the owner saw us leaving, he frowned in disappointment, patted his ample stomach, and said, "Au revoir, belle femme," and then, glancing at me, laughed in what sounded like a whinny, making me wonder if my turkey had once helped some poor Frenchman plow his land.

Our experience at Tintin's was for me typical of Paris. It has always been a city of mixed blessings. The first time I went there I was leading a study abroad class for graduate students, and one of them was threatened by a scar-faced bouncer with a knife in a club in the notorious Pigale section. I negotiated for his safety so that he could exit the "theater" in one piece, but he ended up paying $400 for a glass of grapefruit juice he bought for a young lady in the bar. The bouncer never actually showed a knife, but he kept reaching toward his back pocket as if he had one every time the young man tried to leave the place. I told the student under no circumstances to take out his credit card from his money belt, but after a few minutes of building pressure, beads of sweat popping out on his forehead, he did just that. We got to a phone as soon as we got him out of the bar, and he canceled his card. But I have the feeling Paris left its mark on him, and he never bought a strange woman a drink again.

Like any big city, Paris is a place to be watchful. I've seen a pickpocket in the Paris Metro get caught with his hands in one of my students' pockets and be brazen enough to suggest it was all a silly misunderstanding. In halting English, he said, "I thought I was sticking my hand in my own pocket." So, imagined knife blades and petty thieves were part of the Parisian landscape—as were haughty hotel clerks. On this trip I had a fight with the desk man in our hotel over the bill. We had a train to catch. He had overcharged us, and we nearly came to blows in the lobby before I finally paid what he asked so that we could catch our cab. We missed the train anyway. There is a potential for grace in travel, as well as ill fortune, and Paris has always offered both.

Travel is a lonely business in which a person is always—for good or ill—a stranger in the world, usually without the ability to read the signposts or communicate as he would at home. Years ago, on a train from London to Hollyhead, on our way to catch a ferry to Dublin, Jo-Ellen and I were robbed of credit cards and cash. If it had not been for a kindly English matron who fit the description exactly of Miss Marple cap to stockings and insisted on lending us 20 pounds, we would have been in desperate circumstances as we searched for a bank in the Joycean surreality of Dublin at midnight. It's the angel of mercy we hope for, I suppose, in foreign lands, and in the Montparnasse Station, a French angel on her way to Biarritz appeared and then translated and negotiated for us with the train agents so that we did not have to wait, as they said we must, for twelve hours for the next train to Hondarribia in Spain.

If we looked at travel as Tintin would have, as an adventure that held the probability of bad luck but the possibility of small mercies as well, we might long for the road, despite the dull clicks of the train wheels. Travel is always hours waiting in stations and airports, queuing up to purchase tickets, sitting alongside vacant-eyed travelers or, worse, those who gush with endless talk. But on the edge of this dull waiting, the watching as the clouds sail by, is the potential for surprise and danger—the angel on the bridge, the knife blade glittering in the streetlight, the unexpected enemy or friend. What we search for in travel is, in part, ourselves certainly, and each starts with a different idea of what he might face along the way. Jo-Ellen and I surely looked for different things along the road from

Hondarribia to Santiago in Spain. Our conversations along the pilgrimage path must have sounded at times like excerpts from a fractured version of *Don Quixote*—me seeing romance in slogging down the muddy roads and Jo-Ellen seeing wet clothing and aching joints. In the dormitory bedrooms of the refugios and albergues where we stayed, I saw boyhood adventure. She saw uncomfortable mattresses, common showers, and no hot water. We were twin poles—the dreamer and the realist, the romance of the road versus the comforts of home—held together by nothing short of friendship and love. Usually, that's enough to hold two travelers together. That doesn't mean that we weren't ready to part ways a few times, me to a mountain path and she to a four-star hotel. And it doesn't mean that after a few days we both didn't consider the question "Why go on a pilgrimage along the uncomfortable road when we could be sitting in a café in Hondarribia gazing out across the bay at France?"

Against her better judgment and because I had, for reasons I could not explain to myself, fixed on the idea of walking to Santiago, she came with me. We took the train from Hondarribia to Leon to begin our pilgrimage. On the train, we met our first fellow pilgrim, Royal, a student at Yale, an English major who was writing his senior thesis on the pilgrimage route to Santiago as a conduit of culture in Spanish history. He had started the journey some time before, had gone home for a month to rest up and was back to finish the path. A tall, slim young man with wind-twisted brown hair and an acolyte's sparse beard, Royal was both inherently shy and naturally curious, an innocent eager for experience. Meeting him was like looking into a rear-view mirror, remembering what it was like to want to hurl myself at twenty-one years old into the world with all the radiant mystery it held. In a voice that was at times too quiet to hear over the rattling of the train, Royal talked about the Camino de Santiago, the Way of St. James.

"It's been around for over a thousand years," he said, "and I wanted to be part of something that went back that far, where I could see and feel the connection to the past right there with me. In the Middle Ages, after Jerusalem and Rome, this was the pilgrimage destination for Christians."

He fingered a scallop shell, the symbol of pilgrimage and rebirth associated specifically with the legend of St. James. The scallop shell—we were to see many of them in the next few days—dangled from the front of his backpack in the empty seat next to him.

"I've walked about two-thirds of the 500 miles from southern France, and I haven't met any other Americans. You're the first. I've met people from every country in Europe, though, and some from Africa and Asia."

Even though we knew the history and legend of Santiago de Campostella, he told the story with an appealing brand of bashful enthusiasm that compelled us to listen as if we had never heard the details before.

"Ever since I was a kid, I was fascinated by things like the Crusades and pilgrimages, and I can't imagine a more fun way to do research on all this. One of the things I love about the Camino is that it's loaded with stories. Everywhere you turn there's a town with a legend describing some miracle that occurred there. Even the legend the whole pilgrimage is based on is a pretty good one. In the ninth century, a Spanish hermit named Pelayo saw a bright star and he followed it to a field. He found a tomb there with the bones of the apostle James. I guess there's still some debate over what *campostella* means, 'starry field' or 'burial ground,' but either fits, I think. The religious stuff is interesting, for sure, but how all these hundreds of thousands of people streaming across the mountains and the plains to get to the cathedral changed the economic and cultural life of this part of the world is what I find incredible. After the Reformation, things changed, of course, and by the nineteenth century the Camino had just about disappeared. I'm not sure what it means that the road has come back to life. I don't think people are more religious than they were a century or two ago, do you?"

"Maybe they want to be," Jo-Ellen said.

And that seemed to be as good an answer as any. In the age of Britney Spears and Paris Hilton, it was hard to even imagine such a thing as a spiritual pilgrimage, but perhaps, as Walker Percy suggested, love starts to flower in the ruins. Madison Avenue had not gotten a foothold on the Camino. There were guidebooks and news stories, occasionally, but, for the most part, the only way to experience the pilgrimage path was on foot, by bicycle, or by donkey. There were no bus tours or highway links or ways to make it anything but what it was: a long walk in a mostly rural world.

In the afternoon, our train arrived in Leon. Royal waved goodbye, shaking his wooden staff in one hand and holding the scallop shell in his other. He shouted "Bueno Camino" as he started west. We headed toward the Benedictine Nuns Albergue de Peregrinos, a hostel for pilgrims Royal had told us about during one of his lectures on the history of the Camino, but we probably would not have found the place if it had not been for (and I realize this strains credulity) a carpenter named Jesus. He didn't look much like the iconic image of his famous namesake. Rather, he was beardless and had short-cropped hair. He was tall and lean, though, dark-skinned as Jesus might have been, and had the same gentle manner and encouraging smile we might expect the son of Mary to have had. He lived in Ibiza, one of the Balearic Islands in the Mediterranean, now renowned as a playground for the rich and famous. Perhaps that was exactly what Jesus was escaping. Like the original, our Jesus was thirty-three years old, but even though he led us through the labyrinth of alleyways to the Plaza del Grano and the Albergue de las Benedictinas, he appeared to have no desire to die for the sins of mankind, just to walk the path and help a soul or two along the way.

The albergue had 150 beds for men, women, and children, and the cost was about $3 a person. The old stone building was laid out on two floors with dormitory beds and a small kitchen area crammed next to the stairwell on the second floor. After walking the medieval streets of the old city of Leon and eating tapas in a bar near the majestic cathedral, Jo-Ellen and I sat in the courtyard of the albergue and watched the sun set, light dripping like candle wax on the three storks' nests that sat atop the bell tower of the convent church. The nests, the size of rafts you might imagine Missouri teenagers launching on the Mississippi River, looked ready to set sail themselves on an adventure.

Jo-Ellen and I are not early risers, but we both got out of bed before dawn the next day. It wasn't hard to do. When you sleep in a room with fifty or sixty other people, no matter how quietly they try to gather their belongings and shuffle out the door, you feel the wave of movement around you. At about 5 A.M., everything seemed to whisper *the pilgrimage has begun.* So we hooked on backpacks and fanny packs, picked up our pilgrim's passports, the Credencial del Peregrino, had them stamped, and marched off into the cool, dark morning. We had to walk through the city of Leon, most of its 130,000 inhabitants asleep, past unopened stores and silent apartments, before we got to the lonely open roads that led to Villar de Mazarife, a small town 24 kilometers away. A line of us—a motley crew of pilgrims from around the world—moved in and out of the side streets in the gathering light. I suspect we looked a little like an accordion, one group moving up and another group falling back a few dozen yards. We passed people on bikes and donkeys, but most people were on foot and would say, "Bueno Camino" as we went by. A few miles outside of Leon, the road was just a scar in the open farmland. Then it became a rocky path, shaded on each side, and soon Jo-Ellen and I found ourselves alone, looking for the yellow sign of the scallop, *la flecha de amarillo*, to point us in the right direction.

About halfway to Villar de Mazarife, we met Inigo, a twenty-nine-year-old man from Barcelona whose job there was to work with homeless kids. "Mostly gypsies," he said. "Their parents just leave them on the streets and walk away. Their lives are very tragic. I'm not a religious person. I come here on this pilgrimage to clean my head. You know, to shake the sadness out of it."

The three of us hiked together through a few apparently empty villages—not a car or a person to be seen—and traveled the red-clay roads until we reached El Refugio de Jesus de Mazarife. And, yes, like some reminder that the real world has no obligation to live up to the logic of fiction, Jesus was there waiting for us. He had left Leon at 4 A.M., and although he was not actually *waiting* for us, he jumped up from his seat in the kitchen of the refugio when we entered and greeted us like long-lost friends. That night, the four of us—Inigo, Jesus, Jo-Ellen, and myself—bought half a dozen bottles of *vino de mesa*, a block of manchego cheese, tomatoes, olives, pasta, and sauce, and made dinner in the small kitchen. We ate in the courtyard of the refugio, joining a dozen other pilgrims and sharing food and drink with them. Someone had a bottle of Rioja, and we drank that bottle last, with a slight rain drizzling down on us even though we were half-protected by an overhanging roof in the courtyard.

Our group was like an impromptu United Nations assembly. There was a young man from Madrid who spoke English with a perfectly tuned

Irish accent because he had spent a year in Dublin during high school. There were two retired women from Amsterdam who had walked from the Pyrenees Mountains to Villar de Mazarife. Karl Gandolf could have passed for Santa Claus with his generous girth and flourishing snow white beard if he had not been wearing tight biking shorts, a Michael Owen soccer shirt, and decaying green Nike tennis shoes. He had come from Austria, riding a bicycle and pulling a homemade wagon filled with pots and pans and other accessories. He was on his way back from Santiago, having completed the journey there in June. Another wanderer, a young man from South America, had spent the last six months in Ethiopia "trying to understand what made Africa tick." Now, he said, he was on the Camino to think about what he had seen. There was a Frenchman and an Italian woman, and a young Dane with the blond-haired regality about him of Hamlet. There was a newly married couple from Scotland. The young woman, who looked to be about nineteen, had finished her medical residency in Bristol a few months before and she and her husband were seeing what they could of Spain before they went back to start their careers. "If we go back," he said.

The group of us sat in the courtyard and Jesus passed the wine and jamon and queso from his spot at the center of the table as if it were the Last Supper. We talked of politics and books and music and films—everything from Pedro Almodovar to Bob Dylan to George Bush. Mostly, we spoke in English. For Jo-Ellen and myself, it was a blessing because Italian and Dutch were out of the question. My college French could get me by in a restaurant. For both of us it was our high school Spanish that allowed us to communicate modestly. It was exhausting, though, thinking in another language. Some of our companions felt the same way, and they had more reason to feel the burden because they were much better with English than we were in their languages. At one point, Inigo, no taller than a jockey, stood up from the table, smiled wryly, and stretched his arms toward the black sky. "I can't talk English any more," he said. "My head, it hurts!"

Inigo went up to his bed shortly after that, but if he had stayed I'm afraid his head would have surely hurt more because someone started talking about the war in Iraq. It didn't take long for Jo-Ellen and me to realize that everyone there disliked George Bush, and not one person supported the United States entry into Iraq, a theme that would be repeated through-out the trip in Spain and later in 2006. Once they saw that neither Jo-Ellen nor I supported the decision to invade Iraq, the atmosphere softened. Jose, the young man from South America, threw his arms around me and said, "Now I see what America is, who America really is. I have met you." He hugged Jo-Ellen and me together. "Now I know that America is not George Bush, eh? Let's drink to that."

By the time we got to bed, I felt less like a pilgrim than a partygoer at Mardi Gras in New Orleans. We had only a few hours to daylight, but I slept soundly. Not even the music of the Spanish village—the yips and barks and whines of the Spanish dogs—could keep me awake.

The next morning Inigo and Jesus left with us on the road toward Hospital de Orbigo. We passed through more ghost villages. No one could explain where the people were. "Spain has a reputation for the party, no?" Inigo said. "Where's the PARTY?"

From what we could tell, most of the people, except for a few older men and women, had moved to the big cities and left their family homes to sit vacant until they came back for vacations or retirement. Every now and again, we saw an old woman's face framed by a black shawl staring out at us from the shuttered slits of a ground floor window. A few times I felt like an invader being spied on. The shutters would inch open, and pieces of a face would appear in the shadow—a crow's beak, a crone's obsidian eye—and then the shutters would slowly pinch out the light. There was something eerie about walking through those attractive little whitewashed towns and not seeing a soul stirring. Usually, each town had a mercado or a bodega for us to get a bocadillo or some wine to sip along the way, but for the most part it was like traveling through a postapoca-lyptic landscape where the bomb had left the buildings intact but made everyone disappear.

It was just outside of Hospital de Orbigo, in Santibanez de Valdeigle-sias, that I began to feel the blister on my right foot. The backpack was heavy, and the copy of Don Quixote didn't help, but I still had 100 pages to go, and, besides, I planned to carry it like a talisman the whole way. Band-aids would have been more practical to carry, and lighter, but I hadn't remembered them, and my practical companion hadn't either. We looked at Inigo, but he shrugged his shoulders and cut us slices of manchego. Jesus, now with a few day's growth of beard and looking more like the original, raised his arms out and palm upward.

"I wish I could heal you," he said. "I wish I could give you, how do you say, a second skin."

At first, I thought he was talking about a miracle, something akin to loaves and fishes, until Jo-Ellen explained to me he was referring to a type of band-aid that adhered to a blister as if it were actual skin covering it. It was early afternoon, but my limp was getting worse, so we stopped at a refugio along the way run by Marie Carmen, a sixty-five-year-old woman who had emigrated from Cuba when she was a child. She ran the hostel for her father, and broke into sobs when she talked of her mother's death years before because of a lack of medicine in "Castro's Cuba." But Marie was not all tears any more than her refugio was all spiritual wayside. She spoke to us in a rapid Spanish, pushing back her purple-red hair with a flamenco dancer's flourish, her long silver earrings shaking as she spoke. At first, I tried to get her to slow down, "Habla despacios, por favor. Habla despacios." But the more I pleaded, the faster she spoke. So, in turns, Inigo and Jesus translated in whispers as she talked. In that time, she made a number of things clear—she hated Castro, she loved the United States (even if George Bush were president), and she wanted—more than anything else in the world, she said—to have an American husband.

Jo-Ellen looked sweetly at her, the way an adult would at a child whose wish, if answered, would only bring a brutal end to the fairy tale. With Jesus translating, Jo-Ellen told her that she could do without me for a while, but I don't think Marie fully understood (or the offer wasn't good enough) because all she said in reply was "Jo Helene es muy linda." Who knows, maybe it wasn't a husband she was after. Or, perhaps, like Kathryn Harrison in *The Road to Santiago*, I had "fallen through one fairy tale and into another."

In the midst of Jesus's translating, Inigo whispered to me, "Ah, Cuban women . . . I had a Cuban girlfriend once. Cuban women . . . good for dancing, good for sex, but talking . . . oh, mi Dios, no good. Cuban women never silent." An hour later, when Marie was still talking and Jesus, with the powers of understanding and forgiveness that only a god could muster, was still translating, my mind was so numb I had completely forgotten my blister.

It was mid-afternoon, but I convinced Jo-Ellen we should continue on to Astorga, another twelve kilometers. Jesus and Inigo decided to stay the night. It might have been to soak their feet or for the free Internet connection. Or it may simply have been the novice holy man's intrinsic desire for self-flagellation in the form of Marie's endless conversation.

Two or three miles down the road I realized I should have stayed put. Overcompensating for the blister on my left heel, I put additional pressure on my right leg, and I still carried Cervantes in my backpack. I developed a shin splint, although I had never had one before and at that point all I knew was that it felt like someone had taken a ball peen hammer and hit me a few dozen times on the shin bone of my right leg. Jo-Ellen offered to carry my backpack, which was about twenty-five pounds, or to have me lean against her as we walked, but the pilgrimage had not erased my senseless pride, and I just kept limping forward. By the time we reached the outskirts of Astorga, I was dragging my right leg sideways like a sack of meal to avoid putting any pressure on it at all. At the Santo Toribio stone cross that overlooked San Justo de la Vega, I could see Astorga below in the distance, and I felt like a true pilgrim, in pain, punished for my sin of pride, and hoping for a miracle or at least some Advil. I hobbled the last few kilometers into Astorga, up the last excruciating hill to the Alburgue de Peregrinos San Javier. We had the closest thing to a private room we had seen in days—six bunk beds and ten companions. The shower down the hall had warm water, though, and the man at the front desk gave me a bag of ice (no Advil). They had an Internet station in the lobby. I lay in my bunk, the bag of ice taped to my shin, and Jo-Ellen, a gleam in her pretty blue eyes that told me she felt sorry for me but told me something more as well, said she was going downstairs to write some e-mail. I had an epiphany then. I knew what the punishment for pride was on this pilgrimage: she would explain to all our friends how she was forced to carry her once-athletic husband—the one who was not worried in the least about his ability to finish the trek—the last few miles into Astorga because, well, men are not half as strong as they think they are. She was right, of course, but it seemed unfair to destroy the illusion.

The next day we sat on a bench in the town square near the Gothic cathedral and watched dusty pilgrims march by. At one point, three men and a donkey came along followed by Inigo who told us that Jesus had gone off before him early that morning, perhaps so that he could leave before Marie woke up to offer breakfast and conversation.

"Have you seen him?" he asked us.

We had been there most of the morning, but we had not seen him come past the cathedral or the Palacio Epicopal.

"We'll meet again," Inigo said, but none of us believed it. He took out his pocketknife and cut up some slices of cheese and ham that he shared with us.

"Bueno Camino," he said and he went off, disappearing down the road.

We waited a few days to see if my leg would get better, but it didn't, and eventually we took the train to Santiago. Somehow, it felt right to bend the rules and take public transportation—after all, I was a fallen Catholic, marginally lame, prideful, carrying a hardcover copy of *Don Quixote* when a far less heavy paperback should have done as well, and I had lost Jesus along the way to Astorga.

The route we took from the train station in Santiago to the cathedral led down the cobbled streets of the Porta de Camino, one of the seven original entrances in the walls of the medieval city, to the granite flag-stones that led to the Plaza de Cervantes. From there, the road passed the north entrance of the cathedral and descended a flight of stairs into the magnificent Plaza de Obradoiro. The three spires of the grand cathedral rose like stars in the silver sky. Inside the church, representatives from the entire planet seemed to have gathered. Nuns and priests, sailors and tattooed hippies, grandmothers and college students lined the pews. A group of women we later found out were from Kenya stood alongside a couple from Vietnam who were there to have their sick baby blessed. Pilgrims from India and Turkey and Australia sat side by side with those from Great Britain and Chile. All eyes were on the flight of the botafum-erio and the Portico of Glory. The censer swung from one side of the front of the altar to the other, a huge smoking planet that appeared ready to fly off on its own and beyond the grasp of the half-dozen red-robed priests who swung it by thick ropes. It was like a world on fire, the smoke bringing us all together and at the same time hiding us in our solitude.

I followed what I could of the Mass in Spanish, which is to say I understood little but somehow it seemed like enough. Understanding Spanish would not have made things clearer or changed the undecipherable mystery. The priest's words rose to the vaulted ceiling, but the echo of them hung in the air like memory. It was then that I felt the tears in my eyes as I remembered my mother. It had been three years and I hadn't cried, and I felt the sadness rise in me like a childhood monster lurking in some forgotten closet. I associated Mass and the Catholic Church with her, with my childhood, with so much that I loved and that was now gone. But, as far as I had slipped from those days and those youthful beliefs, I held onto what she had left me with—the things worth striving for—compassion and generosity, courage and honor, grace and faith, love. I might not always find them or be deserving of them, but at least she had given me a sense of what might be possible. Even if God had disappeared, the road was still there. There was always more to come. That's what I had to hope for and have faith in—in the road ahead.

Then Jo-Ellen squeezed my hand to let me know that, whether it seemed believable or not, Jesus had arrived and he was walking up the smoke-filled aisle to say hello.

2006

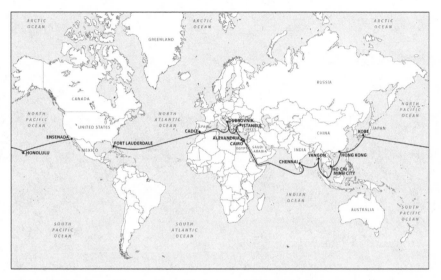

2006. *Created by Donald Emminger, graphic designer, Old Dominion University.*

Setting Sail
San Diego, Mexico, and Hawaii

Is there anyone who has not, at one time or another, awakened from a mesmerizing dream and then gone back to sleep, hoping to recapture it? Going around the world for a second time in 2006 was much like that. Going back to Japan, China, Vietnam, and India felt like slipping into a familiar dreamscape so that I could get the picture clearer the second time around.

In late August, faculty boarded the ship in San Diego, but because the ship sailed under a foreign flag, students had to board in Ensenada, Mexico, a few days later. When Jo-Ellen and I opened the door to our room, we were like two wide-eyed children who got to see our Christmas presents before the adults woke up. The room was bigger than our tiny cabin had been on the 2002 voyage. This one had a marble bath, a sitting area with a couch, and—we held back from giving each other high fives on this—a sliding glass door that led to a deck with a small table and two chairs. Immediately we saw ourselves spending afternoons and evenings gazing at the endless ocean. The ship was only a few years old, and if it hadn't been for the bomb-sniffing dogs at the security checkpoints on the pier, we might have imagined we were vacationing in Catalina.

To me, San Diego was an American Eden, a paradise of opal waters in the sun-dazzled harbor and glittering terra cotta roofs in the surrounding hills. If a bankrupt city could be Eden, San Diego was it—a perfect Mediterranean breeze barely rustling the palm trees, smiling people in light cotton shirts, friendly restaurant workers, healthy joggers, and the lowest crime rate in America for a city its size. The evening of August 26, we sailed south to pick up our students. It would have made a better Biblical allusion to sail east from Eden, but the American continent got in the

143

way of metaphor. We left the gleaming American metropolis for its dingy Mexican alter ego less than a hundred miles away.

Ensenada was a paradise of another sort. Ancient-eyed Indian children sold beaded necklaces, and dark-skinned Mexican teenagers with carefully carved smiles touted one pharmacia or another in the town. Signs picturing old men with canes and huge erections advertised Viagra at a discount. Ensenada was the Shangri-la for those seeking discount drugs south of the border and under the American prescription law radar. American baby boomers filled the avenues and side streets, comparing prices for Lipitor, Celebrex, and Plavix as if they were shopping for winter jackets out of season at the outlet malls in Freeport, Maine. Back at the ship, faculty members queued up, bags of amoxicillin and Valium at their sides, waiting to board but prepared for any toothaches or stresses of teaching to come. With the seals sunning themselves on the buoys and barking out in chorus, faculty discussed their bargains.

When I wasn't teaching or in meetings, Jo-Ellen and I spent a good deal of time on our deck, reading, grading papers, or gazing at the blank, beautiful Pacific Ocean. More than once while staring at the endless rolling vista and yearning for the sight of land, some boundary to give order and shape to my line of vision, I was reminded of Ishmael's words about the dangers of the shore in *Moby-Dick*:

> In the port is safety, comfort, hearthstone, supper, warm blankets, friends, and all that's kind to our mortalities. But in that gale, the port, the land, is the ship's direst jeopardy; she must fly all hospitality; one touch of land, though it but graze the keel, would make her shudder through and through. . . . all deep, earnest thinking is but the intrepid effort of the soul to keep the open independence of her sea; while the wildest winds of heaven and earth conspire to cast her on the treacherous, slavish shore. . . . in landlessness alone resides the highest truth, shoreless, indefinite as God—so better is it to perish in that howling infinite, than be ingloriously dashed upon the lee, even if that were safety!

Shoreless for the better part of two weeks and over 2,000 miles as we sailed from Mexico to Hawaii, we saw nothing but waves and flying fish skimming across steel blue water, and when our thoughts did not soar to

God or to our place in the howling infinite, they went to our destination, Honolulu. When I did have my first sight of Oahu, I knew that Twain had gotten it right a century and a half ago. The population of Honolulu had grown from the 15,000 of Twain's "white town" in 1872 to the nearly 1 million inhabitants of 2006, but his view of it still resonated: "the impossible promontory of Diamond Head rose up out of the ocean . . . softened by the hazy distance."

Now there were high-rise hotels and golf courses competing with the clouds dripping down Diamond Head. But not even high-rise buildings could detract from the strange vision of the place: it could have been a meteor flung into the sapphire-blue waters. Banyan trees stood like statues sculpted in Kapiolani Park, and the air smelled of flowers. Orchids and birds of paradise, all colors of the rainbow—pale greens and soft purples, whites and oranges—flickered in the iridescent air.

We had only the afternoon in Hawaii, and that may have made it seem more like paradise than it actually was, but in that short space of time, the sun shone, the water glistened, and the clean streets looked populated by people who were happy to live there. Everywhere Jo-Ellen and I went—on the city buses, in the malls, in the parks—the people were quiet, gentle, and polite; laughing, playing with their families on the serene beaches.

The only snake I found in the garden was us. On the beach, near Ala Moana Park, as dusk began to fall and the air became slightly cooler after a brief shower, I decided to go swimming. Out about thirty yards, I watched the families interact. The sounds drifted softly toward me in the water. One louder voice broke through the whisperings—"Mother Fuckers!" I looked toward the curve of the shore and saw two SAS students. "I spent $1,000 of my Stanford loan on this fucking trip, but those rich mother fuckers don't have to worry about shit." He went on, including everyone on the beach in his conversation. I started in to shore, and as I got closer, the young man who was speaking looked a lot like one of the students in one of my writing classes. Before I could reach the beach to ask what other words they had taught him at Stanford, he disappeared into the park with his companion. I was left, dripping by the shore, wondering what sort of ambassadors we might turn out to be as we landed in other countries.

Back on the ship that night, we had dinner with Chris Peterson, a retired Portland police officer, a white-haired, mustachioed, barrel-chested cop of the old school—honest, gregarious, soft-hearted—but with the clipped speech and gravelly voice that could make twenty-one-year-olds believe that the sheriff, as everyone onboard called him, could see into their souls. He was the kind of person who could say something like "make my day" without it sounding like an awkward parody of Dirty Harry. That didn't stop the students from trying to sneak alcohol aboard in perfume bottles and inside teddy bears and even in their bras.

"Who's making the money onboard the ship from alcohol sales?" Chris wondered. "And what do these pub nights have to do with the education here?"

Chris also wondered if some of the behavior he had seen already— only two weeks into the voyage—had been alcohol induced. The day before he had seen a student spitting on the harbor pilot as he got onboard the *Explorer* in the rolling seas. He could not identify him for sure, but he had a sense, he said, of who it might have been.

"What's next?" he asked.

Before the journey was over, he would find out—eleven students sent home for infractions of one sort or another, and a twelfth student airlifted from Dubrovnik, Croatia, after she leapt from a cliff into the cold, swirling Adriatic thirty feet below. Chris was a big-hearted man, and he was to encounter many students he admired and respected, but his duty kept him up all night, seeing the netherworld on the ship that most of us slept peacefully through.

It was hard at times, even for those of us who saw things only in the light of day, to view the ship as a "journey of discovery" when it seemed so much like a luxury cruise. One day Jo-Ellen came back from getting her hair cut in the spa next to the exercise room. A male student, no more than eighteen or nineteen years old, Jo-Ellen guessed, strutted in and made an appointment to get his back waxed. He turned to the girl sitting next to him who was there to get a salt and glow exfoliation and a hot stone massage. "I think I'll try a facial next. They do pedicures, right?"

"Maybe that answered Chris's question," Jo-Ellen said to me.

As Twain discovered in *Innocents Abroad,* Chris would eventually find out that there was more indulgence, at times, than intrepid adventure on the *MV Explorer,* and "if a man has good qualities, the spirit seldom moves him to exhibit them on shipboard, at least not with any sort of emphasis."

Japan

A day or so before we reached Japan, a funnel cloud that could have been the afterimage of an atomic blast hung in the tumultuous sky. It seemed as mysterious as foreshadowing from a Haruki Murakami short story. I watched from our deck as school after school of silver flying fish burst from the waves like machine-gun fire. Their pectoral fins spread wide into wings as they scudded over the water. They flew in squadrons about three feet above the rollicking seas as if they were uncertain if they were fish or fowl but knowing the only way to escape the depths and the predators that sought them was to change the essence of their being.

We spent many days in a class called Global Studies (renamed from Core Geography on the 2002 voyage) hearing about the customs and culture of Japan. You needed only two Japanese words to survive in the country, we were told—*ohio* (good morning) and *arigato* (thank you). The English words that were key to modern Japan were *cute, cool,* and *feels good.* Ron Morse, a retired professor of Japanese studies at UNLV and UCLA and now president of Japan Entertainment and Gaming Associates, provided the most unadulterated and politically incorrect information.

Ron was a small guy with a dry sense of humor. He looked uncannily like the cantankerous Mr. Horowitz, a Jewish tailor who chased all the Italian and Irish kids away from his shop in the Bronx when I was boy. Ron scared a lot of people onboard because he spoke his mind, and he seemed tough-edged and cynical. But we became good friends with him and his wife, Jackie, whom Jo-Ellen chose to call *Peanut* because of her size. Ron and Jackie were a match made somewhere outside heaven, both veiling their soft, generous spirits behind a snarling wit.

In Ron's first lecture in Global Studies, a female Japanese exchange student left the room weeping because he described the culture as "shop,

shop, eat, eat, buy, buy, shop, shop." He may have said "herro" instead of "hello" a few times, as well. He certainly detailed much that was positive about Japanese society—"the global imagination's default setting for the future"—socialized medicine, high-quality food and drink, highly refined technology, trains that ran to the minute (if a train came thirty seconds late into the station, the conductor apologized to the commuters).

But, as Ron described the country, it was also a slightly surreal landscape of instant noodles, video games, karaoke rooms, sophisticated digital cameras, and cell phones all coexisting with Shinto shrines and old world manners. In a land of quiet decorum, people politely exchanging slippers for shoes as they entered homes, slurping soup was perfectly acceptable. The number 4 was as filled with superstitious connotation in Japan as 13 was in the United States.

I had been saturating myself in Haruki Murakami's fiction—the short stories and the novels *Kafka on the Shore, The Wind-Up Bird Chronicle,* and *Norwegian Wood*—a world where ordinary occurrences always seemed mysterious and magical, and where the magical often seemed ordinary—fish raining from the sky, young men taking up residence in libraries populated with ghosts, cats and monkeys talking and making good sense—therefore, I was open to some of the mystery and contradiction the country might offer.

If citizens of the United States placed a high premium on individuality and personal choice, the Japanese people valued conformity and social harmony. "They don't like the touchy-feely stuff," Ron said. "Bow rather than shake hands." But, he went on, one had to know how to bow. The higher the person's status, the more respect to be shown, the lower one bent down. If you did someone a favor, he said, get ready for an elegantly wrapped gift. If the favor was big enough, let's say a letter of recommendation that helped a son get into a prestigious American university, then who knows what you might get, but it probably would be more expensive than one of the hundred-dollar watermelons on sale in the upscale markets. Japanese people were quiet and respectful of elders and the limited amount of personal space available in their country, but step into a smoke-clogged pachinko parlor, as Jo-Ellen and I did, and you would experience a level of noise that left you deaf for a half an hour after you exited to the hushed streets. As Ron explained, there were 17,000 pachinko parlors in the country, a \$300-billion-a-year business, ten times larger than that of the gambling industry in his home town, Las Vegas.

In my literature class, we read a few Murakami stories, hoping as we discussed them that not everything would get lost in translation. In the process of helping to ease the students into Murakami's unique world, I gave them some of the details of the novel I was reading at the time—*Kafka on the Shore*. The novel was actually two stories—one about the fifteen-year-old runaway, Kafka Tamura, and the other the slowly converging tale of Nakata, an old man who experienced a strange sleep during World War II. Along with his imaginary alter ego, Crow, Kafka runs from his enigmatically malevolent father, a sculptor who has made an oedipal prophecy about his son, that he will kill the father and sleep with his mother and older sister who disappeared when the boy was four years old.

The stories of Kafka and Nakata run parallel routes. After the accident during World War II that put Nakata into a coma from which he awoke unable to read, he had other skills to take the place of the ones he had lost—the ability to make sardines rain down from the sky or carry on conversations with animals. Kafka too falls into a sleep from which he awakens with elusive knowledge. Kafka's quest and Nakata's are connected in a way that the reader understands is meaningful, even if the reader never fully understands the exact meaning.

This is the essence of Murakami's fiction, puzzles that can never be solved. Kafka's father is murdered, but whether it is Kafka or Nakata or someone else responsible, we are never certain. Kafka does sleep with Miss Saeki, the director of the library where he lives for a time, but it is never clear if she is his long-lost mother. He also sleeps, at least in his dreams, with Sukura, a young woman who might be his older sister. Fantasy and reality coexist seamlessly in Murakami's work. Often, there is no discernible distinction between what might be imagined and what has actually occurred in his postmodern Japan where the hollow consumer world may be more dislocating and alienating than any nightmare.

Kafka is something of an Alice in a Japanese Wonderland. One of the characters he meets, the androgynous Oshima, tells him, "The world is a metaphor, Kafka Tamura." And in Murakami's Japan, that is true.

Chance is a scary thing in his fiction, and most of what can happen does—and seems inevitable, as well. At one point in the novel, he writes, "Reality and dreams are all mixed up, like seawater and river water flowing together." Ultimately, though, the advice that Crow gives to Kafka is the advice Murakami gives to the reader, perhaps: "'You better get some sleep. . . . When you wake up, you'll be part of a brand-new world.' You finally fall asleep. And when you wake up it's true. You are part of a brand-new world."

When we woke up on September 12, the fog surrounding the ship was an eerie absolute whiteness that reminded me of a scene from Poe's *The Narrative of Arthur Gordon Pym*, and although the war still raged in Iraq and much was the same as it had been yesterday, one important thing was different—Kobe sat a few miles away, the construction cranes and high-rises casting shadows over the harbor, the mountains rising somberly behind the city, cab drivers in dark suits and white gloves sitting patiently in polished automobiles. Mechanical birds twittered at street corners to announce to blind pedestrians it was safe to cross, and anything seemed possible, even fish falling from the sky.

With Ron and Jackie Morse and Debbie Clifford, the registrar on the ship, Jo-Ellen and I hiked Mt. Rokko on the northern outskirts of Kobe. Ron was fluent in Japanese, and on the trains, buses, and cabs, he was our personal tour guide, knowledgeable and sharp-tongued. It wasn't beneath him to do a little slapstick, either. He sat in the train car and posed under the poster that read "Women Only," and rested himself on the seat reserved for pregnant women.

In one of the villages near Mt. Rokko, we went to an osento, a traditional Japanese public bath house. A few years ago, millions of Japanese people went to the baths regularly, but now the majority of them use the private baths in their own homes for the same purpose. The bath house Ron took us to was like many modern osentos, a blend of bath and theme park. It had a game room and a shopping mall adjacent to the lockers in the sparkling clean lobby. We put our shoes and valuables in the lockers, picked up our robes and slippers, and separated, the women going through one curtain and the men through another.

Once in the inner chamber, we were given another locker where we left our clothing. There were a series of baths, ranging in temperatures from 105 degrees Fahrenheit to something closer to scalding. Japanese men of all ages clustered in the showers and the many baths. I followed Ron's lead, learning right away that the baths were not for cleaning but relaxing. One used the showers to get perfectly clean before entering the communal baths. So we squatted on the stone seats by the shower and poured cup after cup of warm water over our heads, soaping and shampooing ourselves before we got in the baths. The baths were on the second and third floors, the tubs as large as small, shallow swimming pools. The top floor was on the roof, covered only by a bamboo overhang.

At first, rain was coming down in a cool, fine mist, but before long raindrops plunked like musical notes in the water. The Japanese have dozens of words for rain, just as the Eskimos have many words to describe the snow, and I could understand why. Sitting in the steamy baths for an hour or so, I saw the rain change shape many times, its volume and sound, even the size and direction of the drops. Ron sat next to me in the bath, a white hand towel draped over his head, and recited one of Basho's haiku:

First drops
On parched earth—
Rain

It didn't take long for his recital to deteriorate into a contest between the two of us, both ex–New Yorkers, transforming the haiku into benign mockery, making fun of our political differences or the boroughs of our birth—in his case Queens and in mine the Bronx. Our haikus became more and more heat addled. Steam is a bit like alcohol: it makes you think you're being smarter than you are. The women, Jo-Ellen in particular, were not as lucky or as readily deluded as we were.

When I saw Jo-Ellen in the gleaming lobby, I knew something had happened. Her cheeks were flushed bright red. I sensed right away it had nothing to do with a haiku competition among Jackie and Debbie and herself. From the outset, Jo-Ellen had not been ecstatic about getting naked with two women she knew from the ship and usually saw clothed and in the dining hall line. Naked strangers would have been a lot easier to deal with, she said, but after a little bit of cajoling, she had eventually gone along with the idea.

"What happened?" I asked, looking at her wide eyes and crimson skin.

"You won't believe it," she said, but I knew I would. After thirty-five years of marriage, she had taught me to believe in anything.

"Once I took off my clothes," she said, "I should have just let well enough alone and stayed put in one bath until we left. I'd finally gotten used to seeing Debbie and Jackie without clothes on. Jackie's so small that if she didn't have blond hair she could be Japanese. Everyone looked when Debbie came in to the baths, though. They don't see many six-foot-tall women around here. I tried the hot rocks and the meditation mats. And then I got brave and followed Jackie up to the rooftop bath. The atmosphere up there was pretty Zen-like and I was feeling sort of comfortable. I walked over to the bath and smiled at the half-dozen Japanese women who were sitting in it. I was about to say *ohio* when I lost my balance and plunged face first into the hot water. All that came out of my mouth was the *O* part of *ohio*. Nobody looked at me after I dove in. I'm not sure if they thought this American thinks this is a swimming pool or if they were afraid of what I might do next. I was a little scared of what I might do myself, so I just stayed in the hot water, getting redder and redder until everyone else got out."

It was still raining lightly when we left the public baths, a cool mist and a soft breeze. But Jo-Ellen's face remained bright red after we walked down the hill past the ginko and cypress trees that surrounded the nearby Moonlight Garden Inn and found our way to the bus stop. As gingerly and with as much decorum as a Japanese matron might muster, she touched my elbow and whispered in my ear, "What's the Japanese custom about drinking in the afternoon?" she asked. "I need a sake."

We had to wait until that night, after we had gotten back to the ship and changed our clothes, to head out again, this time with Bill and Sherry May, our friends from the 2002 voyage who had sailed again. We went to a restaurant where Jo-Ellen could regroup after her plunge into the hot springs. Her skin had faded to a soft orange glow, but she still wanted a drink.

We found a sukiyaki place called Hot Pot in Kobe. The four of us sat around the cooktop table, drinking hot sake and trying to figure out what we were supposed to do with the plates of mushrooms and scallions, the thinly sliced strips of beef and pork, and the small bowl of raw eggs. There was a pot of boiling water on the cook stove, but we were not sure what to do with it all. Boil the eggs? Crack them and put them in the water? Mix everything together into some glutinous mass? Talking to the waiters did not help because they spoke English as well as we spoke Japanese. This was a time when *ohio* and *arigato* were not enough to get by. So we continued to drink sake until we had the opportunity to spy on another table and follow their lead—beat the raw eggs slightly in the bowl, dip the food in the boiling water, touch it with soy or ginger sauce, drink more sake. We repeated this process until we staggered out to get a cab back to the ship.

The next day Jo-Ellen had her natural pale hue back, and we decided to see Kyoto once again.

"No baths," she said. "No sukiyaki."

We took the train from Sannomiya Station to Kyoto, around two hours without a cultural miscue or international incident. In Kyoto Station, though, we encountered another moment where *arigato* was not enough to help us translate what was happening. As we exited the train, drawn along in the gravitational pull of the crowd, we came to a stage with a smiling man and woman standing before a microphone, waving enthusiastically and encouraging us to participate in a ring-toss game.

At least, I think they were encouraging us to participate. I couldn't understand a word that was said. I paid 100 yen or maybe it was 1,000, I'm not sure, but I paid and walked onto the stage. *No hot baths, no sukiyaki, nothing to fear,* I thought. And I was right. I tossed the rings from about twenty feet away and twice they floated right onto the pole. The third time I hit it but it rattled off.

A woman with a grin from ear to ear ran from the side of the stage and bowed profusely, handing me a box of cinnamon candy and a bag of grapes so artfully wrapped it could have contained a bust by Michelangelo. We bought green tea ice cream and ate the grapes, feeling as if we had mastered some Japanese ritual that might help us solve other mysteries we encountered.

For a while it worked well. I popped a piece of cinnamon candy in my mouth every time I got a little confused. We found our way around Kyoto, walking the Philosopher's Path again, and getting back on the right train to Kobe that afternoon. In Kobe, we (I use the plural loosely here) were *determined* to find a restaurant we had read about in the Lonely Planet guidebook called Kintoki. It was reputed to be a local favorite with "the cheapest food in the city." In a country as expensive as Japan, the word *cheap* immediately holds the average person's attention. People in Kobe loved it, the book implied.

All we had to do was find it. The address listed for the place was simply Motomachi-dori. Places didn't seem to have numbers. "Look for the blue and white awning" was the advice Lonely Planet gave along with the tempting, "This is a good place to go for a taste of what Japan was like before it got rich." Our street-by-street search gave us a sense of perspective about Kobe, but it never got us to Kintoki. We even spent an hour in the rotating bar at Kobe Tower, pirouetting in super-slow motion to view the entire city, to get a clearer lay of the land. It was early evening by the time we took another turn in the streets. Everyone we asked—*wa doko desu ka Kintoki*—pointed us in a different direction. We made pleading motions, eating motions, said Kintoki with the accent on the *Kin* and then with the emphasis on the final *i*, but all to no avail.

About the time we were ready to give up and eat in one of the mall restaurants that had the plastic models of the food in lieu of a menu, a young man led us to a door that we had passed at least a dozen times in our search. Inside were a few communal tables and about thirty men all smoking cigarettes and slurping soba noodles. For Jo-Ellen, this was a bit like the public baths. With her wavy blonde hair and blue eyes, she could not be missed, even if the men politely avoided staring. There was one other woman in the place, but she looked enough like a man to warrant a second glance to make sure.

I ate noodles because I didn't recognize anything else on the menu. Jo-Ellen wanted to be brave and order fish, but she couldn't make sense of the menu either. So she scanned the room and pointed to a dish a man was eating a few seats away from us. She was never sure what she had asked for or, when it arrived, what she was eating. It came in a large porcelain bowl; it could have been fish or it might have been meat. All we knew for certain was that dozens of solids floated in a murky broth. But if the *what* was a mystery, the *how much* was within our budget, and when I asked if I could buy the miniature beer glasses with Asahi printed on them, they wrapped them up and gave them to me as a gift.

A cat slunk by our table as we were finishing up, eyeing Jo-Ellen's half-eaten fish, and I almost expected it to speak to us as if this were a Murakami tale of the strange ordinary world. When we left the restaurant and were halfway down the street, I turned back just to see if the place was still there or if it had been a dream. I never got to see for certain because two of my students stood in front of me. They were just returning from a homestay with a family in Kobe.

"It was like being inside the story we read, you know, 'A Family Supper' by Ishiguro," the young woman said. "It was so tense between the father and the son, I was afraid to eat the dinner."

The Ishiguro story we had read and discussed in class dealt with a son who returns home to Japan after his relationship with his girlfriend in California unravels. The story begins with these provocative sentences: "Fugu is a fish caught off the Pacific shores of Japan. The fish held a special significance for me ever since my mother died through eating one." The poison sits in the sexual glands of the fish, which must be prepared with precision or else the diner could die. In the story, the narrator goes home to discover that Watanabe, the father's partner in his collapsed business, killed himself and took his entire family with him. The narrator's formidable father appears not to understand the narrator's younger sister or him at all. The sister is a modern Japanese woman, sexually liberated and eager to be on her own, but the father sees her as a traditional Japanese daughter, silent, humble, and dutiful. The son is caught between cultures, less Japanese than Everyman, dislocated and alienated, but the father assumes he has lost his son because he had not brought him up correctly.

As the three of them sit down to eat a fish dinner prepared by the father, we are left to wonder about the levels of the generation gap, the complexity of the miscommunications. Has the father served his son and daughter a final supper? Or has the son from the beginning misunderstood his father's sense of honor? Did the mother commit suicide? What will become of these generations struggling to understand one another amid unspoken emotions and upended codes of behavior? How little do we as outsiders ever understand the society we observe from an unbridgeable distance, however close it may seem to be? Like Kyoko in Yasunari Kawabata's story "The Moon on the Water," we see always through some sort of mirror, one cultural metaphor or another.

The student looked at me with disappointment knitted into a frown. "You know, it was too much like an American family," she said. "The kids rolled their eyes when the parents weren't looking. They made it clear that their folks didn't have a clue about what was going on in the world, and the parents seemed to think their kids needed a better sense of values. I could see that anytime at home in Illinois. The father was pretty stern, though. It made me think about how far he might go with his kids to prove his point."

She paused for a second as three Japanese girls in tight jeans and high heels strutted past us giggling and swinging shopping bags. "The fish was good," she said. "But I waited for everyone else to take a few bites first."

When we boarded the ship that night, we waited in line with dozens of students coming back from days in Tokyo and other cities. Many of them looked bedraggled, as if it had been a long five days. Two girls in particular had a disheveled appearance that suggested they hadn't slept for most of that time. One of them, wearing a tank top about three sizes too small and what looked like a newly minted tattoo on her neck, spoke loud enough for everyone around to hear.

"I spent the whole time with some Japanese students I met in Tokyo," she was saying to the girl next to her. "I don't think we stopped partying for three days. Last night I was so drunk I actually started speaking Japanese, and everyone understood me."

I considered for a moment how drunk one might have to get to become fluent in Japanese, but I couldn't arrive at the precise amount of liquor that would be necessary to achieve that feat.

That evening we ate dinner with the sheriff and his wife, Diana. He told me that one of the students had been sent home. It turned out it was someone from my writing class, a scraggly haired young man who had a soft, feminine gaze that reminded me of portraits I had seen of Percy Bysshe Shelley. He was a quiet-spoken wisp of a kid, shy, almost too diffident to make eye contact. The day we docked in Japan, the young man had come up to me in Purser's Square onboard to apologize for not turning in an assignment on time. He looked sick: snot slid from his nose and his eyes were watery and streaked red. It was not unusual for someone to be sick, though. Seasickness, colds, and sore throats spread around the ship all the time. Something felt wrong, but I shook it off as bad intuition.

The sheriff's story was worse than I expected, making me suspect that a bizarre brand of tragedy had followed us once again to Japan. The young man had signed on to the Semester at Sea program because he thought it would be a good place to kick his heroin habit, away from the college where he had started his addiction. Once Chris told me as much as he knew of the story, I realized that everything had been right before my eyes. I just had not seen what was going on. The watery eyes, the runny nose, the chills and cramps, the dark circles from lack of sleep. The whipsaw thin frame most likely came from a loss of appetite. The occasional yawning in a 2 P.M. class. Everything fit the symptoms of heroin withdrawal. The young man's father had flown in from the U.S. on September 11 to take him home, and that was the last we saw of him.

The ship raced out of Kobe Harbor, changing course away from Quindao, China, to Hong Kong in an attempt to outrun a typhoon that was headed in our direction. I sat with Jo-Ellen on our deck, the winds whistling an ominous warning, the whitecaps snapping against the hull of the ship, and I put down the book I was reading—Murakami's *The Wind-Up Bird Chronicle*—marking my place about midway through. I was struck by one of the sentences: "time wobbled by like a wagon with a loose axle."

Time seemed to be wobbling for us, too. We had been here in Japan before, leaving someone behind, lost, not knowing what would happen to him. It seemed surreal. Would talking cats or skydiving sardines be any more unaccountable than a disappearing restaurant, a coed eating a potentially poisonous fish on a family homestay, or a young man, addicted to heroin, who decided that a ship with six hundred college students eager to party night and day was the best place in the world to break a habit that was destroying him?

Hong Kong

On the way to Hong Kong, we skirted the typhoon but came close to a mutiny. The Global Studies course had gotten toxic after the first test scores were posted. More than half of the students had gotten a D or lower on the fifty-question multiple-choice exam. The professor in charge of Global Studies was looking more and more like Captain Bly to them, although he had an uncanny resemblance to photographs I had seen of Benito Mussolini. When a student at the beginning of Global Studies raised her hand and asked what kinds of questions one could expect on the next exam, the Global Studies guru laughed condescendingly.

"I can't help giggling," he said as she shrunk down into her seat.

The implication was clear: she was to come to class, take notes on everything that was said, even which professor said it, and not expect a study guide to pamper her. In a sense, of course, he was right. There was too much pampering going on, too much grade inflation, on many campuses. However, many of these students were hard-working young people from good universities, and they were struggling to get thirty of fifty answers on the test right. Maybe the questions were trivializing the process. Maybe they should have been given an opportunity to discuss things in the class and not be told over and over again *we don't have time for that in our lectures.* Maybe instead of a daily lecture format for six hundred, there should have been a mechanism for students to convene in small groups and a way for them to address vital questions in essays.

But with an attitude that suggested vital state secrets were at risk, Professor X in charge of Global Studies resisted change for a variety of reasons. Things got worse as the days progressed. Murmurs of dissent became hallway graffiti. Sidelong glances became open sarcasm. Attendance in the morning Global Studies lectures decreased, even after the

Professor X agreed to share the stage with faculty experts in areas other than his own—political science.

It didn't help when some of the lecturers were mind-numbingly boring and students had to prop their eyelids open with pencils so that they did not miss a potential exam question. One professor, for instance, gave a lecture on the weather in a toneless whisper that was all calm before the storm, but the storm never came. I sat in the back, trying hard to shake off the aftereffects of rough seas and a meclizine-induced sleep. After about a half an hour, Jo-Ellen passed me another one of her bad-girl-in-class notes—"Professor X is looking good to me now! I'd rather be insulted in a lively tone than bored to death in a monotone. Where is Fletcher Christian when you need him?"

Fletcher Christian never showed up, but there were a few moments when some of us thought one of his descendents had. After the second test (in which the scores were lower than the first), a demure young woman from one of my writing classes stood up and told Professor X he was insulting and that the course was an exercise in trivia and futility. She didn't just say it. She said it loud and she spoke for a time—until, that is, Professor X demanded she sit down and shut up. It may not have been a bona-fide mutiny, but it was one of those skin-tingling, embarrassing moments that everyone remembers. The moment never found its way onto the multiple-choice test, though.

The protests of the Sixties were a dusty chapter in unread history books for most of the students onboard, and no real mutiny occurred— no sit-ins, no takeovers of the dean's office, no throwing themselves in a pile before the smirking, sleek-haired Professor X. Many of the faculty, though, had fond memories of those good old days, and Professor Y lifted his voice like Patrick Henry asking for death rather than the disgrace of unfair exams. Another faculty member, white bearded with a helmet of frizzled white hair and a voice like a dump truck rumbling along a pebbly path, said that since we were heading to China, we should have a Cultural Revolution of our own. Someone reminded him that the Cultural Revolution hadn't been a total success as of the present: 400 million people in China living on $2 a day, sixteen out of twenty of the world's most polluted cities within its borders, three-fourths of the water supply undrinkable, car pollution rising faster than Chinese slogans.

The subject at hand—fair tests—was lost for about a half an hour in the tangent. Such faculty gatherings, where little is resolved, where people speak as if they were testing out a speech before a mirror or where decisions are tabled until the next meeting, are not unusual. Universities, even ones on the sea, are places where discussion is more prevalent than action. As Vivian Gornick wrote in "At the University: Little Murders of the Soul," such a world can be isolating and soulless—"It is a kind of death in life to which university people become inured."

The faculty protest fizzled into white wine and Dewar's at the faculty lounge over the weeks. But I have to admit that the frizzy-haired revolutionary played the piano with gusto and sang a mean version of "The House of the Rising Sun" after a few highballs. And it was interesting entertainment to watch the business professor who split his time and apparently personality between universities in Holland and Utah, hovering near any nubile coed in the vicinity. His lectures were even more entertaining—an inspired blend of simple-mindedness, bad grammar, and arrogance. It was more fun than watching a *Saturday Night Live* skit.

The student ire drifted away in the same gentle breeze that the faculty protest did, especially after the students understood that the bell curve would transform Ds into low Bs. "After all," I heard one coed say to another, "why argue the principle of the thing when the practical matter is settled anyway? It's best to forget the whole thing. Tonight's pub night, right?"

The skyline of Hong Kong could make one forget many things. In the daylight the buildings rose like opium dreams out of the smog and smoke, and in the night they stood against the speckled lights of the mountains as if steel and glass could last forever. The whole city seemed to exist outside of time, and dull professors and potential mutinies were of little consequence.

I spent my days in the city roaming the back streets with Jo-Ellen, and when I was on the ship I read Martin Booth's *Golden Boy: Memories of a Hong Kong Childhood*. Booth, the author of two dozen books, had died shortly after completing the manuscript for *Golden Boy*. Writing the book had clearly been a labor of love, a way of telling his grown children the story of his childhood in a city that he cherished. He had been a *gweilo*, a ghost or pale fellow, in an exotic world of "devils, demons, and the pan-theon of other supernatural ne'er do wells which every Chinese believed occupied every spiritually inhabitable niche."

Booth's shade was a good one to follow in Hong Kong, and as Jo-Ellen and I sailed on the Duk Ling Junk in the harbor, gazing at the haze-shrouded Victoria Peak, I thought of him as young boy "living on clouds." Sailing on the Duk Ling with a few dozen Chinese, I could imagine how the seven-year-old Booth felt as he watched a ship dock in one of the berths near Ocean Terminal, sliding like a dinosaur on roller skates into a mall parking space, slowly, gently, sideways. The people onboard the Duk Ling "chattered like a flock of migrating starlings" as the Chinese crowds had sounded to Booth.

When we took the Star Ferry across the mile-wide harbor from Tsim Shan Tsui in Kowloon to the business district on Hong Kong Island, I had the same misgivings that Booth had had fifty years before—"Whilst the ferries themselves were perfectly safe, I had my doubts about the ferry piers. Constructed of a wooden deck on wooden piles, they creaked and swayed dizzily as a vessel came alongside. The piles screeched, the deck planking moaned like lost souls and everyone waiting to board swayed unsteadily. What was more toe-curling was the fact that there were gaps between the planks." Like Booth, I watched as my Hong Kong coins dropped from my pocket, slid between the spaces, and sunk into the dirty waters below, where I envisioned Jo-Ellen and I slipping as the ferry leaned away from the dock and the chasm opened to greet us.

The tram to Victoria Peak reminded me of the San Francisco cable cars in a more enclosed environment. The tram ride was so steep that the floor of the cable car was angled so that standing passengers could do just that—stand upright. It transported nearly 100,000 passengers a day, but you couldn't help breathing a sigh of relief when it rattled to a stop at the base of Victoria Peak because, even though it hadn't had an accident since it began service in 1888, the actuarial odds seemed to be building in the other direction. The magnificent view from Victoria, Hong Kong's highest mountain, was probably never absolutely clear.

When Jo-Ellen and I were there, the view shifted from an impenetrable haze to a gossamer smog depending on what direction of the compass we chose to look from. The skyscrapers stretched into the pall like children's building blocks on a playground after the dust had been kicked up, and the thick foliage rolled down the hillsides toward the throbbing life of the city that lay in a separate and distinct world humming below us.

When Jo-Ellen and I ate lunch later that afternoon at the elegant (and noisy) Peking Gardens in Kowloon, I was reminded of the old world atmosphere Booth must have felt having high tea with his mother at the Pen. We ate dim sum with Bill and Sherry May while waiters in dark suits treated us all like English royalty. But Habitu, a restaurant in Ocean Terminal that overlooked the sizzling lights of the harbor, was easier on our Western stomachs—contemporary Italian cuisine and French wines. We ate brick-oven pizzas, sipped cabernet sauvignon, and watched the evening light show spark across the cityscape.

The next day we took the high-speed ferry to Macau with Ron and Jackie Morse who, besides their expertise in all things Japanese, lived in Las Vegas and knew enough about casino lore to fill us in on the gambling there. Macau rose out of the fog like a surreal daydream, the Sands Hotel looming above a replicated village that portrayed the Forbidden City, Venice, and a lava mountain—as if Las Vegas had been transported lock, stock, and meretricious barrel of money in a capitalist building frenzy to the outskirts of a supposedly communist country.

The ferry cost 137 Hong Kong dollars, a bit under $20 U.S., but I won over 300 Hong Kong dollars at the blackjack tables when I got there. In the Wynn Casino in the garish nouveau Las Vegas atmosphere of harbor town Macau, Ron Morse said, "The world moves on money. Money is the real fuel for everything." As I pocketed my winnings, that seemed okay to me because after I deducted the ferry tickets, I still had enough to pay for lunch.

At first, I was surprised by all the new casinos being built on the island, hundreds of feet of bamboo scaffolding rising shakily around one monument after another to gambling. But then I recalled Booth's remarks about the Chinese fascination with games of chance. "Gambling," he said, "and being Chinese were synonymous. . . . To eradicate gambling was akin to prohibiting the eating of rice." As I watched the busloads of Chinese tourists from the mainland unloading in front of the extravagant new Wynn hotel, I realized that Booth had gotten it right then and it had not changed at all. Las Vegas magnates like Wynn probably shivered with pleasure as they dreamed of the 1 billion gamblers on mainland China queuing up to ride the bus across one of the bridges into Macau.

In the Wynn Casino everything was red—the carpets and drapes and chairs—for red equals good fortune in China. Even the Chinese characters for the name Wynn suggested "eternal profit." Of course, everyone—gamblers and casino owners—had a different idea about who would be the recipient of the good luck. Given all the gilt and polished metal in the Wynn, though, I had no doubt who had the odds, and I was happy to get out with a free lunch and head to the Old Town.

Old Town Macau was the original Portuguese settlement. By the sixteenth century, the Portuguese had made it into a vibrant commercial center between Japan and China. When the Portuguese empire crumbled, they left behind their Romanesque and Gothic architecture, their churches, and an instinct for commerce. The Old Town could have been on a different continent from the glitzy casinos and high-rises on the rest of Macau. Just as its history—filled with tales of the blood and faith and brutality of its martyrs and colonizers—is paradoxical, its landscape is a puzzle with abandoned pieces. The banyan trees, the bark hanging like moss, stood as sentinels near the stoic Portuguese fort.

All that remained of the ruins of the Church of St. Paul, designed by an Italian Jesuit priest and completed by Japanese Christian exiles and Chinese craftsmen in the early seventeenth century, was a striking façade. It stood haughtily on one of Macau's seven hills. Once you stepped behind the building, it was like a Hollywood movie set, wearily holding the horizon against grimy apartment towers in the distance. The Portuguese empire was long gone, and the new Vegas colonialists had taken over. I looked at what remained of the stately Portuguese world and shook my head.

"This must have been a beautiful place," I said to Ron.

Keeping his eyes on the skeleton of the Church of St. Paul, he said, "I wonder how long it will take America to be in Portugal's position? We may not get there in our lifetime, but those kids on the ship will see China become the new world power and us just a modern Portugal."

As we walked farther along the sloping streets of Portuguese Macau, a young woman with a child bumped into Jo-Ellen. The child held a balloon in her hand and reached out to show it to her.

"Say hello, Auntie," the woman said to the child. "Hello, Uncle. Say hello."

The child held her red balloon against the chipped yellow façade of the building behind her. The buildings made me feel as if I were in Lisbon, but the crowds were Chinese, noisy and bustling. After being in Japan only a few days before, being in China was like stepping from a silent cathedral into boisterous market. Jo-Ellen turned to me in one of the narrow streets filled with vendors and got that familiar glint in her eye.

"Everything I hear sounds like a variation and repetition of the phrase 'hee haw,'" she said. "I wonder if I could get along here on my own with just those two words?"

"You better stick with me," I told her, but she was resilient and that phrase probably would have worked for her. I think my warning was really for me. I was more worried about what I'd do without her than how she would survive in a Chinese-Portuguese gambling town.

The next few days as Jo-Ellen dragged me down Nathan Street and Temple Street to jade markets and food stalls, the air burning our eyes, the car exhaust clogging our throats, we sidestepped crowds and waved off hawkers. I was still certain she could survive anything, but I wasn't so sure about myself. I saw more dried fish and old coins, more unpackaged underwear and assorted sex toys, cameras, and perfume bottles than I had in any two-day period in my life. I was wilting in the smog, heat, and suffocating crowds. Jo-Ellen just got stronger as the crowds became thicker and the markets denser with items for sale.

On our last day in Hong Kong before our ship sailed, I got my way—no shopping. Instead, we went to a kung fu festival in Kowloon Park. Along with hundreds of Chinese, we watched the Ha Kwok Cheung Dragon and Lion Team perform. I noticed a few people eating what appeared to be moon cakes, even though we were too early for the mid-autumn festival in which they were the main fare. I could not say I was disappointed because I felt as Martin Booth had about the little pastries—they were inedible—

"the glutinous contents had the unpleasant habit of sticking to the roof of the mouth."

We saved our appetites for Habitu and enjoyed the balletic discipline of the kung fu school, dozens of children and adults kicking the air to drums beating and flags waving. Pairs of six- and seven-year-olds flew gracefully into the air, their mouths clamped tight with determination, their eyes slits of fury. The lion and dragon dances were the culmination of the performance, a daring choreography of leaps and flips on a pole to the crashing of cymbals. The carefully stylized lion's head, three times the size of the real thing, had bulging eyes and fur-fringed jaws. The performer held the mask aloft by a bamboo pole and shook it up and down and side to side with a ferociousness that matched the thunderous cymbals and shouts of the kung fu group. The dragon's head was the size of two men and swung up and down in perfect time to the drum beats and cymbal crashes. Its eyes were raised to the pale sky and then with a fierceness that bordered on comedy to the crowd that applauded wildly.

That night we ate in Habitu for the third time since our arrival in Hong Kong. We had the same waiter each visit, an angular young man in his early twenties, a shock of black hair that constantly fell into his squinting eyes.

"Ah, my friends," he said to us, "you are once more here. I'm glad you see me again." He was a familiar face in a city of 7 million strangers. Habitu had a serene atmosphere that permitted us to sink down into soft chairs, breathe the cool conditioned air, gaze at the glittering lights of the city, glimpse the crowds angling along the edge of the harbor, and contemplate with our friends Bill and Sherry May the thousand-mile journey that lay ahead to Ho Chi Minh City. We had received a cyclone warning for the sail to Vietnam, but as we sat there in the safety of Habitu, that seemed fitting.

The word *cyclone* had been coined by a nineteenth-century British captain who witnessed the circular motion of a storm in Mauritius. He most likely hatched the word from the Greek *kuklon*, which suggests a wheel or something moving in circles. We were following a circle ourselves in our journey—so it seemed fair for nature to have a similar plan for us.

Vietnam

As we sailed toward Vietnam, listening to lectures on the four-thousand-year-old history of the country, the myths of the dragon and the one hundred children of the heavenly spirit, the thousand years of Chinese domination, and the many rebellions against invaders over the centuries, we came near once again to a rebellion of our own onboard the ship. The same faculty members who found something disagreeable about not being told how many As, Bs, Cs, and Ds to give in their classes had decided that being leaders on student bus excursions was an onerous responsibility that required something equivalent to a contractual delineation of powers and duties for any faculty member in charge. Common sense, it seemed, was not a viable option for them.

"I mean," one asked, "if a student is late for the bus and we're in Hanoi, do we wait for them?"

"Couldn't you take ten minutes and call their hotel room?" I wondered aloud.

"What if we have a plane to catch? We can't make the whole group late for one."

"No, of course not," someone else chimed in, "but I suppose it's reasonable to make the best effort we can, and if they don't make it, then they have to find a way to the airport on their own."

As is often the case at faculty meetings, the loudest voice made the least sense. It was the bifurcated business professor, the one who trolled the corridors for cute coeds, who raised his voice with the authority of one who has experienced battle. In Japan, he had brought a drunken student home from a baseball game, and he had been patted on the back by many for taking decisive action. The student had puked and urinated on himself and fallen into a stupor in a bleacher seat. The professor took him back to the ship in a cab. He had gone, as he reminded everyone on a subtle and constant basis, beyond the call of trip leader's duty: *he had been PUKED ON and still brought the young man home safe.* I was never sure what his other choice was—leave the student there in the bleachers, unconscious, in pee-stained pants, to find his way back to port the next day?

We sat there in the faculty meeting, one half of the room filled with those who wanted explicit directions about what to do if students puked, showed up late, failed to listen to a guide, or any of an infinite number of possible behaviors that they would happily list for everyone's edification until the sun set. In the other half of the room were faculty who felt there were clear rules already—dock time for lateness, possible dismissal from the program for drug or alcohol abuse—and between the two sides was an empty row of seats that stood like the 17th parallel separating North and South Vietnam. But, unlike the Vietnam-American conflict, we were all non-uniformed combatants, neither side had a devoted and disciplined leader like Ho Chi Minh, and no one was sure what would constitute victory.

One thing I had learned over the years about faculty grievances in meetings: if they talk long enough, they will talk themselves out of the opinion they started with—or at least talk themselves out of the will to act. So, once again, faculty furor faded into dirty looks and whispered insults, and mutineers and militants became malcontents. For those of us who sensed we might be adults and could make a logical decision if called upon to do so, things turned out for the best anyway, even if my love for faculty meetings had not grown in the process.

One reason the academic-political turmoil dissipated was that many of us were about to become millionaires for the first time in our lives. I went with Jo-Ellen to a currency exchange and cashed in $60 in U.S. currency. They gave me a little over 1 million Vietnamese dong. It felt good to be a millionaire. I thought I detected a new respect in Jo-Ellen's gaze. I didn't mind if she wanted me only for my money. I was a successful American tourist, a millionaire, at least for the day. I had some change left after we ate at Lemon Grass Restaurant, gave a donation at Notre Dame Cathedral after Mass, and shopped at the Ben Thanh Market. It wasn't a bad feeling—my body and soul had been well nourished, Jo-Ellen had a dress for herself and silk pajamas for her sister, I had a pair of imitation Ray Ban sunglasses, and I still had 30,000 dong in my pocket.

Saigon was the same city for us that it had been four years ago, even though we had been millionaires for a few hours that morning. That night, we went for a massage at the Rex Hotel. We paid $6 apiece without the tip, but the bill would have been considerably more if I had gone along with the masseuse's suggestion to "massage *everything.*" You'll like it, the young woman argued. *I make feel good.* But I was no longer a millionaire, and Jo-Ellen was in a nearby room. As a matter of fact, I could have sworn I heard her in the hall calling my name.

It was a good thing I held onto the money I had left because we missed the shuttle bus back to the ship, and after dodging motorcycles on all the main thoroughfares, we decided to take a cab. The traffic in Saigon had not changed in our four-year absence. Our experience was the same one that Andrew X. Pham described in *Catfish and Mandala,* his account of his bicycle trip through Vietnam—"The roads are so people-thick I can reach out and touch four other motorists at any moment. Viet works the horn, the brakes, and the gas constantly. The whole time, all I can say is, *Oh, shit. Oh, God. Look out!* to which his reply is a published fact: head injuries resulting from traffic accidents are the number-one cause of accidental deaths in Saigon. I see no helmets and extremely few eyeglasses."

Like Pham, we saw no helmets, but we did see many young women wearing long-sleeved gloves and handkerchiefs over their faces to protect themselves form the sun and pollution. We saw men with their unhel-meted wives and babies riding on the backs of their motorbikes. We saw dogs in cages, farm equipment, bags of rice, cases of bottled water, kegs of beer, window casements, even a motorbike with another motorbike tied precariously over the back wheel.

Saigon was a vibrant city. People never seemed to sleep. They never stopped scurrying around the clogged streets. Children were everywhere selling postcards and coconut milk. Like the language of the country, the city was throbbing with nuance and ambiguity. Right before we found the cab, a scrawny kid on the streets of the Dong Khoi section of the city, trying to sell us books and postcards, said, "All in English. No problem. Vietnamese language not easy for you. *Ma* means 'ghost,' 'mother,' 'but,' 'cemetery,' 'horse,' or 'rice seed.' Have to be careful how you say it, eh? My books all in English, though. Best books all around."

I ended up buying *Paradise of the Blind* by Duong Thu Huong, a Vietnamese writer from Hanoi. She was one of the country's most popular writers, an advocate for human rights for many years, but she had been expelled from the Communist Party, her novel had been banned, and she had been imprisoned in 1991 for her politics. The novel was the story of Hang, a young woman growing up in the unsettling postwar era in Vietnam. The young boy on the streets of Dong Khoi pulled the book out of the thick Saigon air, it seemed, a magician performing a trick for the tourist.

At one point, he said, *Xin chao* and at another *Cam un*. One phrase meant "hello" *or* "goodbye." The other meant "thank you." But I forget whether he was drawing me in at that moment in or telling me to slip away with my controversial book. And instead of saying "thank you," he may have been simply admonishing me, like an American coaxing a reluctant buyer to "come on."

I read *Paradise of the Blind* on the plane flight the next day to Hanoi, and I was eager to see the city that was still the home of a writer so critical of the Communist regime, a city that for my high school and college years had been nothing more than a place for American bombs and a sanctuary for the enigmatic and Spartan Ho Chi Minh. During those years, it was the place we were not supposed to go unless, like Jane Fonda, we wanted to be branded a traitor.

There were two busloads of students with us, and some of their parents had come from the States, by way of Bangkok, to spend a few days with their children in a place they once imagined as an enemy stronghold. But we were all in for a few surprises. The plane flight was smoother, the food better, the attendants more gracious, and the seats more comfortable than any ordinary flight in America. And Hanoi had a shaded old world feel to it. Pham's description of it in *Catfish and Mandala* was accurate still: "Hanoi is a more sedate city than Saigon. The traffic is much lighter, and in the cooler air under tree-shaded avenues, the smog is more tolerable. Hanoi lives on a scale more comprehensible than Saigon. The trees are smaller, more abundant, and not so tall and tropical like those of Saigon. I stroll along the fine mansions, taking in their faded, colonial French glories, their expensive arches, French windows, and wrought-iron balconies. Every structure holds itself up proudly in a state of elegant decay."

Our tour guide, Luu Trung Kien, was in his early thirties, a round-faced, boyish-looking man with wire-rimmed glasses and a crew cut. In his khaki pants and short-sleeved collared shirt, he could have been a social studies teacher at a suburban high school in California. He had earned a master's degree in history and worked, as his father had before him, for the government, but he chose to take a job as a tour guide to make more money. His wife still worked for the government, and their two-year-old child was watched over during the day by his parents.

Kien was a typical Vietnamese phenomenon: overeducated, under-employed, both a citizen and a stranger in his own land. His first piece of advice for us about Hanoi, despite its more genteel atmosphere and wide-open spaces, was this is still Vietnam: "Don't ever run or stop suddenly when you cross the street. Don't make eye contact with the drivers. You might think they crash into you. But don't look into their eyes and you won't be afraid."

Kien was a font of knowledge about Vietnamese history and culture. As we drove in our bus over the Song (or Red) River, which meandered all the way to China, Kien told us that Hanoi, with a population of 4 million, was one half the size of Ho Chi Minh City, and it did not have the same bustling economy. At least one-third of the national income came from Ho Chi Minh City.

"Hanoi," he said into the microphone on the bus, "has been the capital of Vietnam for a thousand years. The name means 'soaring dragon.'" He smiled. "And we hope to soar soon. But we live here in a strictly cash economy. Houses can cost hundreds of thousands of dollars, but no banks, no loans. Everything is cash. Most of the big money in the cities in Vietnam comes from smuggling and corruption. Salaries are often very low, but income can be very high. For most people, living in Vietnam is not easy."

The pink stripes on Kien's white polo shirt suggested that Vietnam had changed a bit in the last decade. He had just finished telling us that before 1990 only four colors were worn by the Vietnamese people—green for the army, blue for factory workers, white for office workers, and brown for farmers. Kien's colors, muted as they were, implied some changes. But much of the Vietnamese culture was the "same, same" as their typical phrase goes.

"In Vietnam," Kien said, "we respect older people. Age means wisdom we need to survive. My father is seventy, but when someone asks him how old he is, he says seventy-one because he wants to be older, and he counts his nine months in the womb. In America no one wants to be older, am I right?"

Of course he was right, and of the three questions that he said all people in Vietnam care deeply to ask—*how old are you, how many children do you have, and how much money do you make*—Americans asked none but would like to know the last.

With Kien, we spent the day seeing the effects of war in Hanoi from the Vietnamese perspective. In the War Museum, we watched a strange film about the battle of Dien Bien Phu in 1954 in which the French were defeated by the Vietnamese. What was unusual about the carefully anti-French film was the lyrical soundtrack of French music that underscored the documentary. Nearby, the Hanoi Hilton, first used as a prison by the French for Vietnamese rebels and called Hoa Loa ("fiery furnace"), was imprinted on my memory for the U.S. servicemen who spent years there. The prison museum was now in the shadow of a new business tower and luxury apartment building, something for Chinese businessmen to gaze down at with blind indifference after a long meeting.

I did not feel superior to those businessmen but aligned to them in discomfiting ways. In 1971, a few months before I got married to Jo-Ellen, Lt. William Calley had been found guilty of murdering twenty-two civilians at My Lai and American Special Forces had unsuccessfully attempted to free prisoners from the Hanoi Hilton, and both were news stories that haunted me with shame and terror—for being lucky and for not knowing with certainty if I would have acted honorably in either situation.

Vietnam was the country of *if* and *might have been* in my life. But with all the questions it brought up for me—and always would, I suppose—the man who led the North Vietnamese through the war seemed a hero who could easily have fit, if roles and nationalities had been reversed, into an American mythology. When we visited Ho Chi Minh's mausoleum and then the simple stilt house that he lived in much of the time from 1958 until his death in 1969, I was impressed as I had been after reading William Duiker's biography of the man and the description of his rise from ordinary beginnings to struggle to make his country free. His story was Abraham Lincoln's or Horatio Alger's. His story was Gandhi's or Che Guevara's—a man of principle who loved his people and his country and the ideal of freedom above anything else. Uncle Ho was an icon in Vietnam, and like all icons there was a story behind the image, but if he were an American patriot, we would have immortalized him as his own people do.

The mausoleum was an enormous stark marble box with columns that controlled the otherwise empty landscape of the wide avenue. We walked around outside the monument watching the Vietnamese flag—red with a gold star—flutter in the hot breeze. Three smartly dressed soldiers in white uniforms marched in front of the wooden doors to the tomb, two of them standing with bayonets in case, I suppose, someone chose to storm the building.

In his will, Ho Chi Minh had requested cremation, but that would not have fit the state's plans to keep his image alive. His preserved corpse rested in a glass sarcophagus in the basement of the mausoleum—that is, except from September through December when it was sent to Russia for maintenance. I was not disappointed that on September 25, when I was there, Ho had flown to Russia for some upkeep. I had already read Pham's account of seeing Ho, and it was not encouraging—"I gawk at him with the rest of the tourists, half of them foreigners decked out in Spandex, cutoff jeans, sports bras, and Birkenstock sandals, the other half Vietnamese, sweaty and hot, quietly suffering in their best Sunday outfits. . . . the hourly event seethes with the subdued giddiness of a freak show."

I was happy when we got back to our hotel and Kien asked me if I would like to take a ride with him around the town on the back of his motorbike. He took me to the Temple of Literature, an oasis in the hot, busy streets, founded in 1070 by Emperor Ly Thanh Tong and dedicated to Confucius. Its five courtyards, separated by walls and connected by a central pathway, constituted Vietnam's first university. Kien drove me also to Hoan Kiem Lake (Lake of the Restored Sword), for Hanoi residents the equivalent of New York's Central Park. In late afternoon, it was crowded with couples and families, children carrying balloons and old men practicing tai chi. The lake itself glistened in the falling light, like a star emerging in the pale sky.

The legend of the lake, as Kien explained it to me, was Arthurian in its shape. In the fifteenth century, the gods had given Emperor Ly Thai To an enchanted sword to fight his enemies, and after the battle ended, he was in a boat on the lake. As he sat there with the sword in his hands, a giant turtle rose from the depths of the water, grabbed the sword and disappeared. Like Malory's Lady of the Lake, the turtle returned the sword to its rightful owners.

From the lake, Kien slithered through the traffic, leaning left and right, with me holding on to the back rail of his bike for dear life. We came within millimeters of stray dogs with patchy fur creeping into the streets; a motorbike with a man, a woman, and two live pigs in a cage; cyclos, bicyclists, and undaunted pedestrians. Many people, like me, rode as passengers on the backs of the motorbikes, but I seemed to be the only one who was terrified. As far as I could tell, I was the only person in Hanoi who did not have absolutely perfect balance or a pure Buddhist faith in my fate—I'm not sure which I lacked more. The others sat serenely, their hands in their laps while mine were clutched, white-knuckled, to the bike.

At one choked street corner, Kien turned to me and said, "There's an old Vietnamese saying—if you want to know the life of the people, you must go to the market. I'll take you there before we go back, eh?"

The markets in the Old Quarter of Hanoi were teeming with life and commerce. People shouted and bartered. The air throbbed with entrepreneurial energy. Each narrow street had its own definition. One was for shops that sold shoes, another for jewelry. There was a street for clothing, others for tin boxes, mirrors, straw mats, herbs, towels, or Buddhist statues. People went to Pho Hang Ma ("counterfeit street") to buy "ghost money" to burn at Buddhist ceremonies. On the food streets, women knelt on the ground over baskets of squirming eels and Styrofoam boxes of small silver fish. They cut raw meat into chunks under the shade of tarps or bamboo roofs. Or they squatted on tiny plastic stools as they ate their bowls of rice and vegetables with quick, skillful movements of their long chopsticks.

Some streets were like still-life portraits—row upon row of colors— flashes of purple, red, yellow, orange, and green; a canvas of bananas, tomatoes, grapes, peppers, carrots, and lettuce. The market had a filthy radiance. Despite its poverty, it had a richness of spirit, a sense of life lived daily, unmediated. Kien turned to me again and spoke.

"This is not America, eh? But if everyone lived like an American, we might need many more earths to live on, am I right?"

He didn't expect an answer, I was certain, because we both knew he was right. I could see he loved the life of the markets. In them, for him, was the heart of the city. We stopped before an indoor market.

"Ho Chi Minh wanted everyone to be able to read," he said. "So he put up a sign outside the entrance to this place. People had to read it aloud before they walked in. If they could not read it aloud, they had to crawl into the marketplace. Uncle Ho shamed them into learning, but like a strict, loving father, he taught them the lesson they needed."

On our way back to the hotel, we stopped and ate a bowl of pho, the traditional, all-purpose, any-meal Vietnamese soup. I had eaten it a few times in the past few days, and my stomach began to feel the consequences as we bounced over the potholed road back to the hotel. When Kien said *chao* to me, it sounded like "chow," and it made me move even faster toward the lobby and my room on the fifth floor.

🌊🌊🌊 The next day we traveled by bus with our students to Halong Bay. Kien turned into a burlesque comedian for part of the two-hour ride.

"Anyone need to stop at the happy house?"

"The happy house, Kien?" one of the students asked.

"You don't know happy house," he said, shaking his head in mock surprise. "You know—Wonderful China—the WC. The toilet. Let me tell you a story of my little cousin. His father looked at him one day and said, 'You're a gentleman now. You must act and speak like a gentleman. When you have to do number 1, that is singing. Just say you want to sing. When you must do number 2, that is dancing. Just say you want to dance. That night the boy's grandmother babysat for him at her house. The boy woke up at midnight and went into her bedroom. 'Grandmother, grandmother,' he said, 'I need to sing, and I think I have to dance, too.' The grandmother said, 'It is late, my dear, if you must sing, go ahead but do it quietly in my ear. And if you have to dance, do it softly on the rug.'"

Kien also offered his explanation of the gender gap in Vietnam. As we passed rice paddies with women stooped over swinging small sickles working the fields or managing water buffaloes, Kien said, "All men want the water buffalo's life. Plow and eat. Work four months a year and rest after that. In Vietnam, women work the fields and men drink rice wine. Men are the banks, women the supermarkets. For women, there are marriage exams. If a girl is to marry a young man, she must go to his house and prepare tea for the boy's family. The water can't be too hot, and the color of the tea must be the same color in each cup. It's not an easy exam."

Much of what we saw in the floating villages of Halong Bay in the Gulf of Tonkin suggested that Kien's view was accurate. Women sold colorful produce from flat boats. The men were fishing—or drinking rice wine—I could not be sure, but they were not around. Halong Bay could have been something conjured in a fairy tale, limestone formations rising like a child's wildest imaginings from the deep green waters of the bay. Literally *Ha long* means "the place where the dragon descends into the water," and the legend said that the dragon who lived there cut a swath through the mountains with its ridged tail, leaving grottoes and outcroppings behind. Kien waved good-bye when we set sail into the bay for a lunch cruise with the students.

In years past, I had associated Tonkin with the resolution that led to the war of my generation, but now the waters of Halong, stretching into the Gulf of Tonkin, looked like paradise. We ate what was probably the best meal we had in our stay in Vietnam on that boat—lemon-scented grilled calamari and shrimp, crisp salads, and hot spring rolls. And we dove—faculty and students alike—joining hands in heart-stopping plunges from the top edge of the boat into the emerald waters surrounded by sheer limestone cliffs, some of them bare rock and others draped with an improbably thick foliage.

I would have always remembered Halong as a kind of paradise if that night Jo-Ellen and I had not gotten lost after dinner and been unable to find our way back to the Asea Hotel on a hilltop overlooking the bay. It was pitch dark, no one spoke a word of English, and every hotel we went in to ask directions pointed us a different way or asked for our passports so that we could register at their establishment. One clerk, who licked his lips each time he spoke, took the passports out of our hands as if to check them and gave them back only after I said I was going to call the police. At one point in our attempt to find our hotel, a man on a motorcycle roared up to us, scattering pebbles at our feet.

"I take you where you want. Where you go? Where you go?"

A quick flashback to my ride on Kien's motorbike made me shudder at the thought of both Jo-Ellen and I riding on this stranger's bike down mysterious streets in the darkness. I saw us in a black alley, his knife glinting in the single headlight of his bike, his friends emerging from doorways. Two other men on bikes rode past us and then did a U-turn, passing us again slowly and turning their heads to eye us. We passed a few sidewalk eateries for locals, and the customers gave the kind of sidelong glances that suggested we were not where we were supposed to be or where many American or Europeans strolled after a certain hour.

The stores became fewer, the lights dimmer, and then everything started to look the same and different at the same time. A few hundred feet in front of us, I saw two large rats dash across the road. Then, not more than a dozen feet to our left, I saw a snake curve into the grass. Without saying a word, I grabbed Jo-Ellen's hand and walked a little faster.

After half an hour hiking up and down the streets and just about when we were both convinced that the hotel didn't exist and never had, we found it. By that time, it looked like a cross between home and the house on the haunted hill, and Halong Bay was no longer the paradise it had been in the late afternoon.

The last time Jo-Ellen and I had been in Vietnam, four years before, we had eaten a snake. This time, in Eden, the snake had glided back and shown us that even though things were not usually as bad as you could imagine, they were generally not as good as you thought they were. The melancholy Dane was right—"There is nothing either good or bad, but thinking makes it so." But at that moment, in our hotel room safe and sound for the night, Jo-Ellen's hand still in mine, the moonlit horizon stretching out in the bay like a broken jade necklace, I couldn't think of any place better to be.

Burma

In our five days in Burma (what the military dictatorship calls Myanmar), Jo-Ellen and I entered an Orwellian reality in which the only thing guaranteed was the unexpected. We broke the law, bought ice cream cones at a Buddhist temple, considered the possibility that we might be spies without knowing it, lived like Rudyard Kipling in the Savoy Hotel, and came within a New York minute of becoming Baptists and then prisoners of the state.

Jo-Ellen and I had some pangs of conscience even going to Burma, in the fear that any dollars we spent would end up in the coffers of the military dictatorship that brutally oppressed the people of the country. We tried to find a hotel that didn't appear to be state run, but finally we settled on the Savoy because it was a small place outside the center of the city. We didn't really know where the money trail led, but we did know that the Savoy was not one of the few monolithic 400-room mega-palaces in the heart of the city.

Burma is the kind of country that makes you feel compelled to do something honorable when you are there. You might not have the courage to sabotage the government, but at least you can try not to support it. We stayed at the Savoy for two days, within a ten-minute hike of the dazzling and opulent Shwedagon Pagoda, a Buddhist temple that looked like a cross between Vatican Square and Disney World.

Burma is often called the land of the pagodas, and it certainly appeared to be a land saturated in the principles of Buddhism. There was a monk or a pagoda around every corner. The people could recite the Noble Eightfold Path (right understanding, right thought, right speech, right action, right livelihood, right effort, right mindfulness, and right concentration), the way a devout Christian could recite the Ten Commandments. The path in Buddhism is known as the Middle Way, the road between the two extremes of suffering and pleasure, the goal being *nirvana*, or extinction of worldly desires. All ardent Buddhists know the Five Holy Precepts the way a Catholic school boy memorizes the responses at Mass—do not take a life, do not steal, do not commit adultery, do not lie, and do not take intoxicating drinks.

We encountered Buddhist monks everywhere we went. At first I thought the country might be one big monastery until I discovered that most Buddhist boys enter monasteries for a short period as monks. It is called *shinbyu*, the time when a boy becomes a novice monk to learn the religious life. Most men in Burma entered the monkhood three times in their lives—once as a boy, once as a young man, and last as an older adult.

The Savoy was no monastery, but from everything we could learn, it was not owned by the government. It was a small pleasure palace, though, in the middle of decaying Yangon, a boutique hotel, thirty rooms of teak, rattan, and marble. It was the kind of place where a waiter put a napkin discretely on your lap before a crumb could tumble from your lips. Attendants observed you from behind half-drawn curtains when you were reclining at the pool so that they could leap forward at the first sign you needed a fresh towel or a vodka and tonic.

The Savoy was the kind of establishment in which expatriates gathered at the Captain's Bar every sweltering night until 3 A.M. talking about how George Bush had bollixed up America and how China would surpass the United States in economic and political power within the next few decades. The expatriates we met—Annabelle and Alex and Richard—from Edinburgh and Brixton and New York City originally, now of Hong Kong and Beijing and Yangon, escaped the wilting humidity by discussing, in turns languidly and feverishly, the fact of America's demise as they sipped a few dozen Johnny Walker and Cokes each evening. Late in the evening, Richard, who ran a telecommunications company in Burma, summed it all up in a few slurred sentences: "Fuck on. Bush has cunted up the whole country and half the world in the process. I don't know if that's a word, but who cares. He's done it, anyway. Fucked everything up."

I realized two things by 3 A.M. of the second evening at the Savoy. First, it was dispiriting to know what many people around the world think of America. It somehow seemed all right to criticize my own country with friends back home, but facing the animus all over the world was heartbreaking, especially when I couldn't reasonably defend some of my country's actions. Second, being an expatriate afforded one the perfect debating position. You had nothing to feel the pangs of loyalty about. Being a citizen of a country is like being a parent. You can't escape the sense of commitment and responsibility, even if you disapprove of your son's or daughter's actions. Being an expatriate is like being a third cousin. You're related but really don't give a damn one way or another. Why should you?

After two days at the Savoy, guilt got the better of us. We felt like Buddhists who had overdosed on pleasure. We'd had enough of the privileged expatriate life—the marble floors and rose petal baths, the perfectly ironed linen napkins beside the plates of naan bread and the "no-nonsense" massages on request, the private pool and sumptuous breakfasts in the Kipling Room—and we took a cab to the Trader's Hotel and roamed around the grimy central part of the city. In the lobby of the government's main tourist hotel, a man sidled up to me and whispered in my ear, "Are you Peter?" His eyes flicked left and right like a man about to cross a busy street. *Peter?* Was it a code word? Was he a government official and this was a test? Did they know we had stayed for two hedonistic days at the Savoy?

This was the kind of country where someone knew everything you did, everyone you spoke with. We had played scrabble with Alexander May and Annabel Allen, two lawyers on vacation at the Savoy. To Jo-Ellen and me, they appeared to be professional players who traveled with their game and a hardcover scrabble dictionary, looking for unwitting tourists to humiliate. We had been beaten badly by them in the late hours at the Captain's Bar, but had we formed any dangerous political words with our scrabble cubes?

After a moment's thought and hesitation, I told him I wasn't Peter. He appeared to be genuinely disappointed and faded into the crowd, making me sorry somehow that I wasn't Peter so that I could have found out who I was supposed to be. Like so many things in Burma, Peter would remain a mystery to me, something whispered, an unanswered question.

Frankly, this may be the heart of modern Burma, the nervous sidelong glance, the unasked question, the whispered conversation. The country has come as close to Orwell's *1984* as any country in recent history. Ironically, of course, George Orwell spent years as a British police officer in colonial Burma in the early twentieth century. He wrote a novel—*Burmese Days* and two classic essays, "A Hanging" and "Shooting an Elephant"— about his experiences there, but *1984* may come much closer to the picture of the place now.

Since 1962, when the military junta overthrew the legitimate government, the people of the country have been brutally repressed. Villages were routinely burned, innocent people beaten, girls raped, nonviolent protesters sent to prison for decades. Children were commonly impressed into military service at anywhere between the ages of eight and sixteen years old. Most of us thought sub-Saharan Africa was where the population of child soldiers was the highest, but that is not the case. Burma had the most child soldiers of any country in the world, we were told. Anyone who spoke out against the government could be sent to prison—and many were. Prisoners were tortured and held without trial.

Burma has the dubious distinction of being the *only* country on the planet to have a Nobel Peace prize winner under house arrest. Since 1988, Aung San Suu Kyi had been imprisoned or monitored by the government. It did not matter that she was the legally elected leader of the country. In the Orwellian atmosphere of twisted logic that the junta had created, she was an enemy of the state.

Most likely, her Nobel award had kept her alive. Those without Nobel Prizes disappeared on a regular basis, some beaten to death in musty prison cells. The military rulers refused to relinquish power, the country got poorer and poorer (the average income was $1,800 a year, considerably lower than in Vietnam and India), and most people knew less about Myanmar's recent history than they did about Hubble's Law.

Burma was a surreal land, and Yangon an otherworldly city. Men in silk longyis (the traditional Burmese skirts) negotiated the muddy streets and stratified sidewalks. The main bookstores had fewer books than I had on my office shelves at home. The bookstores on the side streets sold mainly Xeroxed copies of books that the government would allow them to sell.

That meant the book I was reading—*Finding George Orwell in Burma*—could not be purchased anywhere in the country. When I asked in the Bagan Bookstore if they had any work by Aung San Suu Kyi (and I should never have put them in danger by asking such a question), the clerk said, after an awkward giggle and a furtive glance, "No, no, sir. The government doesn't like, you see. No, no, sir." Then he held out a barely legible Xeroxed copy of Orwell's *Burmese Days*, which I already owned but bought anyway out of guilt.

There was not much traffic in the city because there were only a few asthmatic automobiles coughing their way around town. Motorcycles had been banned some years back after a general's car had been cut off by a scooter; from that day forward—whether they were the most reasonable form of transportation for the Burmese or not—they were banned from the city.

Orwell would have recognized the bizarre world where all the newspapers print only good news. According to the state papers—and there aren't any others—nothing bad ever happened in Myanmar, although plenty of bad things occurred in other parts of the world. Like in *1984*, words in Burma meant what the government said they meant. Big Brother could be your next-door neighbor. As one Burmese man said to Emma Larkin, "The MI [Military Intelligence] are everywhere. They are in the tea shops, in the markets, even the beggars are listening to us talk." As an American official put it to us, Burma is an "outpost of tyranny."

Orwell's experience in Burma in the early twentieth century taught him the real reason for which despotic governments act. In describing himself in "Shooting an Elephant," he described the nature and motives of all tyrants—"He wears a mask, and his face grows to fit it." Losing face would mean losing power, and power was both the means and the end for the Burmese rulers in a country that many reasonably educated people could not pinpoint on a map if it were their final question on *Jeopardy*.

Shaped like a rough-cut diamond, the country is bordered to the north by China, to the east by Thailand and Laos, and to the west by India and Bangladesh. In the south, the country juts out into the Indian Ocean. It is a land rich in natural resources—teak, coal, oil, natural gas, tin, and silver.

But at the same time, as Aung San Suu Kyi wrote in 1985 in a diplomatic understatement in *Freedom from Fear and Other Writings*—"The economy has not been well managed and Burma today is not a prosperous country." From what Jo-Ellen and I saw twenty years after Aung San Suu Kyi made that statement, the country had become an example of criminal mismanagement and totalitarian inefficiency.

There were many languages spoken in Burma, but silence was the language that everyone understood perfectly. The true view was the one that could not be seen. All expectations got confounded, and that was the only thing one could expect for certain. Therefore, as we traipsed around the outskirts of the city late one afternoon, we found not a Gestapo herding innocents into police vans but a peaceful haven known as the Kalaywatawya Monastery. The monastery was a school run by Buddhist monks for children who could not otherwise afford to be educated.

About 90 percent of the population in Burma were Buddhists, and you did not have to hunt to find a monk walking along the city streets or country roads (there were 500,000 monks by last count). We spent some time with the students, all head-shaven novitiates. We were with them at their rice-bowl lunchtime, as they all sat in quiet homogeneity, but rather than seeming alien, it reminded me of my days in Catholic school, all dressed alike, all in rows, all trained in silence and obedience.

Right outside the monastery, Jo-Ellen and I became pied pipers for a dozen Burmese children ranging in age from five or six to twelve or thirteen years old who held our hands as we walked to a nearby pagoda, what Emma Larkin in *Finding George Orwell in Burma* called the center of Burmese spiritual life. "Every town and village has one," she said.

> People visit the pagoda daily or weekly to pay respect to the Buddha relics that are often enshrined there, to meditate, to give alms, or to attend festivals held on religious holidays. The pagoda is considered a place of spirituality and learning. The stairways leading up to the platform are decorated with educational paintings from Buddhist legend, often depicting the moral lessons in the Jataka tales about Buddha's previous incarnations. The peaceful principles of Buddhism, which encourage wisdom and compassion, are instilled through those teachings.

The children who followed us as if we were rock stars appeared eager in their shy way to show us the pagoda in their village. All of the girls had ghostly complexions produced by *thanakha*, a yellow-beige paste that the Burmese made from grinding the bark of thanakha trees and then smearing it on their faces to protect them from insects and the sun.

Along the way we gave them pens, candy bars, hand towels, and notebooks, everything we could find on us. Jo-Ellen took off my mother's scarf, the one my sister had given her the day after my mom had died, and she placed it carefully around the head of a wide-eyed girl with almond skin and long, raven hair. The turquoise cloth had a plum border, and in the setting sunlight, the girl's smile was framed like a painting, one my mother would have smiled to see. We bought each of the children an ice cream cone from a vendor set up near a garbage pile a few yards from the temple. In exchange, each of them in turn gave us the memory of their heartbreaking thanakha-shaded grins.

From the monastery, we headed back into Yangon, what was formerly called Rangoon. Ironically, the word *Rangoon* meant "the end of strife," but the city had seen an enormous amount of unrest in the past few decades. Now it was a crumbling symbol of how quickly a vicious and unscrupulous military dictatorship could run a promising, resource-rich country into ruin. Negotiating the broken streets—dirty, cratered, slick with garbage and rotted vegetables, jammed with pedestrians and diners (most of them sitting on twelve-inch-high plastic stools)—was not for the fainthearted or the unsteady. If the streets did not get you, the heat—a wilting, smoke-clogged inferno—eventually would.

It got to us about 3:30 in the afternoon. That's when Jo-Ellen heard some heavenly music. Once we pinched each other to make sure that heat stroke hadn't killed us and sent us to an even hotter place than Burma—although we doubted there was one—we saw that the Immanuel Baptist Church on Mahabandoola Street stood right in front of us. The service started at 4:30, the sign said, but we decided we'd sit in the back of the building and cool off a bit. It wasn't air conditioned, of course, but there were a few ceiling fans creaking lazily high above our heads, and it seemed as good a place as any to wait out the sun.

By 4:30 the church was packed—both floors—and the Reverend Dr. Paul F. Johns and an entourage of robed assistants stood on a raised platform that constituted an altar. I was listening to the hypnotic whir of the fans when I noticed a somber-faced man in a dark jacket and tie standing in front of me.

"Follow me, sir," he said in a tone that made me suspect I was being arrested or thrown out of the church. I'd just taken a photograph of the portrait of Christ—a Brad Pitt with a brown beard—that hung over the altar.

But we weren't being arrested or asked to leave. We were escorted to the second row, near the Cool Mist fans, immediately in front of the pulpit. There, Reverend Johns gave his sermon, looking at us as we nodded and smiled at every incomprehensible syllable of Burmese he uttered. After about fifteen minutes, Reverend Johns slid smoothly from Burmese to English, saying, "I will speak now for our visitors." He looked at us, as I assumed, all the hundreds behind us did.

"Where are you from? Tell us your story."

One of his assistants handed us a microphone. So I found myself in Burma in the saunalike heat of a Sunday afternoon, a fallen Catholic sitting in a Baptist church, lukewarm mist floating over my head, my shirt clinging to me like a second skin, my digital camera also sweating at my side, the smell of incense mixing with human odor, giving a sermon about Americans traveling around the globe. Jo-Ellen calls herself "micro-phobic," but she spoke for a few seconds, telling the congregation how much she appreciated their welcoming us into their church. Later, she was convinced she had spoken in tongues, but I heard only a half dozen *thank yous*.

When I handed the microphone back to Reverend Johns, he looked out at the congregation and intoned in the well-practiced preacher's pitch, "America, ah, a great country, number one, the land that reaches out its hand to help others. I pray to God to protect them and us from terrorism. I pray for our national assembly, for our leaders writing the constitution. God will answer our prayers. Faithful prayers are *always* answered."

Two and a half hours later, I knew my simple prayer had not been answered. The service was still going on, but we couldn't very well get up and leave, marching past the five hundred Burmese in the pews behind us, after the minister had prayed for our country. *Sorry, you see it's taco night on our ship and we have to catch the shuttle back.* We waited through Burmese and snippets of English, through hymns in a language we couldn't understand but that sounded strangely like sad country tunes by Loretta Lynn and Willie Nelson. We waited until the end when the minister and his assistants flowed down the main aisle, incense drifting from their robes as if they were emerging from a cloud.

As we stepped into the smoky night, tiptoeing along the cratered streets, past the endless rows of Buddhist monks and sad-eyed men and women, I couldn't help but wonder if the minister's advice about the prayers of the faithful always being answered was as much of a harmful fiction as the new constitution that was being drawn up by the puppets of the government.

Perhaps, I considered with the part of my brain not focused on tacos or Willie Nelson or Brad Pitt, the Burmese people needed a Che Guevara more than they needed Buddha. They had Aung San Suu Kyi, of course, who some people had called "Burma's Gandhi," and for the better part of two decades she had fought against government repression, refusing to leave her homeland, for she knew that if she did she would never be allowed to return. In the past twenty years, her husband had died of cancer in England, and she had not been able to be at his side, and her two sons had grown to manhood without her.

Before his death, her husband, the scholar Michael Aris, wrote, "Very obviously the plan was to break Suu's spirit by separating her from her children in the hope she would accept permanent exile." She had stood unwaveringly against the monstrous-sounding and aptly named SLORC (State Law and Order Restoration Council) that repressed the Burmese people. SLORC was an acronym and an organization that seemed more Orwellian than anything the author of *1984* could have dreamed up—a group that allowed political parties to form provided that they never met.

Aung San Suu Kyi followed in the footsteps of her father, Aung San, the first leader of free Burma, who was assassinated in 1948. "For the people of Burma," Aung San Suu Kyi once wrote, "Aung San was the man who had come in their hour of need to restore their national pride and honour. As his life is a source of inspiration for them, his memory remains the guardian of their political conscience." What Aung San Suu Kyi has shown her government and the world is that she is prepared to sacrifice everything she had, everything she loved, for her country. As Emma Larkin in her remarkable account of her travels in Burma pointed out, "Aung San is still a symbol of wise and just leadership, and Aung San Suu Kyi remains an adored figure of hope for many Burmese people." After she won the Sakharov Prize for Freedom of Thought in 1990, Aung San Suu Kyi wrote, "It is not power that corrupts but fear." It seems unimaginable that her sort of fearlessness, if it spread, could be defeated.

Who is to say, though, what such a country of beautiful people, lush landscapes, awful poverty, and suffocating repression really needs, what will make change occur and how fast? Surely, however, religion is founded on *possibility*, and Burma is a country that gives new meaning to the word. It is a country in which anything seems possible. Nobel Peace laureates can be placed under house arrest for decades. Peaceful protestors can be sentenced to jail for years without trial. The grocer on a street corner smoking a cheroot could be an informer, the old man spitting betel juice onto the red-stained earth might be watching every move his neighbor made, the old woman with a toothless grin could be an enemy or a friend. The government benefits from the cloud of suspicion and paranoia it created. Not knowing who the government spies were kept the population cowed and allowed the junta to keep any riches from the country's natural resources for themselves. Burma was pronounced by the U.N. to be one of the ten poorest countries on the planet. It is a country in which a military junta made administrative decisions based on whims and astrological charts. The madhouse, it seemed, was being run by the madmen.

On our final day in Rangoon, Jo-Ellen and I walked down a street that bordered an unkempt park. Over a dilapidated fence hung a large rectangular red sign with white letters:

- Oppose those relying on external elements, acting as stooges, holding negative views
- Oppose those trying to jeopardize stability of the state and progress of the nation
- Oppose foreign nations interfering in internal affairs of the State

• Crush all internal and external destructive elements as the common
enemy

At our embassy briefing onboard the ship before we had stepped onto
Burmese soil, we were warned about a few things. First, the consuls said,
don't ask the people about their government. Such talk could get them
locked up. Just speak about politics with a foreigner and they could disappear for years—or forever. Second, we were warned, don't photograph
anything to do with the state or anything that puts it in a poor light (which
seemed to me just about any part of the infrastructure we viewed).

But in the park, I couldn't help myself. My camera came out of my
pocket of its own volition. It was only when I pressed the "on" button that
I noticed the NO PHOTOGRAPH sign to my left. At the same moment, I saw
two soldiers, rifles slung over their shoulders, walking briskly towards me
on my right. I was ready to have my camera confiscated at best or thrown
in jail at worst.

"Come here," the tall one barked.

"I, uh, well," I stuttered, relying on the speech pattern of an idiot in
the hopes that morons, especially American ones, were sacred in Burma.

"You want a photograph?" he asked, nodding in the direction of the
sign.

"Yes," I said, not certain if he was giving me permission or if it was
a trick question and a *yes* would get me sent to a penal colony where I
would learn to break rocks into assorted sizes.

He nodded again toward the sign. He looked up and down the street,
and then he turned his head to observe the traffic. After a few seconds, he
turned back to face me.

"That's the government. Not us. Take the photograph."

So once again I saw that in Burma anything could happen. As I put
away my camera and headed back to the ship, I reasoned that the next
time I was in Myanmar it might be called Burma again. I might fly into
Rangoon from Bangkok and see a life-sized portrait of President Aung
San Suu Kyi in the airport, get a ride from a garrulous cab driver who was
happy to complain about income taxes, and stay in a family-owned bed
and breakfast. It was like finding a copy of Orwell's *1984* in one of the few

malnourished bookstores in Myanmar. It wasn't likely to happen in the near future, but when such a book found its way onto some hidden back shelf, people would find a way to read it and pass the word along.

The heart of teaching was truth and fearlessness, and as Aung San Suu Kyi had said, "Saints . . . are the sinners who go on trying. So free men are the oppressed who go on trying and who in the process make themselves fit to bear the responsibilities and to uphold the disciplines which will maintain a free society."

Burma was the kind of country that made you paranoid about every move you took, every word you spoke. It was a place that made you look both ways before you said what was on your mind, but it was also a place that made you want to be more truthful and fearless because, ultimately, those were the only natural resources that mattered in such a country—or anywhere.

India

As we approached Chennai, India, slicing across the Bay of Bengal, the moon shone like an antique silver dollar through a veil of clouds. Dark, rumbling seas shimmered in the yellow light. I was sitting on deck with John Allard, a gentle-natured eighty-year-old man who had come on the trip to be a companion to his married daughter, a professor of economics from Madrid, Spain, and her five children who sailed with her.

As we came within sight of the coast of India, John told me, with tears forming in his eyes, about his memories of World War II. He had been barely eighteen years old in 1944 when he fought with the U.S. Army in Brussels and was shot twice, once in the left arm and then in the right shoulder. Only eight of the two hundred men in his platoon survived the battle. In his twin brother's platoon, only two survived. As we spoke, the eighteen-year-olds onboard the ship were enjoying pub night and packing for trips to four-star hotels in India. In Iraq and Afghanistan, young men and women were experiencing the world John had more than sixty years before. He looked at me as if he were reading my mind.

"My brother spent eight months in a POW camp, went from 175 pounds to less than 90," John said to me, not even bothering to wipe the tears that rolled down from his eyes. He just let them fall. With his white hair and trimmed moustache, he looked a bit like photographs I had seen of the older Douglas Fairbanks Jr. A few years earlier and he could have played a double for him in *Gunga Din*, the film set in nineteenth-century India.

"He died a few weeks before the voyage began," John went on. "He's dead, my twin brother, and I'm about to be in India. Seems strange somehow."

Everything about India seemed strange. It had seemed so in 2002, and, I was to discover, it would seem only more so in 2006. Jo-Ellen and I awoke on the morning of October 15, the sliding glass door to our deck open and the smell of burning rubbish and superheated air filling the room. We knew we had arrived in Chennai.

The population in the country had risen over the 1 billion mark in the four years since we had been in India. Marginally, the city of Chennai appeared cleaner. Of course, it was Sunday and much of the swirling stream of people and traffic had the day off. People were waiting for the ship, though, looking to make some money in any way they could. There were thousands of new cars lined up at the dock, waiting to be transported and sold in other countries. New businesses from America and Europe had immigrated to the city since our last visit. It made economic sense. Labor costs in the United States averaged $22 an hour. In India, they were 74 cents. Most of the people we encountered still lived on a dollar or two a day at most.

With Roger Bennett, a communications professor from the ship, and his wife Barbara, we worked our way through the labyrinthine Indian security that was set up from the gangway to the gate by the main road. It was the Indian way—layers of bureaucracy, thousands of gods, dozens of languages, and at least six people to stamp your entry card and peruse your passport. If they had 1 billion people, they seemed to reason, why not use six of them to perform the job that one could more efficiently do by himself. It was a make-work society.

As soon as we exited the main gate and I saw the trishaw drivers leap to their feet and the beggars scurry toward us with the palms up sign for "help me, feed me," I thought of a line from an essay by Seth Stevenson—"Trying Really Hard to Like India"—that we had discussed in one of my writing classes. They were eyeing me "like I'm nothing but an ambulatory wallet." A cab driver ran up to us before the trishaw drivers could reach us.

"We want to go the Spencer Plaza," I said, knowing that was in the center of town and we could find our way around from there.

"Ten dollars U.S.," he replied.

It should have cost about two dollars. We could have negotiated, but we decided to get two trishaws for a dollar a piece. The cab driver followed us all the way to the trishaw line, but before a fight broke out over who would land our contract, we jumped in two trishaws that said they could take us to Spencer. Once we were on the road, though, things changed. Both trishaws stopped in front of a rug emporium.

"Come take a look. It costs nothing to look. Looks are for free."

"We don't want to look at rugs," Roger said. He had an amiable smile but he could snap a tough edge into his voice when he wanted to. And he had the grey crew cut and the steely glint of a retired Marine colonel. But none of this fazed our trishaw drivers.

"Come, come, just one look. Spencer is not opened anyway."

"What do you mean it's not opened?" Roger asked.

"Come, just look. One look."

This went on for five minutes or so. Roger's forced aggressiveness was stripped away and his real nature—soft-hearted and amenable—took over. We followed the Bennetts in and looked at rugs for half an hour. The simple fact was that the trishaw drivers made more money acting as shills for rug and silk emporiums than they did driving people where they wanted to go in the city. It was not easy to escape buying something, for the sales pitch had the same fervor as a time-share presentation for a condo in Hilton Head, South Carolina. We held strong, though the looks on the salesmen's faces turned from congenial to churlish, and we all refused to buy anything.

When we got outside, we demanded to be taken to Spencer Plaza with our trishaws side by side. The trishaws took off together but somewhere along the way in the rush and blur of the Sunday traffic we lost the Bennetts and ended up at a sari store. The Bennetts' trishaw never showed up, and Jo-Ellen and I wondered for a bit if they had been abducted—or if we had. The ten-minute conversation that ensued between the driver and me can be summed up by my final words.

"If you can't or won't take us to Spencer now, we'll fucking walk there." Of course, I had no idea where we were or how to get to Spencer or anywhere else in the city, for that matter. It was a bluff, but sometimes that's all you have.

After more minutes of arguing, the driver reluctantly took us where we wanted to go. When we got there, he wanted four dollars.

"You said two dollars," I told him.

"Two dollars apiece," he screamed. "I said two dollars apiece!"

I knew he was lying and he knew he was. After another five-minute discussion, I wasn't really sure, though, if I was fixated on scruples or rupees. I caught a glimpse of Roger and Barbara walking out the back alley to the mall and decided it was best to just pay and be done with it. India had that ability—to make you feel as if you were ready to be done with it. The Bennetts had been taken to two more rug places and then after protesting had been dropped off in the alley behind the store. They too had been charged more than they had at first been told. We all felt guilty about arguing over a few dollars with people who had so little, but, on the other hand, we felt cheated. But that was just India, and another sentence from Seth Stevenson popped into my mind: "Again, unless you're Gandhi—and you're not—you can't come here without diving headfirst into a salty sea of unpleasant contradictions."

Late that afternoon, parked between two beggars, a goat, and three cows, we found a cab that could fit all four of us in. We negotiated the price, repeated the cost three times to make sure, and took it back to the ship.

We had to get up at 4:30 A.M. for our trip to Delhi, Agra, and Varanasi, the holy city on the Ganges. The morning air in Chennai smelled of decaying garbage. It was thick with humidity, a purplish predawn, smoky and fly-filled. By contrast, the flights were comfortable, the food was good compared to any American airlines—although I wasn't exactly sure what I was eating in the variety of cheese, potatoes, rice, and wheat on my plate—and the attendants were polite and well-dressed. It made me recall my first flights from New York to San Francisco in 1971, when plane travel was not the equivalent of riding a Greyhound bus as it is today.

When we exited the small airport at Varanasi, a dozen soldiers patrolled the baggage area. Outside the airport, a crowd gathered to meet the arriving passengers. Behind them, an armored car with a soldier pointing a machine gun directly at us as we straggled out of the building eyed us as if he were getting ready to fire. The eyes of the Americans—especially the college students—as tired as they looked, invariably sparkled with hope. You could see the anticipation of something wonderful and surprising clicking in their eyes. The eyes of the Indian people were watchful and resigned. You could see it in their dark faces—*tomorrow will be the same as today.*

Varanasi, the city of Shiva, sat on the banks of the sacred Ganges, where Hindu pilgrims came to bathe and wash away their sins. When we got there, long before sunrise the next morning, the streets were jammed with chanting pilgrims and the brown waters were punctuated by men and women in colorful silks. It was the filthiest body of water I had ever seen. Trash and sludge floated alongside dead cows and what looked like human bodies, as well. The river was so laden with filth it looked like anyone could perform the miracle of walking on it.

Varanasi was one of the oldest living cities in the world, and, as Mark Twain said, it looked "twice as old." The cramped streets were cluttered with all forms of transportation—bikes, trucks, scooters, trishaws, camels, water buffaloes, horses, donkeys—and a variety of life Noah would have envied—goats, cows, crows, dogs, cats, dust-covered people sleeping in alleys, women bent over piles of debris like question marks with no answers, and, anomalously, a young boy skipping along in the darkness snapping a stick against the ground as if he had not a care in the world.

In the pinched alleyways, schoolchildren, in blue and white uniforms threadbare from washing in the filthy Ganges, peeked out at our group sliding between cows and mounds of shit on our way to the river. The children's hair looked freshly wet-combed and their eyes were still crusted with sleep and the meager hopefulness of dreams. Their eyes, though, were not the eyes of children we typically saw in America. As the daylight broke upon their faces, their eyes looked as old as the city. It was the children in India and other impoverished countries who broke your heart, their white smiles against dark faces and far-seeing eyes. They made you want to give away everything you had until you faced the fact that there was not enough in your wallet. There were not enough wallets.

"Don't give to beggars," we were told over and over again by embassy officials. "All it does is perpetuate the system of begging. Children are forced to beg. Most of the money they get goes to some Fagin-like boss who teaches them the tricks of the trade. It's a mafia with child labor."

We had heard stories of mothers maiming their babies so that they would be more heart-wrenching targets for tourists, women who drugged their children to make them listless and pathetic sights, but it was difficult to remember the principle of toughness when faced with the little wide-eyed person standing in front of you, head cocked quizzically to the side. Some of our students brought children's sandals to hand out in lieu of money. Others carried crayons or pens or apples or bags of crackers. But there was never enough. There were always more hands reaching up for more, more. So you resigned yourself to a broken heart and kept on the path.

The day before we reached India, our interport lecturer, an Indian women who was a professor in Chennai, argued that the population of her country was not out of control, that they needed more young people to do the necessary work. "After all," she said, "we don't want to end up in the position that Japan will find itself in soon, without a labor force of working-age people." Her ideas were supported by the economics professor from Spain on the ship. But as I walked the filthy, crowded streets of Varanasi and imagined the futures of most of the children I saw, that argument seemed arrogant, the kind of safe theory spouted in the ivory tower but dangerous and delusional in the face of clogged streets, abject poverty, poor sanitation, and high birth rates in a country where cows appeared to live better lives than many people.

With about twenty students, we sat in a boat paddled by a cadaverous man around the floating candles and dead dogs in the Ganges. It was a weirdly spiritual experience, eerily silent in the breaking light of day. It was also weirdly unspiritual. The air smelled familiar. At first, I wasn't sure what it was, and then I realized I was remembering Seth Stevenson's description: "The air smells like twice-baked urine, marinated in more urine."

In Varanasi, there were more than 100 ghats, steps that led to landing places along the banks of the river. Thousands of people gathered along the shoreline, bathing in the river, washing their clothes, brushing their teeth, gargling, floating serenely on their backs, shaving, offering blessings to the gods. Near some of the ghats, stacks of sandalwood stood waiting for corpses. Smoke curled lazily from some of the cremation sites. Our oarsman told us that as many as 60,000 people bathed in or gargled with the feces-laced water each day. The river had approximately 1 million times the safe level of bacteria a body of water used for bathing should have.

I peered over the shoulder of one of our students, who was not gazing out at the people along the shore but reading a tattered paperback copy of Herman Hesse's *Siddhartha*. I could see the top of the page: "When Siddhartha listened attentively to this river, to this song of a thousand voices; when he did not bind his soul to any one particular voice and absorb it in his Self, but heard them all, the whole, the unity; then the great song of a thousand voices consisted of one word: Om—perfection." Along the shore, colorful saris flashed like blue and orange sparks lighting one consistent picture of human frailty and yearning. A hawk drifted indolently on the still air, angling through the smoke and gliding above the monkeys that crawled over the rooftops and ledges of the buildings.

I heard the rattling of beads and then a few voices—"How much? No that's too much. What about that one? Will you take. . . . " Skiffs selling necklaces, bracelets, and plastic statues had pulled alongside our boat, a few yards from the cremation sites. The weight of our boat shifted as half a dozen young women switched sides to look at the trinkets. Money and beadwork exchanged hands. Occasionally, the water bubbled up from decomposing matter in the dark-green depths. A young man with streaks of blond dyed into his black hair turned away from the smoke of the crematory and shifted his seat to speak with the salesman in the skiff. "How much for the blue one?" he asked, his voice rising above the lapping of the water against the hull.

Jo-Ellen got sick on our boat trip on the Ganges. The Indian food or the suspicious bottled water or just the sheer weight of human loss mixing with commerce had gotten to her. One of the students saw her ashen, damp face and whispered to a girl next to her, "Poor Mrs. P, she's so sad she looks like she's about to cry." Then the young woman turned to Jo-Ellen, "Is there anything we can do for you?"

Jo-Ellen sighed deeply. "Help me swim to shore," she said. "And if I don't make it, you can have my necklace."

Jo-Ellen turned to me and put her lips close to my ear. "I'm sick as a dog. Get me out of here. And make sure that girl doesn't get my necklace if I die on the way back to the hotel."

As soon as we got back to shore, I walked with her through the pedestrian alleys until we came to an avenue with trishaws. After a fifteen-minute ride that threatened to twist her stomach into a knot, we got back to the hotel in Varanasi for a cocktail of Immodium and Pepto-Bismol, a breakfast of Ritz crackers, a bath, and a change of clothes before our flight to Delhi.

Delhi, the capital of India, seemed more spacious and British in its colonial grandeur than any of the other cities we had seen. The avenues were wide and the streets cleaner than in Chennai, but despite the monumental government buildings, the tombs, temples, and museums, it was still India. On the way to our hotel, the Ashok, I saw a dead monkey being eaten by a dog on the side of the road. In the large park in the center of town, wild pigs roamed among the untended bushes. Outside our fancy hotel, packs of dogs howled and barked all night long.

That night we ate a communal meal in the hotel restaurant with our students, and Jo-Ellen danced wildly with them to disco music. Actually, she *led* them, taught them a few moves, and was there on the dance floor when the last ones were collapsing in fatigue. It seemed hard to believe that twelve hours before she had been racing away from the Ganges bent over with what she had come to call "Delhi belly." In her case the bard was right—music did have charms to make bad good. Her stomach never bothered her again.

While she was dancing, a few of our students came back from adventures around the city. One of my favorite students, Jess Silver, a sweet-natured young woman who could have passed for Jo-Ellen's younger sister, had come back from some club hopping with two of her friends from the ship. They had spent the better part of the evening at a bar in a nearby hotel, drinking with Henry Winkler, the Fonz. As she should have been, Jess was delighted with the surreal quality of spending the evening in Delhi, India, drinking wine and chatting with Fonzie.

"It was something like spending an afternoon in Philadelphia playing blackjack with Gandhi, I guess," she said.

"Did Gandhi play blackjack?" I wondered aloud, but nobody answered because they were all back on the dance floor with Jo-Ellen.

The next morning we were up before dawn again, this time to catch the train to Agra and the Taj Mahal. The train was late, and we all—

passengers, beggars, dogs—waited in the predawn darkness of the station. People were lying all over the floor, and a few dozen sat in the Upper Class Waiting Room, a dank, unpainted room a few feet away from the equally unattractive Ladies Waiting Room.

We rode in the first class compartment of the train. That meant we got lukewarm water in bottles made of some pre-plastic substance, a cross between cardboard and epoxy glue, and we were offered a tomato soup that was scalding hot and had a blue tint to it. Wisely, Jo-Ellen didn't eat or drink anything on the train. Instead, she watched the scenery through the three broken windows that faced our seat and counted the soldiers with machine guns strapped over their shoulders who marched down the aisles.

I finished reading Jhumpa Lahiri's *Interpreter of Maladies*, getting ready to discuss the final stories with my literature students on the ship when we returned to class. We had already discussed some of the stories before we arrived in India, and although most of them were concerned with bifurcated cultures, with the hyphenated world of Indian-Americans, my students found Lahiri's subtle stories to describe provocatively the meaning of India. Her tales were about loss and yearning, arranged marriages and the caste system, about deceptions and miscommunications.

In an important respect, many of them felt Lahiri's stories spoke to us as travelers and questioned the nature and limits of what we could ever know about another culture or another individual. Lahiri did point out to them the two Indias—the demanding and poverty-stricken life of Boori Ma, the stairwell sweeper in "A Real Durwan," and the privileged existence of the select few in a story like "Sexy," in which one of the characters, Dev, tells another "about his childhood, when he would come home from school and drink mango juice served to him on a tray, and then play cricket by the lake, dressed all in white." Over and over again, Lahiri's stories dramatized the alienation we all shared. We were all homeless, wayfarers, wanderers, hungering for some connection.

When we got off the train, we took a bus, first to Agra and then to the Taj Mahal. In an hour ride we had a hundred near-catastrophic accidents, swerving from cows and water buffaloes, rickshaws and cars and children. I recalled the pilgrims' chanting on their way to the Ganges the day before, but this seemed to me the real spiritual truth of India—the ordinary daily miracle of nerve and good luck that surviving a trip on a public road always was. Every ride was like being in the middle of a symphony orchestra. Every mode of transportation made its own noise. Horns boomed, bells chimed, whistles blew. People shouted. When we got off the bus near the Red Fort in Agra and walked up to the nearby mosque, a woman scurried up to us, holding her hand out. And her voice was Boori Ma's—"brittle with sorrows, as tart as curds, and shrill enough to grate meat from a coconut."

"Your shoes! Your shoes!" she demanded. "I'll guard them."

We paid her to watch our shoes when we went into the mosque, but we were not there long because the salesmen inside the mosque were so intense that they wore us out after a few minutes.

Outside the Taj Mahal, the beggars and hawkers were just as aggressive, but once we got inside, it was only the tourists and the magnificent tomb built by the Emperor Shah Jahan for his second wife, who died giving birth to their fourteenth child in 1631. The marble mausoleum took over twenty years to complete. From a distance, it had a breathtaking symmetry, and once we got a bit nearer, the reflecting pool in the formal Mughal garden made it a metaphor for itself. When we got even closer up, we marveled at the inlaid jewels and the intricate calligraphy from the Koran. Twenty thousand people worked on it, and to insure that its beauty could never be re-created, the emperor had key workers' hands or thumbs amputated. It surely was a monument to marital love, but as P. J. O'Rourke wrote in an essay on India, "If Jahan had really wanted to show his love, he could have cut back on the Viagra."

But if O'Rourke checked, he must have known that there was a poetic justice for Jahan. His son Aurangzeb deposed him and placed him under house arrest in Fort Agra. Jahan spent his final days imprisoned, with his one window giving him a view of the white columns, the marble dome, and the four minarets of the Taj Mahal.

Getting back to the bus, we walked a gauntlet of men, women, and children asking us for money or trying to sell us postcards or beads. We marched along, about thirty of us, faculty and students alike, trailed by dark-haired urchins and wizened old women. It was hot. I took off my shirt and offered it to a young man with slick-backed hair and a dazzling white smile. He shook his head to say no.

"Give me your hat," he said pointing to my Mont-Bell baseball cap.

"I'm not giving you my hat," I replied. "You can have my shirt if you want."

He shook his head again. "I'll take your shoes."

He smiled up at me, and for a moment I was mesmerized into considering his request. But I thought better of walking in my socks the rest of the way to the bus, and the last line of Jhumpa Lahiri's collection of stories looped in my mind: "As ordinary as it all appears, there are times when it is beyond my imagination."

Egypt

Our journey to Adabiya, Egypt, stretched 4,014 nautical miles across the Arabian Sea, longer by ten miles than our trip would be in December from Cadiz, Spain, to Fort Lauderdale, Florida, across the Atlantic Ocean. Along the way, in my classes, we read some of the narrative puzzles of Naguib Mahfouz, the Egyptian author who won the Nobel Prize for literature in 1988, the first Arab-language writer to win the award. He had died a few days after we set sail from Ensanada, Mexico, into the Pacific Ocean to begin our voyage around the world. In particular, my students were enthralled by one of his stories, "Room No. 12." They saw it as the literature of enigma, something like "Kafka in Cairo," one said.

The brief, eerie tale tells the story of a stunning, formidable woman named Bahiga al-Dahabi who takes a room for twenty-four hours at a small hotel in Egypt. She comes with no identity card, just a mysteriously heavy suitcase. She asks the bellhop to move the bed outside the room and to open all the closet doors. Then she calls down to the mystified manager and orders enough food for a dozen people.

Soon people begin to show up asking for her. At first, they are all from the upper crust of Egyptian society—a wealthy couple, then ten more aristocratic people, a female obstetrician, a contractor, and a mortician (who is never admitted to the room). Shortly after the first wave of people arrive, the upper middle class starts to come, asking about the occupant of room 12—a grocery store owner, a sugarcane juice vendor, the proprietor of a perfume shop, a revenue department official, an editor, and a government informer. There are others, and all the while the mortician keeps asking to be admitted, but he is forced to stay in the lobby.

More and more people from the powerful class cram into the room. More food is delivered. Outside, it begins to storm. A large group of common people arrive in the lobby, asking the question that has been reiterated in the story—"Is Mrs. Bahiga al-Dahabi staying here?" But al-Dahabi requests that the common folk stay in the lobby. Confused and frustrated, the manager mutters, "This hotel is no longer a hotel and I'm no longer the manager, and today is not a day, and lunacy is laughing at us in the shape of meat and wine!"

The manager is right, of course. The hotel is not a hotel, but something else. Reading the story, I felt a bit like Mrs. Malaprop, sensing an allegory on the banks of the Nile. The storm, unlike any seen for a generation, grows in wrath, and the rain begins to seep in the roof. People start to vacate rooms, but in number 12 the people are jammed so tight they can't get out. The bellhop tells the manager, "Their stomachs have inflated so much, they can't open the door. They can't even move."

The common people begin to help with the repair of the roof, but things keep getting worse for those in room number 12. The manager shouts his last order, "Concentrate on the roof over the guest rooms—but as for room number twelve, *leave it alone—and everyone inside it!*" The bellhop hesitates before carrying out the order, but the manager "felt his great burden lighten, as his confidence returned with his clarity of mind."

My class read the story as everything from an autobiographical account of Mahfouz's desire to abandon his characters to a psychological tale of the id and the superego. But I thought Jo-Ellen's interpretation (she tutored me in a private session) was the most cogent—a socioeconomic reading of the story in which the upper class gets trapped by its own gluttony and arrogance. If it were an allegory on the banks of the Nile, Jo-Ellen and I were to see in the next few days that Mahfouz's story of the separation between the rich and the poor was a true picture of Egypt. Although the poor seemed to take up most of the space in the picture, the rich took up most of the resources.

Mahfouz is best known for *The Cairo Trilogy,* his mid-twentieth-century masterpiece about a Muslim family in Egypt's capital. But he was the author of hundreds of short stories, thirty-four novels, and dozens of plays and film scripts over his seventy-year career. He was respected as a man of courage, a Muslim writer who spoke out in opposition to Ayatollah Khomeini's fatwa in 1989 against Salman Rushdie. Mahfouz's books had been banned in many Islamic countries over the years, but it was his defense of Rushdie that most likely put him on the Islamic terrorist "death list." In 1994, two Islamic extremists tried to assassinate him, stabbing the then eighty-three-year-old writer in the neck with a kitchen knife outside his Cairo home.

Mahfouz was the man caught in the middle, and he had been aware of his position for some time. In his 1988 Nobel Prize acceptance speech, he said, "I am the son of two civilizations that at a certain age in history have found a happy marriage. The first of these, seven thousand years old, is the pharonic civilization; the second, one thousand four hundred years old, is the Islamic civilization." The world he had described over a long lifetime was the one that Jo-Ellen and I entered in late October 2006, the place Paul Theroux described in *Dark Star Safari* as "the high density city of Cairo—one thousand years of donkey droppings, hawkers' wagons, barrow boys, veiled women, jostling camels, hand-holding men, and hubble-bubble smokers, amid mosques and princes' palaces and a bazaar selling trinkets, brass pots, and sacks of beans."

I envied Theroux his meeting with Mahfouz a few years before he died even though at that time he was "somewhat feeble, almost blind, and nearly deaf." Theroux was part of the entourage that sat around Mahfouz shouting in his good ear about politics and religion and art. According to Theroux, "Mahfouz simply listened and smoked cigarettes and looked Sphinxlike." Every now and again, Mahfouz murmured a sentence that caught everyone's attention, particularly mine as a reader who was about to get as close to the cauldron of violence in the Middle East as I ever expected to come.

Reflecting on the killing in Iraq, Mahfouz said, "The attack on Iraq is like the random attack in Camus's *The Stranger*." As Theroux explained, "The sun-dazed Meursault in that novel shoots a shadowy Arab on the beach for no logical reason." I had read *The Stranger* for the first time in 1968, as a freshman at Fordham University, right at the time of the assassination of Martin Luther King. I knew exactly how Mahfouz felt. I had felt the same way then.

We headed in our bus from Adabiya to Cairo with Hela, our tough little Egyptian tour guide who dressed like a banker's secretary and sold jewelry to her tour customers on the side. Mahari, a thick-necked and silent guard in a tailored dark blue suit that fit perfectly except for the bulge of the miniature assault rifle under his jacket, sat at attention behind the driver. I thought about how close we were in time and space to scenes of indiscriminate violence. On November 17, 1997, six gunmen armed with automatic weapons opened fire on a group of tourists—mainly Swiss and Japanese—killing more than sixty people as they visited the temple of Hatsheput in Luxor, the ancient Valley of the Kings. There had been other terrorist attacks on tourists in Egypt, part of the struggle between militants who wanted to set up a strict Islamic state and the more democratically inclined government of Hosni Mubarek.

As we rode in our bus toward Cairo, some of our students and faculty were on their way to Luxor, recalling, I was sure, that in 1997 SAS participants had been close enough to the gunfire to hear the shots and the screams. None of the SAS people had been hurt, and when they got back safely to the port, the ship raced away into the Mediterranean.

The day before we arrived in Adibaya, I had played basketball with a few students as the ship slashed through the Red Sea. The six of us, regulars on the court, had paused in our game to scan the horizon for Mount Sinai or nomads riding camels across the dunes. We wondered aloud about the origin of the name *Red Sea*. Was it a corruption of *reed* for all the tall grasses that grew by the shore? Or was it the color of the mountains at sunset as they reflected on the water?

One young man named Zach, a student from Morehouse College, a gentle giant who had cracked my ribs twice in the past few weeks, pushed back his dreadlocks, grabbed the ball, and said, "Whatever the origin, it's wild to be here, playing basketball looking at Saudi Arabia." So we finished the game, unlike any we would ever play, the dry, treeless moonscape turning violet in the sunset. On our bus to Cairo, two of those basketball players gazed out the windows at the desert as if it were a landscape charged with grace and good wishes. Zach, I had heard, was on his way with a few others to Luxor, believing, too, perhaps, that the world still had good intentions.

I wasn't heartened, though, by Mahari's clamped jaw, his Secret Service sunglasses, or the awe-inspiring weapon that bulged from his side like a tumor. The police escort leading and following the line of buses wasn't encouraging, either. All the protection made me feel as if someone close by wanted to kill us if the right opportunity arose.

Later, at the American University of Cairo, the assistant provost, a British citizen, put things in perspective for me by saying, "In twenty-five years in Cairo I've never been afraid for my personal safety." He looked at his American audience, his face scrunched into bemusement, and continued, "Egyptians say to Americans, 'You're afraid to come here? You come from the most violent country in the world!'"

He offered us an anecdote about an Australian professor who had come to Egypt to study how the deaf were taught there. After her research was completed, she gave a presentation to the faculty at AUC with her deaf students. For the audience, the students made the sign of a triangle and she asked what they thought that stood for. Immediately, they saw the pyramid as the sign for Egypt. Then her students made the sign for pistols shooting, guns blazing, and the audience did not hesitate—*That is America,* they shouted out. The provost said that in the past year there had been 200 murders in Egypt, a country of 80 million people. There were more murders in any given year in one American city like Detroit. "Your odds are much better here than they are in New Orleans or Newark. So enjoy Cairo."

With close to 18 million people, Cairo was the most populated city in Africa or the Middle East, and Theroux in *Dark Star Safari* called it a metropolis of "bad air and hideous traffic." But nevertheless there was something appealing about it. It was "made habitable, even pleasant, by its genial populace and its big placid river, brown under a brown sky." As Theroux pointed out, many of the people visitors interacted with didn't distinguish between pestering and hospitality, and when they had your attention, they did not want to let it slip away, for that would mean hunting for another source of tourist dollars for that day. In that way, the Egyptians we encountered were like the people in other impoverished cultures—in India or Burma or Vietnam. Generally, Egyptians would be tenacious in getting you to spend your dollars with them, but, unlike many Indians, usually they offered you some service for that money—a camel ride, a carriage tour of the city, a disquisition on how the ancients mummified their corpses, help with your packages—for the baksheesh they expected.

In the Cairo markets, cluttered with fabric stores, hookah stands, and fruit peddlers, I was always treated respectfully and offered "the Egyptian man price." Of course, that was probably because Mahari attached himself to me as I meandered through the marketplaces. Every time I entered a shop, looking for a caftan or a bag of dates, he stood behind me, silent and unsmiling, the gun bulging from his sport coat. But then having an armed guard might make shopping easier in Macy's in New York City, too.

The Cairo Jo-Ellen and I saw on that first day in the city was the same one that Theroux described. It was Flaubert's Egypt too, like being hurled while still asleep into a Beethoven symphony. The roads were clogged with cars and buses, donkey carts and boys herding sheep. At one point, our bus managed a maneuver I had never seen a tour bus accomplish. We were stuck in a traffic jam that appeared to twist on for miles. Our driver turned his eyes toward the sky, hissed *enshaallah,* which I was later told meant "God willing" but took at that time to mean "the hell with it," bounced the bus across a high median in the road, cut in front of oncoming traffic and went up an exit ramp onto the relatively clear highway.

We passed canals in which the garbage was so thick it was difficult to make out the dead horses or donkeys that floated in them. Men on camels plodded along beside our bus. Children played in the dusty streets in the shade of brick buildings squeezed together between a fragment of sunlight. Thousands of buildings had unfinished rooftops, waiting for other family members to arrive but also to avoid taxes. As long as the buildings remained unfinished, Hela told us, no taxes had to be paid.

A few minutes before we arrived at our hotel, within sight of the Pyramids of Giza, our bus nearly crashed into a donkey cart carrying bushels of wheat. The bus had swerved to avoid two young boys who were racing their horses through the busy streets, shouting at us, at the cars, at the universe itself. They turned, smiling, and waved at us as they disappeared around the corner.

When we entered the hotel lobby, there was a Muslim wedding celebration with bagpipes, flutes, and drums in the area by the main stairs. The women stood off to one side and smiled demurely while the men danced in the center of the wedding crowd. The men clapped their hands in a circle, and two of them (one who I assumed was the bridegroom) played a homoerotic cat and mouse game, dancing close to one another and gazing slyly into each another's eyes, their lips nearly touching. The women watched, and I wondered if this boded well for the wedding night to come.

The next morning in the cold, violet desert air a few hours before sunrise, we stood before the pyramids of Giza, the only one of the Seven Wonders of the Ancient World to have survived. It was hard to comprehend that each one of the tombs was created for one person and unknown how many had died moving the massive blocks of stone through the desert. Each pyramid had taken close to twenty years to build, and there were three large pyramids for the pharaohs and a few small ones for their queens. The oldest and largest of the monuments, built by the pharaoh Khufu, was nearly five thousand years old.

Seeing the pyramids in the shifting rose-colored dawn was more affecting than I had expected it to be. I remembered years before being surprised by how much I was moved by Stonehenge when I assumed it would be meretricious, something once splendid turned into a tourist trap. But the Giza pyramids, like Stonehenge, had a power that all the light shows and camel rides could not diminish.

Standing guard over the pyramids was the Sphinx, known to the Arabs as Abu al-Hol, the "father of terror." Its shattered visage recalled Shelley's poem about Ramses the Great, "Ozymandias," and the ironic lines reflecting on the ephemeral character of life: "Nothing beside remains. Round the decay / Of that colossal wreck, boundless and bare / The lone and level sands stretch far away." The Sphinx, its nose shot off by Ottoman raiders or Napoleon's soldiers and a piece of its beard worn away by the sands and winds, stood over sixty feet high and had been carved from an outcrop of natural rock. The Arabs were right— the Sphinx held the area with a terrible authority even now, nearly five thousand years after its creation. It was awe-inspiring enough to change even Mark Twain's sarcasm in *Innocents Abroad* into unadulterated admiration:

After years of waiting it was before me at last. The great face was so sad, so earnest, so longing, so patient. There was a dignity not of earth in its mien, and in its countenance a benignity such as never anything human wore. It was stone, but it seemed sentient. If ever image of stone thought, it was thinking. It was looking toward the verge of the land-scape, yet looking *at* nothing—nothing but distance and vacancy. It was looking over and beyond everything of the present and far into the past. It was gazing over the ocean of Time—over the lines of century waves that, further and further receding, closed nearer and nearer together, and blended at last into one unbroken tide, away toward the horizon of remote antiquity. It was thinking of the wars of departed ages; of the empires it had seen created and destroyed; of the nations whose birth it had witnessed, whose progress it had watched, whose annihilation it had noted; of the joy and sorrow, the life and death, the grandeur and decay, of five thousand slow revolving years.

Jo-Ellen and I sensed what Twain had felt, that we were standing before the oldest man-made structures on earth, that life stretched out endlessly behind and before us, that time was so short but Time was never ending. And that spell was not broken until the sun rose fully and a few of our students came galloping by on horses, scarves streaming from their heads and shattering the desert quiet with their squeals and shouts.

That afternoon, before we headed back to the ship in Abadiya to tran-sit the Suez Canal, our guide, Hela, took us to the Mosque of Muhammed Ali, built in the early nineteenth century. In hushed tones, she explained the essence of Islam that she felt most Westerners misunderstood in their focus on what they thought was the inequity between men and women in Muslim countries.

"Women are not second-class citizens in Egypt," Hela said.

At the risk of being rude, I asked her why men could have more than one wife and women could not, why married women's faces should be hidden and their husband's not, why a man could divorce a woman who could not bear him children but a women could not divorce a man for being sterile.

"Who would want more than one husband?" she asked, laughing at the thought of such absurdity, but she never answered my questions, and I didn't ask again.

Outside the mosque, a gaggle of young head-scarved girls asked Jo-Ellen to be photographed with them. I took the picture of their smiling faces framing hers, and, except for the scarves, they could have been a gathering of teenagers in any American city.

That evening, we had a dinner cruise along the Nile, what the explorer John Speke called "the holy river, the cradle of Moses." For us, it seemed more spinning than spiritual, though, with dervishes twirling at giddy speeds and belly dancers gyrating to ecstatic music. But it didn't stop us from eating as if we were to be thrust into the desert to fast for forty days and forty nights. We ate hummus, plates of feta cheese and tomatoes, baba ghanoush, aish, koshari, bamiyya, stuffed vine leaves, pieces of lamb and chicken, fuul, filo pastries, and chocolate cakes. And then we stepped outside into the cooling Egyptian night as men in loose-fitting robes and grimy turbans held out their calloused hands and implored, "Effendi, let me show you the nightlife of Cairo," and pointed toward gaunt ponies and rusted carriages with oil-stained seats.

Alexandria had all the grittiness and poverty of Cairo, but it had a European atmosphere to it, as well. Stretching twelve miles along the Mediterranean Sea, the city was founded by Alexander the Great in the fourth century BC, and it is the second largest metropolis in Egypt. It rivaled Rome for a few hundred years before it began to fall into the aristocratic decline that left it looking like a movie goddess whose sagging lines have taken over her former beauty. One of Naguib Mahfouz's characters described it as "the tongue of land, planted with palms and leafy acacias, that protrudes out into the Mediterranean. . . . Lady of the dew. Bloom of white nimbus. Bosom of radiance, wet with sky water. Core of nostalgia steeped in honey and tears." It was all that and more.

In the nineteenth century, after the Pasha Mohammed Ali brought the city back to life by linking Alexandria to the Nile, its renewed prosperity brought thousands of Europeans and the decadent atmosphere their presence created. Alexandria seemed a postdecadent city now, a city whose history was bleached white like an old black-and-white photograph left too long on a window ledge.

The Bibliotheca Alexandrina, once the greatest library in the ancient world, had been rebuilt as a modern cylindrical monument of glass and granite. The sunlight shimmered from the glazed roof onto the seven tiers of chairs in the 2,000-seat reading room. Architecturally, it was a wonder, and I saw many people ogling the library as if they were observing some pharaonic masterpiece, but I saw few people actually sitting in one of those seats reading. Nor did there seem to be many books on the few shelves in the cavernous spaces.

From what I could tell after a day or two roaming the city, the library— once a symbol of Alexandria's glowing past—was like much else in the city. We saw the shadow but could not find what present reality cast the image. The Pastroudis café, once the hangout for writers like Lawrence Durrell, was now a shaded spot with streetside tables, nothing more. The Pharos lighthouse, once one of the Seven Wonders of the World, was nothing but a few blocks of stone discovered by recent underwater excavation.

It was a city of faded memories and shadows cast by the invisible past. The U-shaped Corniche that curved along the eastern harbor fronting the Mediterranean Sea, a sun-dazzled avenue of cars and tall buildings, was the spot where Jo-Ellen and I found the point that modern Alexandria intersected with the past. Or, rather, we bumped into Yusef, a man we had tried to avoid for twenty-four hours. We had met Yusef on our first day in Alexandria. He stood by his bedraggled horse and patted the cracked leather of the seat in his cart.

"My friends, I will take you for a ride. I will show you my city."

When we said that we preferred to walk, he did not argue, but rubbed his stubbled cheek and gave us a wide yellow smile.

"You are British? German?"

When we told him we were Americans, something we had been advised to downplay in our journey around the world, he waved his white baseball cap in the air and patted his horse, Tiger.

"You see, Tiger," he said. "I thought they might be Americans. What did I tell you?"

The horse tilted its head in his direction, and for a moment I thought perhaps it was going to nod twice or pound its hoof against the ground, some Egyptian driver's trick. But it remained still, an ordinary horse. Then Yusef turned back to us.

"Americans are the best people in the world. I love Americans. Not the American government. Not George Bush. But he is not the American people, am I right?"

We told him we hoped he was right and listened to him talk about the last five American presidents. He knew more about American politics than the majority of high school students in the United States would know. But this was a phenomenon we had encountered before—that is, the person in a third world country in a menial job being well versed in American politics and culture when most Americans could not name the head of that person's country or say much about its politics.

"You speak English well," I said to him.

He put his calloused hand on the cracked black leather of his carriage. Then he patted Tiger's ribs.

"This is my school," he replied.

His Harvard and Yale, I thought. Yusef had learned English from the tourists. He knew some German too, but he didn't like the Germans because they were not as generous as the Americans—or as smiling. We disappointed him, though, because we did not hire him right then and there. He gave us such a sad face that we said we would hire him the next day. It was a lie, the kind of untruth people tell others every day, to save their own feelings as much as the other person's. Jo-Ellen and I reasoned that Alexandria was a big city, we would not run into Yusef again, and if we did, he would have forgotten us in a day's time.

When we ran into him the next day, we discovered we were wrong on every count. He was waiting for us in the same spot on the Corniche that he had first met us. He saw us walking down the avenue and waved his white baseball cap in the air jubilantly. My heart sank because I guessed we were doomed to be conned gently but surely on our last afternoon in Alexandria. It would have taken too much effort to resist, so we just smiled, got in the carriage behind Tiger, and let Yusef carry us around the city past billowing laundry hanging from iron terraces, along dirt-caked alleyways close enough to scrape the chips of cement from the deteriorating buildings, and into back streets that had been his home for nearly sixty years.

Yusef gently flicked the reins and turned sideways, letting Tiger follow his own path. Yusef talked to us, every now and then waving and greeting a friend on the street, *"Assalaamu aleikem,* these are my American friends." Then he would point to us and smile broadly.

We spoke with him about how the world, in the midst of the war in Iraq, seemed to view Americans. "It's dispiriting," I said.

"Keep spirit," he told me. "Egyptians love Americans. Our hearts are broken by what happens. Beautiful American boys killed. Throats cut." He held his dirt-caked hand sideways against the grey stubble of his own throat. "Why? Why? Why Americans no speak to the president?"

I had no answer for him. But I had learned something from him. He had not conned us in our afternoon carriage ride. When he brought the carriage to a stop back at the port where our ship was anchored, he kept to his original price. He reluctantly took the tip I begged him three times to take. Then he bowed to Jo-Ellen and hugged me.

"Muslims and Christians are one," he said. He placed one of my hands in both of his, rough as sandpaper, dirty, but warm and gentle. "We are brothers."

Turkey

Our original departure date from Alexandria was postponed because of gale winds and fifteen-foot swells in the Mediterranean Sea, so we left a day late, but the ship sped through the still-rough seas at twenty-four knots and we arrived in Istanbul on time anyway. Weeks before, we had been told our ship was the fastest of its size and could outrun any pirate vessel in the Strait of Malacca. I was a little seasick en route to Turkey, but I was confident we would be safe if we happened to encounter pirates in the Aegean.

The morning of Tuesday, November 7, 2006, five years to the day after my mother died, we sailed from the Sea of Marmara into the Bosphorus Straits, the bodies of water, along with the Dardenelles, that separated European and Asian Turkey. Istanbul laid claim to being the only city in the world straddling two continents. Only three percent of Turkey was in Europe and 99 percent of its people were Muslims, but the country—or at least Istanbul and its more than 10 million residents—was spilt between Islamic fundamentalism and European secularism, the old and the new worlds in an uneasy balance represented by the women in head scarves in the markets and in tight jeans and high heels in the cosmopolitan Beyoglu section of the city. Turkish writers, even those of the stature of Orhan Pamuk, had been brought to trial for insulting the state in their work. Istanbul, Pamuk's home, might be the bridge between Europe and Asia, the place where Christianity and Islam met, or it could become the dividing line between the two cultures.

A little after sunrise, the sunlight competing with a rusty pall that was probably a familiar part of autumn days there, I stood on the deck of the *MV Explorer* and surveyed the skyline of Istanbul—a time-wrenching landscape of domes and minarets. The ship berthed at the Karakoy

Terminal, a short walk to the Galata Bridge, which spanned the flooded estuary of the Golden Horn, and I stood there thinking about how much my mother would have loved being in this gorgeous city or even seeing it through my eyes.

The wave of sadness that swept over me caught me by surprise and sent me reeling back to a passage from Orhan Pamuk's memoir, *Istanbul: Memories and the City*. He wrote, "In Istanbul the remains of a glorious past civilization are everywhere visible. No matter how ill-kept, no matter how neglected or hemmed in they are by concrete monstrosities, the great mosques and other monuments of the city, as well as the lesser detritus of the empire in every side street and corner—the little arches, fountains, neighborhood mosques—inflict heartache on all who live among them."

As Pamuk sees it, the mysterious air that foreigners sense in Istanbul, something they feel but cannot name, is *huzun*, which in Turkish means "melancholy" but also implies the inward-looking soul of its people and their acceptance of failure, indecision, defeat, and indigence "so philosophically and with such pride, suggesting that *huzun* is not the outcome of life's worries and great losses but their principal cause."

In part, this melancholy could be understood only by acknowledging the city's deep-rooted past. The first human settlement there dated back thousands of years, but its famous recorded history began with the Greek settler Byzas who immortalized himself in the name Byzantium. Over the years, Byzantium survived attacks by Persians, Athenians, and Macedonians, becoming a synonym for culture and civilization. In the early twentieth century, William Butler Yeats wrote two poems—"Byzantium" and "Sailing to Byzantium"—about the city, sculpting his vision of it into a symbol of art and the imagination in which the poet at one point dreams of becoming what he creates, to "set upon a golden bough to sing / To lords and ladies of Byzantium / Of what is past, or passing, or to come."

By the second century AD, Byzantium had become part of the Roman Empire, and before the middle of the fourth century the Emperor Constantine made the city, now called Constantinople, the heart of his realm and the launching point to bring Christianity to the region. Instead, the empire surrounding Constantinople fell in bits and pieces as the Ottoman Turks carried the Muslim faith across Asia. On May 29, 1453, Sultan

Mehmet II marched into Constantinople after a fifty-four-day siege, and Istanbul was born as the capital of the Ottoman Empire, a myth-saturated culture floating in stories of sultans, harems, palaces, and powerful pashas, a civilization that Orhan Pamuk has transformed, as Yeats suggested in his two poems, into a landscape where art and life are inextricably linked, forever mysteriously and inseparably entwined.

After World War I, the Ottoman Empire was broken up by the European powers and remained fractured until Mustafa Ataturk, still adored today by his people as the father of modern Turkey, declared the country a secular republic, abolishing the sultanate, separating church and Islamic state, reforming the Arabic alphabet with a Roman one, and creating legislation that granted women greater social and political rights. It was Ataturk's Turkey that we entered on November 7, 2006, a land in which East and West held a precarious balance.

At the embassy briefing shortly before we got off the ship, a young vice consul, so handsome that the young women onboard sat in a circle at his feet and sighed deeply every time he brushed back the curly hair from his forehead, told us about the country.

"Earthquakes, terrorists, scam artists, cab drivers who cheat you on the fare, traffic accidents . . . but you'll have a great time."

He reminded us of something we had heard many times before, that in Turkey we were between two worlds, a country in which 68 million of the 70 million people were Muslims but a place Westernized enough to be on the verge of entering the European Union. Bordered by Syria, Iraq, Armenia, Georgia, and Iran to its Asian east and by Bulgaria and Greece to its European west, Turkey was at the junction between the past and the present.

Or at least Istanbul seemed caught there, as cosmopolitan as New York City and as grimy in spots as Cairo. All you had to do was spend half a day at the futuristic Kanyon Mall, noting the chic men and women who could have strolled off Park Avenue a few minutes before, and then wend your way to one of the city parks, seeing the weather-lined faces of men with drooping moustaches and skull caps and the dowdy women in head scarves. It was just as common to hear the click of a pair of Prada heels in the Grand Bazaar as it was to see a pair of women in black burkas with only a slit for their eyes.

Jo-Ellen and I spent the day roaming the spice and fish markets and sipping hot tea in rug shops in the Grand Bazaar as swarthy men with megawatt smiles who understood every word in the *Oxford English Dictionary* but "no" flicked rugs before us as if they were magic carpets waiting for us to ride. We were killing some time before we kept our date with a friend of a friend, Ipek Cankat, who had arranged to meet us in a restaurant in the Beyoglu section of the city. We said we didn't need a rug, but of course we bought one, a silk prayer rug—and a set of glasses, a teapot, some necklaces, a few simits (the pretzel-shaped bread coated with sesame seeds that the sellers balance on their heads), a shirt, a jacket, and a piece of fabric that could have been used to make a caftan or a tent for a child.

That night we would have been lost on the train if it had not been for a gracious young woman who spoke English well and looked as if she had stepped from the pages of *Vogue*. She came on the train with us and showed us where to exit in Taksim Square, the equivalent in Istanbul of Times Square in New York City. The restaurant, Leb-i-derya, was not easy to find either, and we were swept along the pedestrian-only Istiklal Caddesi in the chill dusk until we could find someone who pointed us down a winding alleyway.

The restaurant was on the rooftop of an anonymous-looking apartment building. Ipek was waiting for us, a beautiful wisp of a young woman, conversing with the little man who ran the coat check. He made spice wine on a hot plate in his tiny room, and we hugged her in greeting and drank the warm wine. In an important way, Ipek seemed to be Istanbul, the modern woman in the changing world of Turkey. She was smart, ambitious, politically aware, and dressed as if she had spent the day in Kanyon Mall. It felt to me like more than a coincidence that she had the same name as the long-lost love of the poet Ka, the protagonist of Orhan Pamuk's *Snow*.

The Ipek we met at Leb-i-derya had the sort of ethereal beauty that a character like Pamuk's Ka might immediately romanticize into a poetic vision. In my literature class on the ship, we had spent the days before we reached Turkey reading *Snow*, and in the weeks before that I had saturated myself in Pamuk's work. *Snow* was a challenging novel with an elaborate, experimental plot, an unnerving mix of farce and poignancy, a postmodern hall of mirrors where Pamuk reflected the questions that had been dramatized in his other novels—what is the relationship between art and life, and is it possible for an individual, let alone a country, to come to a sense of a true identity?

I was surprised at how much the students loved *Snow*. A few of them even tried to get to Kars, the town where the novel was set, but even the most resourceful couldn't figure out a way to get to the Armenian border town and back to the ship in five days. Many of them saw the book, as I did, as an incisive portrait of the schism between the secular and the religious in Turkey but also as a sad, funny probing into the nature of art, politics, and individuality. Pamuk's winning the Nobel Prize a few weeks before we docked in Istanbul added to his star status in Turkey and with my literature students. For many of them, *Snow* became the key to unlock the Turkish mystery.

Originally published in Turkey in 2002 as *Kar*, both the name of the town that serves as the principal setting in the novel and the Turkish word for *snow*, the story centers upon the forty-two-year-old Kerim Alakusoglu, a melancholy, self-referential poet who prefers to be known by his initials, Ka. After living for twelve years in Germany as a political exile, he has returned to Istanbul for his mother's funeral. While he is home, he learns that a former college classmate, the dazzling Ipek Hanim, has gotten divorced and is living in Kars, a bleak, snowbound city in northeastern Turkey. Although Ka has not thought of Ipek for years, when her name is mentioned he remembers how beautiful she was, and the "prospect of love" fills him with longing for her.

It becomes clear, as the plot thickens with snow and enough reflexive switchbacks to dizzy even the most careful reader, that Ka's "only thought was for poetry." Ostensibly, he goes to Kars to report on the rash of head-scarf girls in the town who have committed suicide rather than shed their symbol of Islam. But Ka, often unable to separate the dancer from the dance, finds himself incapable of distinguishing the line between art and life, poetry and politics. Like the snow that covers every aspect of the story with a symbolic whiteness as intense as anything in Melville's *Moby-Dick*, the human mystery at the heart of the narrative is as undecipherable as life itself.

Snow is the most political and controversial of Pamuk's novels. It raises many questions that Turks might prefer to leave unspoken—the treatment of the Kurdish minority, genocide against the Armenians during World War I, the country's love-hate relationship with the West, and the highly charged conflict between religious values and secular interests. There is a quality of *huzun* that permeates the book, a sadness as mysterious as the snow itself. But there is also a farcical brand of comedy in which Pamuk satirizes everything in his sightline—the media, secularists and Western intellectuals, Islamic terrorists, religious extremists, politicians, military leaders, and writers like himself who by necessity separate themselves from the fury of the world in order to write about it (the effaced narrator of the novel who parts the curtain and steps onto the stage late in the story is a novelist named Orhan).

Like Ka, Orhan falls under the spell of Ipek's beauty, perhaps as every writer becomes a slave to beauty. The relationship between art and life gets wonderfully confused in the novel, and it becomes difficult to tell which reflects what, art life or life art. Newspaper stories predict what will happen rather than recounting the events. Ka writes most of his nineteen poems (of precisely thirty-six lines each) simultaneously with the political, religious, or sexual actions they describe. And Ipek, Ka's Maud Gonne, becomes idealized symbol and real woman in ways that are both hypnotic and hilarious. In one diary entry, like a character in an eighteenth-century novel by Samuel Richardson, Ka records the nuances of his lovemaking with Ipek in such a way one wonders how he had time to make love to her with all the scribbling.

Pamuk's ambivalence toward his homeland is Faulknerian and portrayed in his picture of a society at odds with itself. For this reason, perhaps, there are so many love triangles and doppelgangers in Pamuk's work, *Snow* included. He is a master of stories within stories, reflecting the malleability of truth and the difficulty of turning multiple realities into one that can be accepted by all. In *The Black Book*, he compresses one of his main themes into a question that a barber asks the protagonist: "Is there any way a man can be only himself?" In Pamuk's world it is not an easy trick, but in *The Black Book* the main character is offered a piece of advice that speaks to the question: "It's not for nothing that they say it's important to see the world through someone else's eyes from time to time. Because that's really when you start to understand the mystery of life, not to mention other people's secrets."

In a place like Turkey, in particular, what one of Pamuk's characters describes as "an oppressed, defeated country," it is a struggle to find one's identity. But that truth just reminds Pamuk of another story, "in which the hero discovers that he can only become himself by first becoming someone else or by losing himself in someone else's stories." Therefore, the question near the end of *Snow*—"How much can a man hear another man's voice inside him?"—seemed to me not only the most pertinent question for citizens of Turkey but for any traveler as well.

However, when I asked Ipek Cankat, our new friend in Istanbul, what she thought of Pamuk's work, she said that he had done a disservice to their country. She was too gentle a spirit to support the trials, prompted by political conservatives, of writers like Pamuk who had been accused of insulting Turkishness, but she refused to read his books anymore. As we exchanged opposing views of the meaning and value of Pamuk's work in the stylish Leb-i-derya, the lights of Beyoglu and the crowds below us, the dark descending as Pamuk might have phrased it "like a poem in the pale light of the streetlamps," I tried to understand this well-educated and modern Turkish woman's view of her own world. I tried to hear her voice inside of me, to lose myself in her story. And she, I'm sure, was doing the same with me.

The next few days in Istanbul Jo-Ellen and I saw all the magnificent sites of the ancient city. Ipek reserved a room for us at the Hotel Sokul-lupasa, negotiating for the "Istanbul resident rate." The hotel had a frayed sort of charm, and the window of our room peeked between the houses and mosques that angled down the hill to the Bosphorus. The hotel was a few yards from a small mosque, and five times a day the muezzin climbed the minaret to chant from the Koran and call the faithful Muslims to prayer. Actually, I don't think he climbed the minaret but used a sleep-shattering loudspeaker that forced us on the third day to return to sleep on the ship.

The hotel was close to the Blue Mosque and Hagia Sophia in Sulta-nahmet Square, two architectural wonders that faced each other across the leafy quadrangle of the hippodrome. Hagia Sophia was inaugurated by the Emperor Justinian in the early sixth century AD. In the fifteenth century, the Ottomans converted it into a mosque, adding the minarets. It may be the most modern of Turkish symbols, at once Christian and Muslim with its Byzantine mosaics and baptistery holding a fragile balance with ablution fountains and a kursu, the raised chair used by the imam while he reads excerpts from the Koran.

The Blue Mosque is singularly Muslim in its character. Built in the early seventeenth century by Mehmet Aga, the sultan's architect, it took its name from the millions of blue Iznik tiles that decorate the interior. As with all traditional mosques, there are no human or animal images in the building. The praying space was uncluttered with pews or Stations of the Cross. It had a stark grandeur. I had grown up with the gold and silver ornaments, the unending images of Christ and Mary, in the Catholic Church. The mosques I saw, even one as breathtaking as the Blue Mosque, had an unornamented straightforwardness that put the emphasis for conscience and conduct back with the individual.

It was a cold day, and it made me colder to watch the Muslim men wash their feet at the taps outside the mosque before they entered to pray. Inside the mosque, men knelt on prayer rugs and bowed their heads to the ground. Off to one side of the main room, behind a lattice partition, was a shadowy section in which veiled women prayed. A few SAS students entered the big hall, chattering until they became aware of the silence around them.

One was a student from my literature class, a young man with a dog-eared copy of *Snow* sticking out of his back pocket. Slowly, he drifted from his group, and as Jo-Ellen and I left the mosque, I saw him standing by himself gazing at the muezzin mahfili, the raised platform used by the principal mosque official, as if he were waiting for some words of wisdom.

We spent the rest of the afternoon at Topkapi Palace, a Turkish Versailles built in the years between 1459 and 1465, around the time Constantinople became Istanbul. A series of pavilions enclosed by four large courtyards, Topkapi was, for me, the Arabian Nights configured in stone. Each pavilion and courtyard had its purpose in the Ottoman government—the circumcision pavilion, the garden of the white eunuchs, the barracks of the black eunuchs, the harem, the courtyard of the concubines—and the rooms not set aside for the pleasure or pastimes of the sultan were storehouses for jewel-encrusted jugs and daggers, silk caftans, and holy manuscripts adorned with gold filigree.

The harem, most particularly, reminded me of my boyhood reading of the Arabian Nights, with its ancient Arabic connotation of all that is forbidden. Beside the eunuchs, the sultan and his sons were the only men allowed in the harem. In the same complex as the harem were a series of rooms known as the Cage, where the sultan's brothers were kept locked away to avoid succession conflicts.

In the heyday of the sultan's harem, there were more than a thousand women from all over the Ottoman Empire housed there. It must have been a cauldron of political-sexual-social intrigue. At least, that was the way Mark Twain saw it in *Innocents Abroad.* Describing the situation in Istanbul, he said, "Mosques are plenty, churches are plenty, graveyards are plenty, but morals and whiskey are scarce. The Koran does not permit Mohammedans to drink. Their natural instincts do not permit them to be moral. They say the Sultan has eight hundred wives. This almost amounts to bigamy. It makes our cheeks burn with shame to see such a thing permitted here in Turkey. We do not mind it so much in Salt Lake, however."

After Topkapi Palace, Jo-Ellen and I stopped at Sultanahmet Square to see the Basilica Cistern, a fascinating Roman artifact. I have to admit that I wanted to see it principally to hold it alongside my memory of watching the James Bond film *From Russia with Love* in which Sean Connery battles some spies in the cavernous aqueduct. While Jo-Ellen lingered at the cistern, I went to an ATM in the square across from Haghia Sophia. When I got my money and was reaching to place it in my money belt, I felt someone brush up against me to steal my Turkish lira.

My mind was still firmly planted back in the RKO Fordham in the Bronx in 1964 as I watched Connery throw a punch. With a muttered curse, I turned to do the same to the thief. That's when I heard Shauna Sweeney and her boyfriend, Mario Mangiardi, two of my students from the ship, giggling a few yards away. Shauna had seen a chance to play a practical joke, and her half Chinese and half Irish heritage not only made for a beautiful dark-haired young woman with an oval face and freckles, but it produced a deadly combination as a practical joker. It was the one time I have been grateful that age had slowed me down. In 1964, I would have knocked the person reaching into my pocket to the ground. I had been too slow to do that now; therefore, the most sensitive and subtle writing student I had taught in years survived to enjoy the rest of her trip and graduate from UC-Berkeley. And I had been saved from the newspaper headlines. *Professor Dreaming of Harems and James Bond Knocks Out Brilliant Student Writer: Eliminating Future Competition?*

On our last day in Istanbul, Jo-Ellen and I hiked the Ballikaya Mountains, walking the mud-slogged paths alongside sheep and waterfalls. We ended up at a gorge that seemed as far from the street life of the city, the mosques and prayer beads, the simit sellers, and loudspeakers chanting the Koran, as one could get and still be able to return for a dinner date that night.

We met Ipek at 6 P.M. at a ferry to take us from the European side of Istanbul to the Asian part of the city where she lived with her brother and parents. Their apartment had four bedrooms—one room for the parents, another for the brother, Ali, Ipek's room, and the maid's quarters—and a spacious living room that opened onto a wide terrace overlooking the Sea of Marmara. Both parents spoke basic English, and we talked about American politics, religion, and education around the world. They were the Westernized, secular individuals that Pamuk often wrote about, the residents of Istanbul who were ready to enter the European Union. Like their daughter, they might not have read Pamuk, but they were the new Turkey that was one half of his story.

Ali and Ipek took us to their parents' yacht club, a short walk from their apartment. Ali, a slight man in his midtwenties with thick, neatly barbered hair and a carefully trimmed beard, entertained us with his sly sense of humor, teasing us about helping him to meet an American coed from the ship, and Ipek acted the perfect hostess, ordering sea bass, Circassian chicken, kebabs, dolmas, calamari, yogurt soup, hummus, Turkish pastries, and more food than we could do anything with but taste to experience her beloved land. Ali, a twinkle in his eye, ordered raki. "Lion's milk," he said. It was a clear, anise-flavored liquor that turned cloudy when water was added to it and burned less than I expected as it went down my throat.

They drove us back to our ship, even though we insisted we'd take a cab, showing a graciousness and good will that made me even more convinced that the European Union should stop delaying Turkey's entrance into it. When we got to the port gate, Ali and Ipek got out and hugged us good-bye, but before we could wish them well, a cab screeched to a halt alongside of us. One SAS student, her makeup streaked from the rain and her golden hair in disarray, stumbled from the cab, banging against the door. The other was slumped in the back seat. Her friend had to carry her to the gate that led to the ship. The cab driver, a narrow-eyed man with a few days' growth of ash-brown beard, ranted in Turkish. Ali, looking slightly embarrassed, translated. "He says that the girls didn't pay for their ride."

Ipek said, "Don't trust what he says. He may just want more money. Don't get involved with him."

We looked at the girls, now staggering in their expensive dresses and high heels past the guards toward the ship. The cab driver was still yelling, gesturing, imploring, hoping perhaps that we would be shamed into offering him money. Ipek got back in the car, and Ali, who no longer seemed interested in a date with an American coed, got behind the wheel.

Jo-Ellen and I waved to them as they drove off into the dark, drizzling, melancholy Istanbul night, their lights flashing on people hunched against the wet wind and maybe even in opposition to an invisible fate, and I wished that I could call them back to explain that not all American students were like this, too much money and too little sense of balance. I wanted them to understand my country. I wanted to understand theirs. But all I could recall were some more words from Orhan Pamuk's *Snow*: "How much can we ever know about the love and pain in another's heart? How much can we hope to understand those who have suffered deeper anguish, greater deprivation, and more crushing disappointment than we ourselves have known?"

Croatia

The red-tiled roofs and the sun-splashed white walls of the houses in Dubrovnik came into view in the early morning of November 14. It was home for the captain of our ship, and as we sailed along the rocky Adriatic coast into his harbor, he blasted the bone-rattling horn three times, announcing to his family and neighbors that he was back for a short stay. I was sitting on our deck reading Josip Novakovich's *April Fool's Day* as daylight began to glint off the terra-cotta tiles of the houses and had just come to a passage in which the main character, Ivan, after years of warfare, thinks about the dreams he once had for his country: "He used to imagine that once Croatians ran their own country, the economy would prosper and there would be jobs. Croatia would become a southern Norway, with a coastline full of fjords and efficient factories with an excellent workforce; Croats would come back from Germany and Australia and with their wonderful working skills turn Croatia into the promised land."

Looking at the carefully tended whitewashed houses along the jagged coastline, I wondered if Ivan's dream had come true. Once Jo-Ellen and I stepped ashore onto the gleaming stone streets of the walled city of Dubrovnik, we had many reasons to think it was as close to the promised land as a person could come. There were no homeless or disaffected in sight. The buildings, despite a few mortar or bullet holes from the recent war, were freshly painted and in perfect repair. Everyone we met was pleasant and appeared happy to be living in such a beautiful land.

We had been given few warnings by the embassy administrators before we left the ship. Violent crime seemed nonexistent, and even petty thievery was rare. A tourist was more likely to suffer from sunburn than from being pickpocketed. Croatians, from all accounts, were peaceful and courteous, they loved their country, and took their stewardship over it seriously. They treated their visitors with a gentle ambivalence, knowing they needed tourist dollars but not always relishing the crowds that came as the price of such an economy. The streets were clean, the waters crystal clear, the air pure, and the people content. It could have been, to use Milton's phrase, "a heaven on earth."

Of course, a few years back things had been different. The history of Croatia is byzantine in more ways than one, with Moslem and Christian influences that go back to the Crusaders and the Ottoman Turks, with a connection to Hungary and Yugoslavia, struggles with Italy and Austria and the surrounding countries. Croatia, like its neighboring republics of the former Yugoslavia—Bosnia-Herzegovina, Macedonia, Slovenia, and Serbia-Montenegro—had multiple identities, ethnic, religious, cultural, political, and they all got twisted together. Now, three-quarters of the population was Croat, a little more than 10 percent Serbian. Nearly 90 percent of the country was Christian, mostly Catholic. Only a small percentage was Muslim. It had been part of Hungary, part of Yugoslavia, a country forever caught between opposing worlds and conflicting cultures.

A thousand years before the birth of Christ, the Illyrians, known for their love of commerce and piracy, settled in Croatia. They were followed by the Celts and then the Greeks. In the second century BC, the Romans conquered the country, subduing the coastal towns so that their merchant ships would be safe in the Adriatic. What the Romans left behind when the Huns and the Vandals swept in were their roads and walled fortifications that one can still find remnants of along the coast and in towns like Pula and Split.

The Ottoman Turks moved in alongside the Romans, Croats, and Franks and lived in relative peace until they were conquered by and subsumed into Hungary. By the early sixteenth century, the Turks under Suleyman II claimed most of Hungary and Croatia as theirs. By the nineteenth century, Croatia had been stitched into the Austria-Hungarian Empire. After World War I, Croatia became part of the kingdom of Yugoslavia, held together under the iron rule of Tito until his death in 1980. When the Republic of Yugoslavia dissolved in 1991, Croatians had already experienced a long history of conflict, invasion, and shifting identity. They proclaimed their independence but had to fight a faction supported by the

Yugoslav People's Army and the Serb minority, and it was not until 1995 that the Croat army liberated its country.

Dubrovnik was surrounded, held under siege, and bombed for seven months, but there was little evidence of that as Jo-Ellen and I, along with the sheriff, Chris Peterson, and his wife Diana, walked into the sparkling town looking for a cab to take us up to the island of Korcula. Our cab driver, Sergen, was the only sign that the war was not far removed from the where we stood. He was about my size—slightly shy of six feet tall—but much stockier. He looked like he had been a fullback in a small midwestern college in the United States and then spent years in the military working his way up to drill instructor.

But when you looked closely at his weatherworn round face, mapped with stubble and wrinkles, the way he scratched the back of his thinning brown hair, the manner in which he sat with us when we stopped for coffee on the ride to Korcula—like an enlisted man among officers—you saw someone if not tamed by experience at least made gentle-hearted by it. He had fought in the war for years. His English was not good enough to detail his experiences, but even if it had been, you could tell he was not the sort to say much. War changes people's eyes, and it had done something to Sergen's, but war can temper a man's fierceness or make it deeper. For Sergen, he looked like he had seen enough cruelty to make him believe that goodness could only be discovered in honest work and standing at attention to the world.

It was hard to imagine Korcula, reputed to be the birthplace of Marco Polo, being touched by war or even as a place that someone would leave. It wasn't the Bronx, the kind of landscape that induced dreams of escape. Rather, it was the sort of island people dreamed about finding. It was an island of olive groves, vineyards, and dense pine and cypress forests, thirty miles long and seven miles at its widest, with mountains that ran the length of it rising to over 1,800 feet in places.

The main town, Korcula, was a walled village on an isthmus in the northeast corner of the island, built in tiers on the hills rising up from the harbor and overlooking the Adriatic and the backbone of mountains stretching along the Dalmatian coast. Narrow stone streets twisted through plazas and between buildings into the hills above the town. One street intersected with another in a complicated pattern that made the town seem bigger than it was and forced the wind to tack its way up the hills on a breezy evening.

When we got off the ferry, Dani (who pronounced his name "Johnny") met us at the dock in a wheezing white van and drove us to one of his houses overlooking the harbor. Like many people in Korcula, or Croatia in general, Dani had an eclectic career. He owned a tire shop, rented houses to tourists, and was a travel agent of sorts.

When he met us, he was wearing a grey jumpsuit, which, like his fingers, was stained with grease and oil. He had a scraggly dark grey beard, a mouth full of crooked teeth shades of yellow and brown, and a smile that displayed them often. His hair, a darker grey than his beard, sprung unselfconsciously from his head like an untended bush. In his left hand, between his index and middle finger, he held a cigarette that either never went out or that he relit with a magician's dexterity, for in two days I never saw him without it between his oil- and tobacco-stained fingers.

Dani put the Petersons in one place and us in a nearby apartment. Before the night was out, Chris and I sat on our terrace like old Croatian neighbors, drinking wine and eating cheese, sighing at the glittering lights of the town and harbor below us, and daydreaming about how we could make this a permanent way of life.

"I could wear a jumpsuit like Johnny's," Chris said. "I wonder if they need private detectives here?"

After Chris retired from the Portland Police Department, along with Diana (a nurse by profession), he opened a private investigation company. I could see Chris getting along in Korcula. He lived on an island right now in the Columbia River. How different could it be? Besides, Chris was the type of guy, I was convinced, who could get along anywhere. He was an old-fashioned beat cop, a tough exterior but too compassionate to pass anyone with a hand extended without reaching into his pocket. He had already bought his landlady a dozen roses and tipped every bartender and waiter in town enough to make them hug him before he walked out the door of their establishments. He had the same tough round face as Sergen and the same lines of experience chiseled around his eyes, the kind of guy anyone would want to have alongside him in a fight but the kind of man who would much rather tell a joke than make a fist.

"Hey, this may be paradise to us," I said, "but I bet they still have cheating husbands and people scamming the insurance companies. I'm sure you could find a job here, but would they need someone who could teach a course on the modern American novel?"

That evening, in his bucking van, Dani took us to Maslina Restaurant, a local place high up in the hills above the town and probably not coincidentally a few yards up the road from his tire shop—all part of his part-time job, perhaps, as a tourist agent. It was the best meal we had in Croatia—plates of olives and tomatoes and cheese, grilled shrimp, homemade ravioli, fresh-baked bread, manistra (a soup made of pulses and vegetables), strudel, and palacinka (a pancake filled with chocolate)—and it cost us about ten dollars apiece. That included bottles of Ozujsko beer and glasses of local red wine.

We didn't want to leave Korcula any more than Marco Polo did (if he had any sense), but we spent our last day in Dubrovnik near our ship. They were used to tourists in Dubrovnik. Cruise ships docked there in the summer sometimes two at a time in the tiny port. In late November, though, we were the only tourists around. SAS students had the gleaming streets of the walled town to themselves. The old section of town was all polished stone, a treeless mélange of restaurants, churches, book stores, and jewelry shops. In half a day, most people felt as if they knew every corner. The hills surrounding the town rose above the clock tower on the eastern side of the main square, making you feel, as you sipped coffee in one of the ubiquitous outdoor cafés, that the modern world stood out there waiting if you ever needed to enter it for some unfathomable reason.

Old Dubrovnik was small enough that Jo-Ellen and I felt we were still onboard the ship. SAS students walked around the town in packs. There were more of us there than there were Croatians. To shake the familiar crowds, as we had done for a few days in Korcula, some students went hiking in the hills, despite the fact that they had been warned about unexploded land mines left over from the Yugoslav war in the 1990s. Eden had its dangers. Nearly a quarter of a million mines were still planted in fields and forests. In recent years, 260 people had fallen victim to them, adding an adrenaline rush to any off-road hiking. But adrenaline rush was what so many SAS students seemed to hold as the sole criterion for a meaningful experience in a new world.

So they hiked through the unmarked territory, hearts beating a bit more quickly at each twig snapping. And they found the same swimming hole that we did. We had heard about it from a friend in Virginia. A small door carved in the walls of the city led to a café that sold drinks and allowed access to the cliffs jutting out into the seething Adriatic. As Jo-Ellen and I bent into the opening, we saw that a dozen students had found the place before us. They stood on various levels of the cliffs and yelled to us as we stepped into the sunlight. The waves crashed against the craggy shoreline. The students jumped and dove and flipped into the crashing waves. One young man and woman held hands and jumped from fifteen feet. Another jumped from twenty. One dove from twenty-five. And it escalated, as if it were a drug and each time a bigger fix was necessary.

"Professor Pearson, are you jumping with us?" one young woman asked.

"Depends upon what you mean by *jump*," I replied.

With Jo-Ellen, I walked down to the lowest level, a three-foot drop into the swirling sea. That was more than enough of an adrenaline rush, as the Adriatic was freezing in November, and I discovered that getting back onto the rocks from the pulsating water was not an easy trick. I was swept back and forth by the rough water a few times, remembering my near-drowning in Brazil and wondering if I'd ever get to the age where I learned from my mistakes.

But I was lucky again, and a few minutes later, my hands scraped raw from being slammed by the waves into the sharp rocks, I climbed back up to a flat surface to spend the rest of the afternoon drinking wine, eating cheese, and reading Ivo Andric's epic of Balkan life, *The Bridge on the Drina*, thinking that these cliffs, like Andric's bridge, would outlast invading soldiers or tourists. No matter what "fresh storm . . . burst over the town, overturning and tearing up by the roots its ancient customs, sweeping away living men and inanimate things, the bridge remained white, solid, and invulnerable as it always had been." Like Andric's bridge, the cliffs would silently record all that had happened and was to come.

A few hours after we left the cliffs, we found out that one female student jumped, landed the wrong way, and damaged her spine. Her journey around the world on the *MV Explorer* ended there. We were told that she was flown to Vienna where they had doctors able to do the necessary surgery, attaching a steel rod to her spine so that she could walk again.

That night in the Square of the Loggia, in front of the Church of St. Blaise, a line of men, women, and children marched holding candles that they placed in the square to make certain they remembered the war and the bombing that had ended a decade before. After the children were led home by their parents, the candles flickered in the empty plaza, gleaming red and yellow light left in a heart-shaped pattern of glass containers. There were things that everyone should remember, even in paradise, if only as a reminder that, despite Milton's words, there was no heaven on earth.

Spain

On Wednesday, November 22, the day before my mother's birthday, we celebrated Thanksgiving onboard the ship. The day was grey and drizzling, and the silhouette of the mountainous coast of Spain lay off the starboard. I focused my attention during that meal on the students who reminded me of her in one way or another—because of their curiosity or innocence or instinct to know, their toughness of spirit or largeness of heart, their passion for the unmediated world.

The students I sought out that day were Dustin Burke, from the University of Oregon, who crashed into the world as if he were exploring it for everyone who would not have the opportunity. Or Nick Parker, from Stanford, who looked at everything around him—in books and in the world—as if his life depended upon seeing it clearly. Or Marie Gassee, who called both San Francisco and Paris home and studied at UCLA, an exotically pretty young woman who, despite her fragile appearance, gave one the sense that she was strong enough to face the world wherever she landed. These were the students I saw on Thanksgiving—the ironic and sharp-witted Jeff Phillips from Colorado; the ardent-hearted Shadiya Lim from my alma mater, Fordham University in the Bronx; the splendidly eccentric Rosemari and Forest, who ranged the world as if they were Adam and Eve, newly thrust from Eden; or Patrick Healy, the engineering student from California who was more passionate about literature than any English major I had ever encountered. Those students reminded me, as my mother once had, that we all live in the past-laden future, and that experience and memory are as indistinguishable as waters flowing into the same stream.

It was still dark the next morning when we sailed into Cadiz, which claims to be the oldest city in Europe. Historical records said that the

Phoenicians established a settlement there in 1100 BC, but legend said that Hercules founded the city. The city was occupied, in turns, by Carthaginians, Romans, and Moors, was sacked by Sir Francis Drake, and for a short time was the capital of Spain in the early nineteenth century. A few miles southeast of Sanlucar de Barrameda, the fishing village that was the point of departure for Magellan's circumnavigation of the globe in the early sixteenth century, Cadiz eyed the Atlantic Ocean as if it still was the great unsolved mystery of our planet.

We had been on the ocean long enough, though, and the mystery for us was Spain. So, with Bill and Sherry May, we rented a car and headed toward Seville, Granada, and the pueblos blancos in the hilltops of Andalusia. Bill, a professor of bioethics at USC, was about to retire the next semester. A youthful grey-bearded man in his midseventies, he had a playful sense of sarcasm that was one of the things that made him seem younger than his subtle limp suggested. Sherry, a few years younger and already retired from her position in the university, was an attractive redhead with a smile that convinced you she had once been a nun and still believed in saving souls. Jo-Ellen and I found ourselves sneaking a peek at them occasionally, trying to see what life might hold for us if we were lucky.

After we picked up our rental car, discovered I had forgotten my license on the ship, and realized Bill would have to be the chauffeur, we drove the two hours to Seville. He made a fine driver, I told him, and he asked me if I planned to tip him at the end of the day. In lieu of a tip, when we got to the cramped side streets of Seville, I took over the driving and used my New Yorker's natural-born talent for parallel parking to slide the car into a space half its size. Growing up in New York City had taught me a few life lessons, but the most valuable may have been how to park in three seamless moves.

Once we dropped our bags off at the Acoba del Rey, a boutique hotel with a Muslim flavor, we ate supper in a tapas bar name Robles, casting aside vegetarian pretensions as any reasonable person must do in Spain and eating chorizo, jamon iberico, and pescado frito along with manchego cheese, giant olives, and gazpacho.

Before the food was brought to the table, Bill entertained us by explaining what a bioethicist actually did. In his deep newscaster's voice laced with good sense and mischief, he described working with pharma-ceutical businessmen and medical doctors. He tested us with questions about coeds trading eggs for the price of college tuition, young men sell-ing sperm for a week's worth of gas, and compelled us to think about the consequences of our new technologies.

Recently, Bill had been working with doctors who had had their licenses suspended for mistakes or inappropriate actions. They took his course the way a driver with too many points on his license is forced to take a driver reeducation class with the DMV.

"So," Jo-Ellen asked, "if people stop behaving badly or stupidly, you're out of work, then?"

Bill got a look in his eyes that he often did, the glint of a vaudeville comedian whose straight man had just given him the line he'd been wait-ing for. He paused in appreciation of the gift, letting the silence beat a few times, welling up to his remark.

"I keep some ethical issues unresolved," he explained, "so that's it's only an almost-perfect world. I wouldn't want to eradicate all the ills on the planet. That wouldn't be good for business and too dull, besides."

As if on cue, as soon as Bill stopped speaking, a well-dressed, middle-aged man entered the restaurant, bumping our table with his hip as he passed toward the bar. He walked with the uncertain gait of a drunk and had a few days' growth of beard. Just before he reached the bar, he turned back to our table and looked unsteadily in our direction.

"No like vida, entiende?" he said, as if rattling our table demanded some explanation of his feelings about life.

This was not a conversation that would have been easy to engage in, no matter what language we used. So we played more ignorant of Spanish than we were.

The man sliced his hand like a knife blade across his unshaven throat. "No manana for me," he proclaimed.

Our waiter, Lupe, raised his eyebrows, a sign that he had heard it all before, and Bill nodded as if this were just what he was talking about. The world would never be dull.

The next morning, as we stood before the tomb of Columbus in the Seville Cathedral, I wondered about our well-dressed drunk, if he had sobered up and whether the world looked better or worse to him. Right before we left the hotel room, I had finished rereading Hemingway's *The Sun Also Rises* so that I could discuss it with my literature class. I considered that the drunk man might have been like the character Jake Barnes, and I recalled his conversation with another Bill, the one in the novel. He encouraged Jake, who was feeling despondent, to have another drink. When Jake worried that another would not do any good, Bill said, "Try it. You can't tell; maybe this is the one that gets it."

I had my doubts, but maybe our drunk had found the drink that got it for him. I'd never know, of course, any more than I would know for sure if Columbus was actually buried in the artful tomb that displayed the four kings of Aragon, Leon, Castile, and Navara carrying his casket on their shoulders. Columbus's bones had been moved from Spain to Santo Domingo—and supposedly back—but some claimed that it was his son Diego who was buried in Seville and that the renowned explorer was lost in Santo Domingo as he had often been lost in his life.

Bill was no Columbus, and by that I mean he always knew where he was going, how to get there, and where we were when we arrived. The road to Granada was punctuated by rolling hills and clusters of olive trees. In the far distance we could just pick out the snow-covered peaks of the Sierra Nevadas. We stopped briefly in the town of Loja supposedly because it was on the Washington Irving Route, but *The Tales of the Alhambra* was less on our minds than good wine and getting to Granada in a few hours.

In Granada I parked the car on the narrow street near the Casa de Federico, which we had convinced ourselves was the last residence of the poet Garcia Lorca before he was taken away to be shot during the Spanish Civil War. I'm not sure where I got the idea, but when I asked the clerk about it, he dismissed me with a shrug and suggested I get a good night's sleep so that I could beat the tourists to the Alhambra the next morning.

We decided to make it an early bedtime and found a tapas bar near the hotel. But we had not figured on encountering Omar and Inigo, a bartender and waiter who kept us plied with free drinks and tapas late into the night. Omar was a tall, sleek Argentinean who spoke enough English to tease his customers by imitating their accents.

"I have the British and the Australian down," he said, "but can you help me with the New York accent? It is too hard for me, I think."

What followed was short course in saying hello to New Yorkers.

"Say 'how you doin','" I instructed him.

"How are you doing," he said, tilting his head in imitation of my head movement.

It took a while, but by the end of the night he sounded like a native of Brooklyn. "How ya doin'," he kept saying to us until I begged him for mercy. Then he called over the diminutive waiter, Inigo, whose father had run a foreign language school in Granada for years. Inigo spoke English, German, and Italian along with his native Spanish, and was about to venture out into the world for a year or so, first to Australia to work ("Shrimp on the barbie, eh mate?" Omar said) and then wherever the spirit took him.

"I'll be glad to get rid of him," Omar lied. "He's little but he's *insupportable*, you know, a pain in the ass."

Inigo laughed and said, "I will miss you too, amigo."

I drank *tinto de verano*, a blend of cheap red wine and lemon soda, we talked about bullfights, and I quoted lines from *The Sun Also Rises*—"A bottle of wine is good company" and "Nobody ever lives their life all the way up except bull-fighters"—until the group kindly asked me to shut up. Bill and Sherry wisely had gone back to the hotel a while before I began quoting Hemingway, and Inigo, perhaps on the theory that if my mouth were full I could not recite lines from American authors on Spain, kept bringing plates of olives and cheese and ham and placing them in front of me.

The next morning, when I woke up with my clothes smelling charred and my head throbbing, I knew I was not made for the fiesta. Bill and Sherry asked if we had enjoyed ourselves after we left. Jo-Ellen said *yes*, and I resisted the temptation to quote Hemingway one last time—"Isn't it pretty to think so?"

By the time we reached the Alhambra at 8 A.M., my head had cleared a bit in the chill, windy day. Built under Muslim leaders in the thirteenth and fourteenth centuries, the parklike collection of palaces and gardens was an attempt to create a sense of paradise on earth. As my head unclouded, I saw that they had accomplished their goal as well as any group of architects could. The baths and fountains and intricate gardens were framed by graceful arcades. The ceiling of the Saloñ de Embajadores, once the throne room, represented the seven heavens of the Muslim cosmos. The pool of water in the Patio de Arrayanes reflected daylight into the surrounding halls of the throne room and the Baños Reales, the baths of the king.

In general, the Alhambra, which literally means "the red," referring to the sun-dried bricks used to make the outer walls, was a labyrinth of quadrangles that connected rooms of one palace to another. The wind and warmth and light of the sun moved unimpeded from one section to another, from the Palace of Charles V to the Palacio de Partal. Each building had its own rectangular garden or pool of water. The fortress was a labyrinth of great banqueting halls and wooden ceilings, fresco paintings on the walls, alabaster lamp stands and devious mosaics, honeycombed domes, spurting fountains, and rows of cypress trees. It was both Christian and Islamic, two cultures soldered together by war and history, joined peacefully now as the battle lines were drawn elsewhere but in much the same way they had been in the thirteenth and fourteenth centuries. For a long time, it had been an embattled place, but in the late fall of 2006, gazing out at the foothills of the Sierra Nevadas and the gypsy caves that lined the hills, it could have been whispering Coleridge's lines from "Kubla Khan" to the crowds of visitors who waited to enter: "a stately pleasure dome . . . gardens bright with sinuous rills . . . and incense-bearing trees."

I would have guessed there was not a more beautiful spot within hundreds of miles, but once again I was proved wrong within twenty-four hours. The next day we drove along the Costa de la Luz to Malaga and up into mountains where the pueblos blancos, the white towns of Moorish heritage, sat like hallucinations in the blazing sunlight. No one else in my group cared about such things, but I wanted to see a bullfight. The closest I could find, though, in late November in Spain was the *plaza de torres* in Ronda, reputedly the oldest bullring in the country. It was a beautiful small amphitheater that had been transformed into a museum except for the first week in September. During that week, some of the best matadors in Spain came to fight, and the crowds followed them.

The legendary bullfighter Pedro Romero (the same name Heming-way had given his young bullfighter in *The Sun Also Rises*) changed the nature of the sport there in the eighteenth century. Before Romero, it had been traditional for the matador to fight the bull from horseback. Romero stood his ground on foot, though, and modern bullfighting was born. I asked if it were possible to get tickets to the bullfight in advance and was told that there were no advance tickets except for those who had them in their families.

"People come two weeks before and sleep on the streets to get tickets, my friend," one hotel clerk said to me.

"How about reserving a room for next September?" I asked.

"Impossible," he told me. "You can call in August and see if anyone has canceled. Everything is sold out, always."

That day we were lucky to find a place—a lovely one—in the Hotel San Gabriel, one of the handsome mansions of the town that had been turned into a small hotel for tourists. The family still owned and ran it, and we felt as if we were guests at the home of a "propietario rico." It had about twenty magnificently furnished rooms, a library, a tiny screening room to watch movies, a dining hall, and a garden area—but as a family home, it had the sort of grandeur that made me contemplate the life that the individuals in it had once lived.

The old section of Ronda was one of the most memorable towns I had ever seen. Built on a triangular plateau in the Andalusian Mountains, Ronda was a white village hanging from a dramatic escarpment. From the Puente Nueva or a dozen other locations in town, there were dizzy-ing views of the 500-foot-deep chasm, the valley below, and the Serrana de Ronda Mountains in the distance. The cobbled streets wound past stately homes squeezed together as if in memory of the long-gone days when the Moors watched for enemies from the massive outcrop of gran-ite and limestone.

Our two days in Ronda were a pleasant dream. I strode around the *plaza de torres* and imagined the crowd's roar, and we got lost on the narrow streets, ate and drank, and gazed at the nearly uninhabited world crawl-ing far below us. For me, it was a replication of Hemingway's description in *The Sun Also Rises* of Jake and Bill's fishing before the chaos of the fiesta in Pamplona. Like them, we had little to think about but the pleasures of the moment, we were with friends we admired and enjoyed, the scenery was dazzling, and death and war seemed too far away to be real, for the time being, at least.

 When we returned to the ship, we had one day left in Cadiz before we sailed back to America. Cadiz was once the starting point for so many who dreamed of finding a new world. The town had a tough, honest character, like a prideful old Spaniard who accepted his decay as a sign of outlasting his enemies.

Jo-Ellen and I spent our last day on our own, walking along the Campo del Sur, the field of the sea, the rim of road that followed the curving bay that outlined the city. Most of the old part of the city was on a peninsula that jutted out toward the wide, mysterious world. The surrounding water made it impossible to get lost in the twisting streets. We could always find the ocean and the ship. Like many of the cities in Andalusia, Cadiz had a Moorish feel in its maze of narrow, winding streets that opened into small, lively squares. No matter where we were, though, we imagined we could find our way home.

On that last night in Cadiz, sitting with Jo-Ellen in a streetside café overlooking the emerging lights around the harbor, I had the feeling that I was as close to home as I would ever come—comfortable as a stranger, a traveler—and I would have been content to stay there for weeks or months or years with her, looking out at the bay and thinking of the new worlds beyond.

But 4,000 miles away through rough December seas, America beckoned. It was time to wake from our dream. Even Rip Van Winkle had to awaken eventually. But we did not want to open our eyes like Rip and see the world had changed without our knowing it. The question was what lesson did we return with, what had two trips around the world given us? For me, it had made me fall in love with my wife again—and again. It had made me feel the grace and responsibility of the teacher's vocation. It forced me to recall one of the primary lessons my mother had demonstrated in her life—to live always as a traveler, to see everything with a child's fascination. Remembering that would mean never forgetting her. Remembering would mean trying to see even familiar landscapes with new eyes.

For the last week of classes, I discussed Hemingway's *The Sun Also Rises* and discovered that many students read it as a guidebook to drunken revelry in Spain. They followed it the way others read a Lonely Planet guide. I did my best to dissuade them of the notion that the novel was an artful example of a bartender's guide.

The last few days onboard the ship we discussed Yann Martel's tale of shipwreck and self-discovery, *Life of Pi*. Using that provocative novel as a point of departure, we talked about the varied cultures and countries we had experienced, contemplating Pi's eclectic spirituality, his inclination to say "Jesus, Mary, Muhammad, and Vishnu" when facing Richard Parker, the Bengal tiger with whom he shared a lifeboat. Martel offered at least two versions of Pi's adventure, and each reader could choose the one best fitting his or her vision of the world.

The danger Martel pointed to was clear to most of my students—watch out for becoming too entranced by "dry, yeast-less factuality," for it was an easy way to "miss the better story." Our journey around the world would transform itself, as everything did, into stories. Sparked by Pi's narrative, one of my students wondered in class whether we could see the connections between one religion and another, one culture and another? And if we could, wouldn't that be the better story to tell?

Before I packed up all my books to ship back to Virginia when we landed in Florida, I glanced once again at Emma Larkin's *Finding George Orwell in Burma*. My gaze fell on this passage: "Tormented by these Burmese ghosts, Orwell began to look more closely at his own country and saw that England also had its oppressed and nameless masses in the form of the working class." I realized that, for good and ill, these two trips around the globe had filled my life with memories and ghosts, and I wondered if they would help me see my own country as a new land and live in it with the intensity and enthusiasm of a wayfarer among fascinating strangers.

One book I kept out of the box to be shipped, and I read it for the tenth or eleventh time right before we landed in the United States. *Death Comes for the Archbishop* by Willa Cather had been one of my mother's favorite novels, and it had become one of mine, a portrait of friendship and love and courage, a picture of the American spirit. Near the end of the story, the main character, Archbishop Latour, is old and retired, and the young priest who is caring for him worries about his catching a cold and dying. The archbishop's wry response suggests his contentment and wisdom: "The old man smiled: 'I shall not die of a cold, my son. I shall die of having lived.'"

The archbishop's lesson was my mother's lesson as well, the lesson that any traveler should learn: when our time comes, we all want to die of having lived fully. Earlier in the novel, the archbishop suggests how one might achieve that kind of life: "Where there is great love there are always miracles. . . . our eyes can see and our ears can hear what is there about us always."

When Jo-Ellen and I got back to the United States, we were scheduled to go Santa Fe, the locus of Cather's imagination, the archbishop's city of holy faith. From there, we would head back east toward *home*. Even if I wasn't perfectly sure where that was or what it meant, I had my own faith that our only chance was to discover it together.

A Random Reading List

The Sea, Explorers, and Travelers

The Discoverers. Daniel Boorstin
The Four Voyages of Christopher Columbus. Ed. and trans. J. M. Cohen
The Mysterious History of Columbus. John Noble Wilford
The Travels. Marco Polo
Over the Edge of the World: Magellan's Terrifying Circumnavigation of the Globe.
    Laurence Bergreen
Life of Pi. Yann Martel
The Sea Around Us. Rachel Carson
The White Nile. Alan Moorehead
The Mapmakers. John Noble Wilford
Captain Sir Richard Francis Burton. Edward Rice
Moby-Dick. Herman Melville
Billy Budd. Herman Melville
The Innocents Abroad. Mark Twain
The Global Soul. Pico Iyer

Burma

Burmese Days. George Orwell
Essays. George Orwell
1984. George Orwell
Animal Farm. George Orwell
Finding George Orwell in Burma. Emma Larkin
Freedom from Fear and Other Writings. Aung San Suu Kyi

Brazil

Dona Flor and Her Two Husbands. Jorge Amado

Canada

Selected Stories. Alice Munro

China

The Good Earth. Pearl S. Buck
Waiting. Ha Jin
Ocean of Word. Ha Jin
Under the Red Flag. Ha Jin
The Bridegroom. Ha Jin
Soul Mountain. Gao Xingjian
Shanghai Baby. Wei Hui
Tao de Ching. Lao-tzu. English translation by Stephen Mitchell
Golden Boy: Memories of a Hong Kong Childhood. Martin Booth

Croatia

The Bridge on the Drina. Ivo Andric
April Fool's Day. Josip Novakovich

Cuba

Waiting for Fidel. Christopher Hunt
Cubana. Ed. Mirta Yanez
The Old Man and the Sea. Ernest Hemingway

Egypt

Miramar. Naguib Mahfouz
The Seventh Heaven: Stories of the Supernatural. Naguib Mahfouz
Out of Egypt. Andre Aciman
Dark Star Safari: Overland from Cairo to Cape Town. Paul Theroux

India

Interpreter of Maladies. Jhumpa Lahiri
Love and Longing in Bombay. Vikram Chandra
Siddhartha. Herman Hesse
The God of Small Things. Arundhati Roy

Japan

Kafka on the Shore. Haruki Murakami
The Wind-Up Bird Chronicle. Haruki Murakami
Norwegian Wood. Haruki Murakami
Blind Willow, Sleeping Woman. Haruki Murakami
The Sound of Waves. Yukio Mishima
Acts of Worship. Yukio Mishima
Hiroshima Notes. Kenzaburo Oe
Snow Country. Yasunari Kawabata
Hiroshima. John Hersey
The Art of the Story: An International Anthology of Short Stories. Ed. Daniel
    Halpern. A wealth of superb stories from around the world, among
    them tales by Ishiguro, Murakami, and others.

Kenya

Out of Africa. Isak Dinesen
Green Hills of Africa. Ernest Hemingway
Weep Not, Child. Ngugi wa Thiong'o (James Ngugi)
Dangerous Beauty: Life and Death in Africa—True Stories from a Safari Guide.
    Mark Ross

Malaysia

Modern Secrets. Shirley Geok-Lin Lim

Spain

The Sun Also Rises. Ernest Hemingway

For Whom the Bell Tolls. Ernest Hemingway
Don Quixote. Miguel de Cervantes
Homage to Catalonia. George Orwell
The Basque History of the World. Mark Kurlansky
Picasso's War. Russell Martin
Blood Wedding. Federico Garcia Lorca
Selected Poems. Federico Garcia Lorca
The Road to Santiago. Kathryn Harrison

South Africa

Cry, The Beloved Country. Alan Paton
Disgrace. J. M. Coetzee
The Rights of Desire. Andre Brink
Selected Stories. Nadine Gordimer

Turkey

Snow. Orhan Pamuk
The Black Book. Orhan Pamuk
My Name Is Red. Orhan Pamuk
Istanbul: Memories and the City. Orhan Pamuk

Vietnam

The Things They Carried. Tim O'Brien
Going after Cacciato. Tim O'Brien
Catfish and Mandala. Andrew X. Pham
Paradise of the Blind. Duong Thu Huong
The Sorrow of War. Bao Ninh
Ho Chi Minh: A Life. William J. Duiker